My
Not-So-Shameful
Sex Secrets

Girl on the Net

For content notes visit
www.girlonthenet.com/content

Book Layout © 2016 SexyLittlePages.com

My Not-So-Shameful Sex Secrets/Girl on the Net. -- 1st ed.
ISBN 978-1-530363315

For the one who's atomic, the one who's insignificant and above all the one who's not in it.

CONTENTS

I Didn't Listen To The Lyrics Of 'Teenage Kicks' Because I Was Far Too Busy Masturbating

If you'd asked thirteen-year-old me what I wanted to be when I grew up, hovering somewhere near the top of the list alongside 'astronaut' and 'writer' would have been 'wanker'. When I was thirteen, I wanted to be a wanker.

I suspect the same could be said of many teenagers—that moment when you discover that touching yourself like *that* can make everything else in the world seem dull, shallow and unimportant, is a moment that many of us spend the rest of our lives trying to recreate.

Since then I've been chasing that feeling—that desperate, horny kick you get when something strikes you in just the right way. When a guy says 'come here and bend over', when he puts one arm tightly around my waist and uses the other to pull my knickers down, when he leans over and whispers in my ear, 'I can see your nipples getting hard through that top.' Every single time my cunt twitches and I feel that stinging lust in the pit of my stomach—they're all descendants of that initial spark.

The first thing I ever wanked to was a book.

Not a book with any particularly saucy images on the cover, or, as a surprising number of my male friends have confessed, a hardback compilation of 'arty' Pirelli calendar shots. To my utter adult horror, my first teenage wank came about via a sadomasochistic novel that belonged to my dad.

Allow me to explain:

My parents were divorced. Not in an 'oh God, why must they tear the family apart?' way, but in a 'well, that seems to have calmed them both down' way. No doubt it was agony for eight-year-old me, but I'm sure she'd forgive twenty-eight-year-old me for being a bit blasé about it, given that both of my parents subsequently settled down with lovely partners, neither of whom hit me or made me sweep out cinders from the fireplace.

It's well documented that post-divorce many children cash in, and benefit from having two of everything: two Christmases, two birthdays, two trips to the special cake shop to be congratulated on not fucking up your GCSEs. And it's also well documented that this isn't a great idea, and can leave your children well and truly spoiled. Luckily for me my parents read the documentation thoroughly and decided to do their absolute best not to fawn over, bribe, or otherwise pander to any of their children. This means that my brother, sister and I have all grown up relatively balanced, if a little light on presents.

I did get one special treat when I visited my dad, though: my own bedroom. Initially this meant peace and quiet, personal space and the ability to lie in on Saturday and read book after book after book. Eventually, though, as I grew up and discovered the brilliant things I could do to myself given enough 'alone time', I started to look on weekends at my dad's house as simply forty-eight hours in which I could wank to my heart's content.

During the week I'd share a bedroom with my sister, which was split according to the rule that says 'she with the loudest voice gets the biggest space', so I got the crappy space.

Late at night my sister and I would have feisty rows over why I'd borrowed her good hairbrush, then settle into our respective beds to recharge our energy for tomorrow's big fight. She, I imagine, would fall instantly into a deep and unshakeable slumber, while I would focus on learning to wank without moving the bedsheets.

It's trickier than you think.

First you have to manoeuvre your body into a position that befits wanking yet also looks like it might be a way a human would sleep. If, like me, you sleep lying on your front, this means bunching the duvet up around you so you can ever so slightly raise your arse from the bed to make enough space for one hand to fit between your legs.

Don't jump the gun, though, my hand is not between my legs yet. First, I have to lick my fingers. I have to coat them in spit in a way that makes absolutely no sound whatsoever. Try it at home. In a silent room, in the dead darkness of night, coat your fingers in spit without making any lip-smacking, finger-sucking sounds. Tricky, no?

Having achieved this Herculean feat, next you must move your hand under the bedsheets without a) wiping any of the spit off or b) letting on that you might be about to do something inappropriate. It is impossible to do this without rustling the duvet, so don't even try. Instead, make sure your movement appears casual and insignificant—a slight shift in sleeping position, a scratch—you're just getting comfortable, that's all. Under no circumstances must the movement be done with the gleeful eagerness of someone who is about to have a wank.

Next comes the good bit—the actual wanking. And this works much the same as a full-on, adult, 'I've got my own sofa and I'm not afraid to rub one out on it' wank, only with much smaller movements.

As an adult I'll wank openly, joyfully, safe in the knowledge that not only is an Englishman's home his castle, but that if anyone looks through the window of my particular castle, they have no right to judge me. All I'm doing is having a nice, healthy wank. Like almost everyone does of a Saturday afternoon when something hot strikes them and there's nothing on the telly. Rubbing frantically at my clit, without guilt or fear of being caught, I can bring myself to an express, functional orgasm within about thirty seconds.

Sadly it wasn't so for teenage me. Very slight movements and delicate rubbing built to an infinitesimally gradual increase in pressure as I tested whether the duvet could withstand small vibrations without giving the game away. And I won't lie—it didn't always work. Sometimes I'd lie there, tensing every single muscle in my body, rubbing in tiny tiny strokes with just one finger as hard as I'd dare. My nipples hard, my fingers slick, my forehead creased into a frown of agonising concentration... and still I couldn't come. I knew that with just a bit more pressure it would work. I just needed a slightly faster rhythm, longer strokes, or to have my other hand free to pinch one of my nipples or grab at myself more tightly. On those occasions I'd cough, get out of bed, wrap a towel around myself and retire to the well-lit bathroom with its heaven-sent door lock, and lie on the floor with my legs open, frigging myself to a twitching, guilty climax.

But that was rare. Having had plenty of practice, the silent wanking was usually a success. Fixing a fantasy in my head (pirates tying a willing wench to the mast of their ship, and whipping her with the cat-o'-nine-tails, since you asked), I'd rub harder, push harder, and feel the first waves of orgasm tearing through me.

There were no post-climax sighs, no groans, and very few rustling noises as I took my hand away and shifted back into a sleeping position. Exhausted after the effort, I'd nod off to the sound of almost-silence: the quiet, steady breathing of my sister, curled up tight in bed, definitely not wanking either.

But that all comes later—younger me didn't quite understand what wanking was. The closest I'd come to coming was when I'd act out scenes with things that happened to be lying around my room—books, stuffed toys, marbles. I'd move objects around like a general directing a battle and inevitably the childish stories—man rescues woman from the clutches of evil kidnappers—would evolve into slightly more adult plays as my mind got that bit filthier—man rescues woman from the clutches of evil yet sexy kidnappers. Eventually, as I started growing up, the players in my games would more frequently end up in contrived situations that gave me a sexual thrill.

There was always a kidnap victim, lost princess, stepdaughter, or pirate's wench who would inevitably have to be punished. The leaders were eager—never reluctant— to punish the wrongdoer. She was always female. Usually surrounded by a group of pissed-off men. The men would threaten to punish her and she'd be more than stoic—like she'd got into trouble deliberately just because she wanted to hear the word 'thrash'. As in 'I'm going to thrash you for that.'

Thrash.

That word still does good things to me. The sound of someone being thrashed, the sight of a guy's arm, holding a whip or a belt, tensed ready to strike, gives me a dark, hot feeling deep in my stomach.

In more literary books people talk of 'sexual awakenings' where the world becomes more vivid, where you notice things you'd never noticed before and suddenly become alive to your sexual sense. It all sounds very poetic and meaningful, without the sordid stains that come with our actual, real-life awakenings. I'm not going to lie and tell you that any of this filth was poetic. The truth rarely is. What I'm telling you is that I lay on my bedroom floor with a bunch of marbles and quimmed my pants at the word 'thrash'.

Thrash.

Shudder.

Having worked out that this word did weird things, I experimented with other words. 'Beat'. 'Whip'. 'Spank'. 'Hit'. 'Thwack'. Each of them resonates with me, conjures stark and immediate images of men straining at the shoulder, bearing instruments of stinging pain. Beat. Whip. Thwack. 'I'm going to beat you now.' 'I'm going to whip you.' All so good that just writing them makes me shudder. But no other word gives me that kick in the gut quite as hard as the word:

Thrash.

But despite these words giving me that trembling feeling, I didn't know how to keep it going. Other than repeating the scenes over and over in my head, I was at a loss. Insights garnered from TV shows that I watched late at night had given me the impression that I should stick my fingers in, but I'd done that before when I was practising with tampons, and it had just given me a vague feeling of medical-grade discomfort. Touching my insides seemed wrong, and putting my fingers in my cunt seemed about as arousing as poking at an open wound. Moreover,

I had no idea what I was supposed to do once my fingers were there. Should there be a side-to-side motion? A swirling motion? An in-and-out motion? Not a bloody clue. I could have done with a handbook, or at the very least a nudge and a wink and an explanation that 'fingering' could be done in many different ways.

So I'd got hot, got wet, got horny, and yet still hadn't actually wanked—until I found the book.

It wasn't deliberate, I'm sure of that. My dad is quite a liberal guy, but still prone to saying 'oh, deary me' in a jovially uncomfortable way when adverts for sanitary products appear on TV. He left the book in my room, certainly, but I know he didn't leave it there on purpose.

On this occasion I went to visit Dad, and spotted that things had been moved about a bit in my room. This was reasonably unusual. My room was seen as my space, so unless they'd had guests who needed a bed, no one would go in, let alone start moving my stuff around. Dad felt the need to explain, as I dumped my weekend rucksack on the bed, that he had a bad back and had been borrowing my bed for a few nights during the week.

I found out later that it was because he and my stepmum had had a fight. Not just a 'why do you never do the washing up?' fight, but a full-on, storming-out, 'I can't bear to share a bed with this twat' row. Hence the book, I suppose. If I were my dad, and had found myself suddenly and temporarily wifeless, I'd have taken the time to catch up on my wanking too.

I set about putting my things in order—rearranging my room, taking out the clothes I'd packed for the weekend, and putting my own book into the bedside drawer. And that was where I found it—Dad's.

I can't remember what it was called, but I'm sure it was something French-sounding. The action was set in Parisian streets, and the images in my mind are of people in vaguely old-fashioned clothes cavorting with each other and talking in strong French accents, but any one of these memories might be incorrect. The key thing I took away, having flipped through a few pages, was that it was dirty. Filthy.

Not dirty like the pictures of shining, pink-mouthed topless women that the boys at school pored over, not even dirty like the scenes of thrashing that whirled round in my head, but dirty in ways I'd never imagined before. On the first page I flicked to, a woman tied a man flat to a board, teased him into a throbbing erection, then encased his cock in a condom-like sheath that had hundreds of tiny spikes on the inside.

I told myself I should put this down. I thought I'd discovered the edge of filth, the world's end, and that nothing dirtier was possible. I tried to close the book, reasoning that nothing could be worse than the passage I'd just read. Then I read the very next paragraph, in which she sat down upon the sheath, letting it slide slickly inside her, and watched the anguished looks on the guy's face as his dick throbbed with pleasure and pain.

OK, I should definitely put this down, I thought again.

But instead I settled myself back onto the bed, resting one hand casually on my crotch outside my jeans. Pushing with gentle pressure at the place where the waves of heat were coming from.

'I'm going to put this down now.'

The woman started sliding up and down the guy's dick—the sheath smooth on the outside and adding precious thickness to his erection. The book described in detail her arousal—her cold, solid nipples stiffening as she rode him faster. It drew a detailed picture of her muscular thighs, clamping him tight as she rocked back and forth. It went into lengthy detail about the mechanics of the act—how every time she sat down, sliding his cock deeper into her, the tiny spikes would push more heavily into his skin, pricking his prick so he'd moan in pain.

Without making a conscious decision to, I was touching myself. My hand on the outside of my jeans, my legs spread wide so that the seam pressed heavily on my clit, I rubbed hard with my fingers through the strong fabric.

'I should definitely put this down.'

But I didn't. I couldn't. The hot, topless woman was riding the guy with such need, such a desire to come that she'd hurt him more than she meant to.

I was gripping the book in my left hand, rubbing harder with my right, trying to mirror the passion and the need of the woman in the book. I cared even less about the embarrassment of wanking than she cared about the pain of the guy sat beneath her. I rubbed myself, and I felt what she felt—her clit rubbing against something, her cunt getting wetter, and finally—just before I had to turn a page—that powerful gut-wrenching kick that marked the first rush of the first wave of the very first orgasm I'd ever had.

A few years later, I found another book in my room: the *Osborne Book of Teenaged Bodies*. Nice try, Dad. Nice try.

Having discovered the dirty book and spent a few happy weekends holed up in my room frigging myself crosseyed, I eventually came to the realisation that wanking—contrary to almost everything I'd previously been led to believe—was not just for boys.

The references to it were everywhere: jokes about boys being boys, talk of crusty bedsheets, sniggers and whispers if a guy had his hands in his pockets for too long. Not just at school, either. TV programmes and teen flicks were filled with not-so-subtle nods to the fact that boys just couldn't get enough orgasmic alone-time. I could understand why they liked it so much—given thirty minutes on my own, I'd be able to knock out five orgasms in quick succession and still have time to do my homework. What I couldn't quite fathom, though, was why no one ever mentioned that girls did it too.

No one ever made jokes about me if I spent too long in the bath. No one questioned my almost constantly jiggling knee —the friction felt pleasantly soothing on my clit, and was a nice way to get through IT lessons until it was time for a bathroom break. Most surprisingly, girls themselves didn't even talk about it.

I remember spending hours with girlfriends as a teenager dissecting whether this or that particular boy fancied so-and-so, exactly whose hand was where during the slow song at the school disco, or whether Ricky Martin would ever be likely to shimmy his oh-so-hot and definitely-not-gay-just-flamboyant ass over to the UK to do bad, bad things to my best friend.

But never once did we talk about wanking.

We must have all been doing it, and none of us were particularly squeamish. There was just a feeling that no one should ever say. That we'd be breaking some sort of unwritten rule if we owned up. We were demure, delicate creatures. Creatures who were waiting to be defiled behind the bike sheds and wanted to maintain some semblance of innocence so that we could put on a shocked face when boys tried to touch our tits.

We could be in love, we could have crushes, and we could be curious. But we couldn't actually have *desires*, for God's sake. That would be cheating. A whispered discussion about what cocks were like was all well and good, but the powerful, wet, angry lust that we actually felt was a bit freakish, a bit wrong. No one ever had to tell us this, we just knew. We were allowed to have giggles and sleepovers and secret codewords and whispered gossip and posters of be-coiffed boyband members. But wanking? Wanking was for boys.

I'd like to say that things have changed now that I'm a grown-up. We live in a more liberated time, when we can wander into a bookshop and buy filth like... well... like this. Or read magazines that give sex tips alongside fashion advice. Or give a friend a dildo as a 'sorry you got heartlessly dumped' present. But I don't think we're really much further along the track.

Dildos and rabbit vibrators have made girl-wanking OK, but only in quite a specific sense. Women are allowed to experiment with wanking because now there's a way to market it. You can have a vibrator or two, you can joke about having some 'alone time' with your rabbit, because discussion is no longer about the act of wanking, but about the accessories. We're still ever so slightly weird about the idea of teenage girls locking themselves in their room and frigging themselves raw through their jeans.

Girls can be horny now; they can be hot and wet and desperate for a fuck. Their cunts can twitch and ache with longing and desire. They can feel that deep, angry kick-in-the-gut that signals something has triggered the naked, rutting, cavewoman instinct inside them. But they must do it all with a giggle and a smile and a wry sense of how liberated they are. They can read *Fifty Shades of Grey* on the bus, but when their friends ask they'll say they're only reading it to see what all the fuss was about, and they didn't like it and it was badly written and they didn't rub one out to it, honest.

I've heard men complain about this with smiles that say they're only half joking. 'Why is it OK for women to read porn on the bus but I can't flip open a jazz mag without commuters running in terror?' They can't sit on the back seat with a copy of *Penthouse* flipped open, casually perusing the weekly selection of tits on their way into work. And they're right, they can't. Partly because—for fear of stating the blindingly obvious—*Penthouse* has actual pictures, for the love of Christ, and they might terrify fellow commuters. But primarily because men are seen to have a different relationship with porn than women. When a woman looks at porn people raise their eyebrows, and assume she's just curious. People don't think about her cunt getting slick or her nipples getting hard or her heart pounding or stomach contracting. They don't imagine her lingering over the hottest paragraph, the one where our hero finally succumbs to his own desire and bends the heroine over a desk, spanking her as she writhes and moans and pushing his engorged cock into her spit-lubed ass. No. When women read porn there's a vague assumption that they're doing it ironically.

Men can't read porn on the bus, but that's not because we hate your porn, or think you're a filthy pervert. On the contrary, it's because we feel like you're the only ones who truly understand it, who get what it's for. Women can look at porn in public because strangers assume that they must have a motive other than the simple desire to get off. Men: you might not get to read porn on the bus, but at least you have the benefit of the doubt. When you say you're horny, when you say you like sex, when you get hard over porn, we believe you.

I don't think porn played a huge part in my teenage years. There was one computer, and it was in the dining room—even the bravest of teenagers would have to take quite a leap of faith to pull their trousers down in confidence that their parents wouldn't walk in just as you got to the good bit. More importantly, I'd have had to ask permission to actually use the internet. Each minute you used it cost money, and all you'd get for your investment was a clunky image of a woman's nipples, loading slowly down the screen, line by agonising line.

Whichever way you look at it, the 90s weren't an ideal time in which to learn about sex, and all the filthy, spunk-covered, hair-pulling ways in which people do it.

But I tell you what we did have back then—imagination. Acres and acres of it.

To this day I rarely watch porn to have a wank. Occasionally, I'll browse through a few of my favourite websites, clicking through videos to find the best moments, or I'll read a book with the specific intention of putting it down halfway through, conjuring up the images in my head, gritting my teeth and then coming all over my fingers.

But more often than not I can come up with better images on my own. I don't need porn to spark them off. Why? Well, the filthy naked people in my head always do just what I want them to do. No one's going to put me off by saying something dodgy at the wrong time, or changing camera angle just when I was getting into it. Nor am I going to be wracked with guilt and worry that the people in my imagination might be being exploited.

Exploitation makes me careful about the porn I'll seek out. I wouldn't want to watch something that looks like it's been filmed covertly, for instance. There are enough blurred videos of me sucking someone's dick that I don't want to encourage any more sex-tape-leaking than there is already. But the main reason I don't like porn is that it can only take a tiny thing to completely kill my mood.

For instance, using the word 'pussy'. As in 'fuck my pussy' or 'you've got a nice wet pussy'. Just say it—say the word to yourself, and try not to shudder. 'Pussy'. 'Wet pussy'. It's like something you might step in, not something you fuck. Likewise 'hole'. Everyone has different words that they find hot, but the porn people in my head always talk about 'cunts'.

Similarly, no matter how hot the porn scene, I can be instantly turned off by a switch to a close-up camera angle. Not that there's nothing beautiful about a nice, thick, porn-star cock, but when I'm watching two—or three, or four—people fucking, I want to actually see them fucking. I don't just want to see the bumping, wet smack as one small part connects with another. Just as I wouldn't go to Disneyland and ride nothing but Space Mountain, likewise with porn I want to see the full show: the slaps, the grabbing, the facial expressions. In real life we know that a fuck is about much more than rubbing the right body parts together, but for some reason pornographers have forgotten that. They show us the dismembered bits: part A fitting into slot B, like a crude jigsaw puzzle. I want to see the whole thing. I want to watch as he bends her over the sofa, see his hand settled firmly in the small of her back. I want to see him reach forward with his other hand and grab at her hair or squeeze her tits. I want to see her throw her head back with desire when he does this. I want to watch her pushing herself back onto his dick, to feel the full, thick length of him. And I don't get any of this if you just show me her cunt in close-up.

And finally, crucially, the main thing I hate about porn is that it so rarely reflects how actual sex happens. Even with amateur porn, or BDSM porn, or any kind of specialism, most of the videos will follow a reasonably tried and tested formula.

Guy meets girl, guy kisses girl, guy removes her flimsy top and firmly rubs her tits. Girl strips sexily. Guy removes her knickers. Guy plays with her cunt for far longer than the average guy would play with a cunt. Guy licks her clit, she sucks him off, they fuck in a minimum of three positions, he pulls his cock out and wanks onto her face, the end.

With slight tweaks to the details, this story runs through almost every porn film that's ever been mainstream. It might be popular, and it might do good things for some people, but it's frustratingly formulaic. Sex, actual sex, just doesn't work like that. And it's a bloody good thing, too. Actual sex is hot and fun and sticky and sweaty and it all happens out of order. If we followed a manual like the one they give to the porn industry we'd all die of boredom before we reached the come shot.

But I digress. When I was younger none of this occurred to me. I'd never seen any porn, I'd never watched anyone else fuck, and even the launch of Channel 'we show tits late at night' 5 only gave me some vague soft-core humping that didn't quite press the buttons worth pressing.

My obsession was still with the word 'thrash', and derivatives of it, and the stories in my head were far more tailored to this personal quirk.

As I lay in bed with my duvet bunched around me, rubbing gently at my clit with silent movements, full-colour, scripted porn masterpieces would play out inside my head.

Angry, horny men would crowd round a girl and call her a slut. She'd groan with arousal, delighted to be the focus of so much desire. She'd twitch her cunt around the dicks she was being fucked with, or bend over a desk to get beaten with a thick, black belt. The guys around her would be pushing in, trying to get closer—to touch her, to grab her, to slap her arse and see how firm it was. To push their dicks into her mouth, her cunt.

One guy directs them all. He tells them this girl is good, that they'll all get a chance, but that he has to punish her first.

Thwack.

'You're a filthy girl.'

Thwack.

'I'm going to punish you...'

Thwack.

'... and then I'm going to fuck you.'

Thwack.

'Let's see how wet you're getting.'

Thwack.

'Oh, you filthy girl.'

And as he makes the next stroke she cries out in pain, and one of the other men steps forward, tilts her head back by grabbing a clump of her hair, and forces his dick into her gaping mouth.

Thwack.

She's flagging, the strain of keeping silent, of not making choking noises, is hard for her to cope with. Her breath catches and spit runs from her mouth to her chin to her chest. The guy with the belt pushes down on the small of her back, bending her further, pressing her to the table, squashing her tits against the cool smoothness of the desk while from the other end his friend takes grunting pleasure from her mouth. He draws his arm back ready for another stroke.

Thwack.

At that stroke the leader moves in, using his free hand to rub his already rock-solid dick. She bucks and writhes as he forces it into her, choking out a moan against the cock that's already in her mouth.

'That's it. Take it. Good girl.' He raises his stroke hand. 'Are you ready for one more?'

She tries to nod; she wants to nod. She knows that this will be the final stroke of the onslaught, the last fresh wave of pain that might push her through to orgasm. But she can't nod, her hair's held tightly in the grasp of the other man, and the leader has her pinned from behind, holding himself and his thick cock still, teasing her cunt while he waits for a response. The guy at the front starts thrusting harder, pushing her back onto the other man's dick. Making strangled grunts in the back of his throat. She knows he's going to come, can feel him start to come, can feel his dick twitch deep in the back of her throat as she makes a muffled cry.

Thwack.

So this is what I did through my teenaged years. In between trying to pass exams and not get too bullied at school, I wanked. Frantically, furiously, and with a passion and commitment that the world tried to tell me was just for boys.

I'd sit in lessons and think about wanking. I'd eat dinner on my lap in front of *EastEnders* and think about wanking. I'd get into the car to visit my dad and spend the twenty-minute journey thinking about wanking. How much can I get done between now and Sunday night?

Perhaps the world's not yet ready for the slick and desperate wanking power of teenaged girls, but I wish it were. I wish it had been when I was young. Because although it occupied most of my waking thoughts, actually doing it made me feel weird. Not like an excited explorer stood on a cliff-edge of opportunity, but like a lonely hermit in a cave, scared of what the outside world would think when she told them about her discovery.

I'd learned how to wank, which made my life immeasurably more fun. It gave me something interesting and free to do with my spare time, and let me explore the disgusting things that went on inside my head. But I'd also learned to keep as quiet as I could about it. I'd learned not to talk about it or dwell for too long on the things that happened inside my head. Every other thing about me was normal—tediously so. But this secret thing I did was a bit unfeminine, a bit abnormal, and certainly not something I should openly discuss.

It took me a good few years to unlearn that lesson.

CHAPTER TWO

Sometimes It Is Necessary To Give Someone Crisps So That They'll Grope You

The problem with adult men is that they just don't touch my tits enough. I've never met a straight man who says he doesn't like tits. And yet as grown men they miss out on a million opportunities to touch them up. I can think of no occasion when I've been relaxing with a guy on the sofa that wouldn't have been immeasurably improved if he'd had one hand idly exploring the inside of my shirt.

Teenage boys were fantastic, for countless different reasons, but the most fantastic thing of all was their obsession—their pure and complete satisfaction—with touching my tits.

I wasn't particularly popular at school. I was the geeky kid, the one who did well in exams but badly with the boys. The 'good' one, for whom detentions were so unthinkable that the one time I did get one my mum reacted as if there'd been a terrible miscarriage of justice:

'Oh, you poor thing. Is there an appeals process?'

But despite the surface impression of being a good girl who'd pass all her exams with flying colours and have little time for boys in between, I was burning up with lust, with heat, and, above everything else, a desire to have my tits touched by boys.

Many of my girlfriends were the same. To greater or lesser degrees, all of us wanted to find someone with whom we could retire to a quiet alleyway and experiment with a bit of tit-touching. When you're young, the jolt of electric surprise when a hand brushed a nipple—even through the bra—is as powerful as a passionate fuck might be to someone older.

And yet none of us wanted to be the one suggested it. No girl could actually say, 'Hey, guy who is one of our friends but who I don't technically fancy, would you mind just rubbing my tits for twenty minutes or so until I slick my knickers?' So we made things happen. Stealthily, subtly, without ever suggesting we might be 'up for it', we made things happen.

One summer, my friend Amy and I went on a mission to get our tits touched. We didn't discuss it but we both knew that was the plan. As reasonably unpopular girls, we understood that no matter how short our skirts or how much make-up we inexpertly applied, we'd never hit the teenaged jackpot of an actual boyfriend. So we settled for the next best thing—we lowered whatever expectations we'd been foolish enough to have and headed straight for the guys who seemed most willing.

At school there was a group of boys rather cruelly known as the 'untouchables'. These were the guys who would never get slow dances at the discos, the boys who were a bit pervy or nerdy and were generally given a wide berth. The bullied kids always stuck together, so we gravitated towards this group, and would spend countless hours swigging cheap cider with them in parks, swapping the right answers for our homework, and occasionally getting them to touch our tits.

That summer, Amy and I picked a pair of them who were quite good friends, and spent our time engineering situations in which we could get them alone. We didn't want to shag them, and weren't even bothered about snogging particularly—an activity which I'd found to be relatively unsexy and to require far too much post-snog facial wiping. So, no shagging, no snogging, as little conversation as we could get away with—all we wanted to do was get their hands on our tits.

Darren had his own bedroom, furnished with a bunk bed left over from the days he'd shared with an older brother, and a cheap TV/VCR in the corner on which he and his friend Rob would watch endless shit B-movies to pass the time until evening. Every morning for a couple of weeks, I'd walk to Amy's house, knock on her door, and we'd set off to Darren's.

Plastered with more make-up than was realistically necessary for a day spent sat in a darkened room, we'd knock on Darren's door and ask him if Rob was around. He usually was.

'You watching films today?'

'Uh... yeah.'

'Can we watch them too?'

'Umm...'

'We've brought Pringles.'

'Come in.'

Eagerly, we'd rush into Darren's room, where a poorly scripted horror film would be playing on the TV and Rob would be reclining on the top bunk of the bed. Even when our visits became routine, he always looked surprised to see us.

By unspoken agreement, Rob was mine, and Darren was Amy's. I'd swing up into the top bunk, she'd settle into the bottom one, and we'd all sit in silence and pretend to watch the film.

An hour and a half was never quite long enough. It would take half an hour for Rob to get over his nervousness and make a move on me. Long after all of the movie characters had been introduced, and thrown into whichever perilous yet implausible situation the film required, he'd shift slightly towards me and brush against me with his arm. I'd respond eagerly, brushing back against him with slightly more pressure, and angling my chest so that the next move he made would have him pressed against the side of my tits.

'Are you comfortable?' he murmured. This was my cue.

'Not really, can I sit in front of you?' I replied, so quietly that the rustling coming from the bottom bunk would almost drown out my whispers.

He gulped, nodded, and I slid in front of him, so that his back was pressed against the wall and my back was pressed against him.

With our eyes still firmly on the TV, he'd make tiny, gradual movements to shift his arms so that they were holding me around my stomach. I watched the film, taking in nothing except the feeling of his hands moving ever so slowly towards my tits. The on-screen heroine would scream and flee from the latest danger, and I'd be screaming inside my head, 'Go on, up a bit.'

I was dripping wet. Feeling the soft, gentle touch of his hands on my top would drive me mad with lust. That kick-in-the-gut feeling of need was eating away at me, and I willed him to go further.

He started breathing more heavily behind me, shaking a bit with the heady excitement that a girl was letting him touch her. She was actually, unless he was very much mistaken, shifting slightly to move her tits closer to his hands. Pushing back against him so that she could feel his jumpy, throbbing erection pressing into the small of her back. He wasn't watching the film, just seeing the pictures. And as the people on the screen grew more terrified of whatever B-movie monster was chasing them, he was getting ever closer to having both of his hands cupped around the soft, jumper-clad, erotic holy grail—an actual pair of tits.

He wasn't mistaken. I was doing all of these things. Subtle gestures made way for more direct ones, as I leant back and felt his hard, aching dick pressing into me. My nipples were rock solid and stood out clearly even through a bra and a thin jumper. I wanted him to touch them. I pressed myself against him and shifted to bring them closer to his hands, willing him to feel them, to be determined, to squeeze them nice and hard through the fabric.

Finally, just before the climax of the film, he'd cup his trembling hands around the actual curve of my tits, and I'd shiver with satisfaction, a wave of lust spilling more wetness into my already soaking crotch.

As steadily and silently as I could, I reached my right hand behind me to feel his hardness. I felt, rather than heard, the gulp in his throat as he realised what I was doing, and he squeezed my tits harder, clinging to them as if otherwise I'd move away. And I looked down at him running his hands all over them, as I grabbed at his dick through his trousers.

His cock wasn't thick, but it was long, and so so hard. It twitched in my hand as I rubbed at it through his thin sports trousers. The fabric was slippery to touch, and I could feel a spreading wetness at the tip as he leaked excitement out through two layers of cotton. He'd grip me harder, using his first two fingers to trap my nipples in his grip. With every touch we'd both get wetter and I'd be willing him to come. I wanted to know what it felt like—to give a guy that feeling.

Eventually, with a sore arm, soaking wet knickers and a desperate need to feel Rob shoot spunk through his trousers, the film credits would start to roll. Everyone sat up straight, moved apart, and pretended we'd done nothing as Darren got up to change the video.

Then the whole process would start again.

I have Rob to thank for a lot of things, but mostly the tit-touching. Having proved to myself that no matter how thick my glasses or how depressingly lanky my hair, some boys would still allow me the pleasure of a mutual grope, I moved on to other boys, to see whether they'd do it too.

To my unending delight and gratitude, they did. Late at night in the park I'd join in games of spin the bottle, hoping whichever boy I landed in the spin would slip a hand up my top while we kissed. Guys at school would give me friendly hugs, and grab my tits in what I was often disappointed to realise was a joke. One boy, who I sat next to in maths classes, would run a vibrating pager over my school shirt, watching as my nipples got hard beneath it. He'd grin and get hard and then turn it on under the table, sliding it under my skirt and gently over the crotch of my knickers. I was amazed, delighted, and desperately horny to find that if I jokingly suggested to boys that they touch my tits or grab my crotch, they would.

Unfortunately, the only one who wouldn't was the one I wanted most of all.

My First Love was a boy I met in English class. A skinny, witty, Irish boy, who for some reason just didn't like me at all. I hated him at first too. His wit and his volume were too similar to mine, and I didn't appreciate the competition. I'd make a joke, then he'd make a louder one and win approval from our giggling classmates. So I'd make a joke at his expense, and get a louder laugh. He'd reciprocate, and escalate, and make me seethe with competitive rage from behind my exercise books. This war continued until he called a truce, and the passion and hatred of our frequent fights developed into a warm reciprocal friendship.

Instead of fighting, now we'd sit next to each other in classes, making quiet, secret jokes to each other. We'd spend hours on the phone at weekends, dissecting what had happened during the week. We'd open up a bit about our habits and lusts, and what our rampaging hormones made us want to do.

Not to each other, you understand—despite my desire for him I knew that he'd never be mine. He was slightly cooler than me—not popular, but cool. And with my high test scores and big glasses and ignorance of popular music, I most definitely wasn't. I settled for simply being friends, projecting an air of calm platonic happiness, while in secret I fell hopelessly in love with him.

'Can anyone tell me what the difference is between weight and mass?'

I daydreamed during science classes. It was one of the few lessons in which First Love would sit further away from me and I could watch him from my desk, as he laughed and wrote notes to the guy sat beside him, ignoring the teacher until just the moment when he'd be called upon to answer.

'Come on, anyone? Mass versus weight, anyone?'

It was during a science class that I realised I loved him. I was watching him writing notes, admiring his long, quick fingers, his thick forearms accentuated by a chunky watch.

I looked at his hands and was struck by a powerful image, of him pushing me roughly against the wall in an alleyway on the way to school, using both hands to push at my tits as I hiked up my school skirt.

I felt that deep, throbbing lust and I squirmed on my stool. I could feel myself getting wetter, as I kept my eyes on his hands and wished I could be alone to touch myself. That quick snapshot—the roughness of his grip and the force of him pushing me against the wall—was the first genuine fantasy I'd felt for a real person. I don't think I imagined us fucking at that point, I just pictured how desperate he'd be to come, how hard he'd rub himself against me, and how his hands would stray from my tits to grab my arse through my knickers and pull me forward against his dick.

I ran straight home from school that day, not speaking to him, or even to my friends. I waited until my sister was safely settled in the lounge, unlikely to return to our shared bedroom, and I wet my fingers, touched my clit and thought of him, him, him.

'You need to be careful,' said Dad. 'I know it might seem like a platonic relationship to you, but boys are different. It's hard for a boy to stay platonic. He'll be thinking of you in other ways, so you need to make sure that he knows how you feel.'

Listening to my dad telling me that First Love wanted to fuck me was almost as painful as hearing First Love tell me he didn't.

Both of us would protest if asked whether anything was going on. 'Oh no, we're just friends. It's not like that.' But I'd watch him during school, I'd speak to him whenever I could, I'd hang on his every word like each one was a magical secret, and I'd go to bed at night wishing he would touch me. 'Honestly, we're just mates. Nothing's going to happen.' But God I wanted it to. He was as interested in girls as I was in him, but for some reason I could never give him that feeling. We'd play-fight and we'd hug and sometimes we'd sit so close on the sofa that I was scared he'd hear the throbbing of my cunt, but he never touched me.

Other girls were more interesting to him. My friends. My girlfriends. Amy. He'd snog Amy with slobbering, desperate passion then turn to me, with a semi-hard dick, and let me know all about it. And I'd smile, and congratulate him, my potent, lucky best mate. Well done, man. Good on you. You got some. And then go home to sob silently into my pillow, and relive the times when—in my head—he'd fucked me.

Dad, again: 'It's not that boys are only after one thing. It's just that they're often thinking about this one thing. They want sex even if you don't, so you have to be careful not to lead them on.'

I sat through the lecture with gritted teeth and a determined smile. I smiled as hard as I could to stop myself from crying. My dad was telling me how inevitable it was that First Love would try to fuck me, and I was replaying in my head all the times he'd told me, 'No, I don't feel that way about you. Let's just be friends.'

My dad told me that as a woman, I'd be irresistible to anyone with a penis and a pulse. Men have erections and they need someone to fuck. And of course First Love had erections, and he wanted to fuck too. But no matter how fun I was, how young and horny and wet and eager I was, he still wouldn't fuck me. As I listened to my dad telling me to push First Love away if he made any advances, I remembered all of the ways in which this boy had rejected me, and I felt an actual physical pain in my chest.

'What I'm getting at here is that he'll be thinking these things about you all the time. I want you to be careful. It's not that I don't want you to be friends with him, I just don't want you to break his heart.'

And it broke my fucking heart.

After years of friendship and countless hours of longing, masturbating to the thought of him rubbing his erection against me, First Love eventually moved away. I still spoke to him every weekend—languid hours spent lying on my bed, one hand comfortably down my knickers, listening to him tell me about his new life, his new school, the girls who were much prettier than me who might or might not be interested. But I could at least forget him for a while during the week and focus on finding that lustful feeling elsewhere.

I made rather awkward friends with a gang of laid-back stoners. Although I wasn't keen on everyone in this new, scruffy group, it opened up plenty of new opportunities to have my tits touched. I still thought about First Love, and whenever I met a new boy I'd be looking for elements of his character that reflected Him—a quick wit, a dirty smile, lovely big hands or a penchant for chatting about wanking. And he remained the only real-life person who had ever featured in one of my fantasies. He'd left an impression on me that I realised would never go—the first person who'd got me hot and wet and then fucked off without giving me any release.

But my new friends were fun as well. We'd hang out in shy groups after school, arguing over the artistic merits of Kurt Cobain, smoking lopsided joints and feeling better than everyone else.

They introduced me to a lot of new things, some of which (like smoking and super-noodles) I'll never forgive them for. But they also helped me to lose my virginity.

'Ow... ow... ow... please sto—oh, you've stopped.'

I lost my virginity in a shed. That's right, I was classy. But I wasn't that different from others in the group. Without parents willing to host big parties, we spent most of our evenings swigging cheap cider in parks and frotting in darkened alleyways until the tension would build up and we'd find a place to fuck. Any place to fuck. Fussiness about these things was considered bad form. At the time you'd be seen as 'stuck up' if you insisted on a place that had walls, let alone an actual bed.

I met number one just before my sixteenth birthday. He was tiny—around five foot five—with soft skin and bright green eyes. He wore torn jeans and smoked roll-ups and spoke with a slight, shy stutter. Best of all, though, he was not fussy. He was horny and willing and desperate to have a girlfriend. He didn't just want to hang out on the outskirts of parties and kiss the girls who were drunk enough to fancy him; he wanted to be at the centre of it all, one of the couples. The couples didn't have the same rules as everyone else. They didn't have to get wasted at the beginning of the evening and then try to pick out the second drunkest person on which to try and experiment. The couples would just drink for pleasure, occasionally excusing themselves from the group to go and fuck in someone's parents' bedroom.

The first time we had sex was at his birthday party, the night before my own sixteenth. Friends milled around in his garden exchanging dares and competing to see who could be the most visibly drunk. Number one and I joined in for a while until my desire and his pressing erection made it difficult for us to sustain conversation. We slipped away from the party and into the shed.

It sounds drab, but really it wasn't that sort of shed. We weren't dodging spiders and secateurs. It was effectively a converted room—painted walls, carpeted floor, and enough cushions strewn around that eight or nine teenagers could sit in a huddled circle with a reasonable degree of comfort. I'd been in the shed with number one many times before. We'd go there with friends after school and he'd sit awkwardly behind me to hide his pressing erection. When they'd all drifted home for their dinner, we'd snog for endless hours, enjoying the distraction that meant we didn't have to talk. But this time when we entered it felt more purposeful. We weren't just going to snog, it was his birthday, after all. Something different, something better was going to happen.

We took the key.

I locked us in from the inside and settled down on a pile of cushions. He double- and triple-checked the door, then lay awkwardly on top of me. We could still hear the party going on outside.

As with all teenage sex, it began with some excessive and enthusiastic snogging—dripping tongues, heads moving frantically from side to side, jaws working against each other. We sank into the familiar rhythm of the kiss, and I pushed myself against him, parting my legs to rub myself on his dick. He frotted back, pushing urgently against me, running his hands up under my clothes. He pulled down my bra and slid his fingers over my aching nipples.

I unzipped his trousers and rubbed him incompetently. He pulled at my tights until they were halfway down my thighs, trapping my legs together uncomfortably, but affording him just about enough clearance to push his fingers into my cunt.

I sighed. I squirmed. I wished he knew how to do this with more purpose. Not just a fumble or a feel or a token gesture, but to actually fuck me with his hands. To make me come. It takes time to learn that there's more to first, second and third base than just ticking off a box on the way to a home run, and neither of us had quite realised this yet. Although the contents of someone else's pants is unrelentingly fascinating when you're that age—and, if I'm completely honest, it still is even now that I should be concentrating on more adult things like mortgage payments and regrouting the bathroom—the fun of touching them is far outweighed by the fun of rubbing the contents of your own pants against them. Eager though we both were, neither of us could be said to be giving a proper 'hand job'—at best we both pulled off a 'mediocre-rub-job' accompanied by a lot of belt-jangling and catching of zips.

I moaned with one part desire and at least four parts frustration, and he pulled away, reaching for a condom in the pocket of his jeans.

OK, I'm going to lose my virginity now.

This revelation was not particularly nerve-wracking, but it was a surprise. Despite my status as the least experienced person in my group of friends, few people I knew had actually had sex. It seemed unfair that I'd get to be the first one.

'Are you sure about this?'

He nodded and put the condom on, with an ease that showed he'd been practising with the free ones. After only a bit of fumbling with my tights, he slipped inside me, gasped, and I wasn't a virgin any more.

Apart from the thought that I was no longer a virgin, there were plenty of things to occupy my mind for the five or six seconds between penetration and ejaculation.

Am I bleeding?

Does it get better?

Has he ripped my tights?

What should I be doing?

I can't wait to tell First Love about this.

Treacherous thoughts. I tried not to think about him, about how I'd wanted it to be him who was doing this. It wasn't that I needed the moment to be special, but I was sure his hands would be steadier, his cock thicker, his arms even tighter around me. I held my legs as far apart as my tights would allow and tried to push thoughts of First Love right out of my head.

It hurt a bit, he grunted a bit, and then it was finished. I hadn't come but I had felt his cock nice and deep inside me, scratching an itch I hadn't realised I could scratch. He'd replaced my virginity with an interesting, different feeling. For the first time ever I felt full, satisfied.

He kissed me and pulled out, careful to hold the condom on tight to avoid telltale spillages. We awkwardly rearranged our clothes, smiled shy smiles and walked hand in hand back to the party. Despite first-time nerves, it had been a roaring success. We'd fucked without embarrassment, tears or noticeable staining on the carpet. No one's mum had burst in, no one's friends had shouted 'Oi! What are you two doing in there?' and above all neither of us had been too drunk to remember what happened.

He picked up a two litre plastic bottle of cheap cider and offered me the first swig. I took a gulp, passed it back to him and we joined in the chat. Whenever we'd catch each other's eye we'd smile conspiratorially, delighted that we'd thrown away our virginities together, astounded that we'd done so well, and aching to do it again.

OK, he wasn't First Love, but he'd do.

CHAPTER THREE

Apparently There Are Things You Can Do With A Boyfriend That Don't Involve Sex

Inevitably, number one and I set about having as much sex as was humanly possible in the often very short times we'd be together. I'd head straight to his house after school, and had a curfew of 9 p.m. This meant we had roughly five hours in which to consume as much as we could from the all-you-can-fuck buffet.

Naively, I'd assumed—based purely on a passing reference in that classic educational film *Grease*— that sex took around fifteen minutes. My assumptions around that were shattered in the five seconds it took number one to jizz away our virginities, so I modified my expectations and assumed that fifteen minutes was the average recovery time between quivering ejaculation and the next enthusiastic hard-on.

I was swiftly proven wrong.

'What are you doing?'

'I'm sucking you off.'

'But... we've only just had sex.'

'Yeah, about fifteen minutes ago. Now can we have sex again?'

'Umm... how about we watch telly for a bit?'

To paraphrase everyone's parents: I wasn't angry, just disappointed. Everything I'd ever read, seen and heard about sex, including the rather memorable chat from my dad, had promised me that men were constantly on the boil. Sure, they'd occasionally neglect their erections to leave the house and hunt for food or Xbox games, but realistically there was very little chance that a man would turn down sex with a woman he fancied. Some publications—notably *FHM*, which I devoured as if it were *The Idiot's Guide to Men* even went as far as to suggest that your chosen man didn't need to fancy you that much. Consequently, I believed guys just needed a spare half-hour and a structurally sound erection and, Bob's your undiscerning horny neighbour, a shag would be all mine.

Poor number one.

Not only did he have to cope with a girlfriend who was far more confident—and for 'confident' read 'loud, horny, and unafraid to mention it'—than him, he was also solely responsible for battling years of ingrained stereotypes about his gender.

Sometimes he had a headache. Sometimes he was tired. Sometimes it would get to 8 p.m. and he was simply empty of spunk, having managed to successfully live up to my expectations for a good four hours already. He'd shyly ask me if I wanted to watch TV or listen to some music. He'd offer me food, cigarettes, a refreshing walk in the sunshine, or if things were getting desperate he'd play his guitar, staring earnestly at me to try and tap into a romance that neither of us was old enough to be comfortable with. Occasionally, when all else had failed, and his attempts at distracting me simply led to comments about how I loved watching his hands as he strummed his guitar and could we have sex now pleasepleaseplease, he'd lead me into the kitchen and encourage me into protracted conversation with his parents just so that he had a chance to rest.

It's not that I'm insatiable, I've never been insatiable. Thanks to my superlative wanking skills, I'll happily go without sex for a while. And as an adult I'd happily see this situation for what it was—a slight mismatch in sex drives that could easily be solved by a bit of conversation and compromise from both parties. But I wasn't an adult, I was sixteen, and as such I was devastated. I was a sixteen-year-old girl who had been told that all men would want to fuck her, that they were only after that one thing, and it was I who'd have to feign headaches and manage expectations just to get a decent night's sleep.

Having been conditioned to believe this, it was humiliating to find that this man—*my* man, my *teenaged boy*—who should by all rights be an insatiable sex pest, was immune to the sexual temptation I threw at him.

I'd whisper filthy things, dress in cheap Ann Summers lingerie, strip naked for him and beg him to touch me. My attempts at seduction were as ham-fisted and incompetent as his undiplomatic rejections, but that just made things worse.

Late at night, after another failed attempt to tease an erection out of his exhausted cock, I'd lie next to him in his single bed, beneath a poster of Shirley Manson looking like teen-punk sex made flesh, and cry myself to sleep.

As an adult I know these lies for what they are—not all men want sex all the time, and not all women will punch the air in celebration if they receive a 'get out of sex free' card. People are just different, with different drives and needs and desires. I didn't understand that back then, but I wish I had. It would have saved me the misery and heartache of trying to work out why I wasn't sexy enough for my boyfriend, and it would have saved him the humiliation of having to explain to his sixteen-year-old lover why he couldn't maintain a fifth erection in one night.

It's important to challenge the assumption that 'men are only after one thing', because publicly recognising that it is definitely not true helps all of us feel a bit more normal. If young women grow up thinking that all men want to sleep with them, we're not giving them the gift of insight, we're telling them an outright lie. A lie that will lead to humiliating disappointment for our daughters, and—most importantly for my poor first boyfriend—give our sons a reputation that they could never possibly live up to.

But I shouldn't complain about number one. As I say, it was mostly the fault of the weird expectations I had about male libido that led to my sexual frustration. I don't mean to cast aspersions on his manhood—he was actually incredibly good. I am gobsmacked that we managed to have quite as much excellent sex as we did given that neither of us knew much beyond what we'd been told by teachers, parents and the aforementioned well-thumbed copies of *FHM*.

So although the sex wasn't quite as copious as I'd have liked, it was certainly decent, and I won't complain just because the poor guy hadn't yet managed to overcome the limitations of biology and started producing six gallons of jizz per day from a permanently erect penis. We'd still shag a lot—at his house, at my house, at parties. In sheds, behind bushes, in tents. We learnt enough about each other's body that we could frig each other to simple, gleeful orgasms during snatched moments—on buses, in his parent's kitchen and, of course, in the darkest corners of the local park. On one memorable occasion, we shagged in a treehouse, learning two lessons at once, namely that a) sex is much better when your friends aren't standing nearby shouting 'Timbeeeeer' and b) it's impossible to remain aroused when you're within three feet of a garden spider.

Our parents soon learned what we were up to, and were given ample opportunity to lecture us about condoms, carelessness and conception. The Talk came earlier for me than for him, and certainly far earlier than my mum would ever have expected:

'Can I stay round his house this Friday?'

'What, in his bed?'

'Yep.'

'Umm... we need to have a talk. I don't want you sleeping with him until you're completely ready.'

I thought it appropriate to cut the chat short early to save embarrassment. 'I already have.'

'You have? But... when?' For some reason as soon as they have children parents forget that sex can be had in places other than beds, and at times other than night time. I have not yet met a single teenager whose parents haven'tt insisted on placing restrictions on couples sleeping together. As if without the sleeping there can be no sex.

'Yesterday. And a few days before that. And every time I've been at his house for the last few weeks.'

'Oh. Well, are you using condoms?'

'Yep.'

'That's good.'

In hindsight, it might have been cruel to spring things on her so quickly. My sister, who was eighteen months older, had showed no signs of wanting to rampantly hump anyone, and I felt like I was jumping the queue.

I was clearly opening doors that my mum hadn't quite been ready for me to see behind, and I got the distinct impression that she felt like she'd let me down. Like she'd missed out on the chance to talk to me about sex before I actually did it. Still, after she'd shed a few tears for my lost innocence, and warned me to be careful, I hopped up and went to get ready for a night at number one's house.

'I'll be careful. We've got loads of condoms.'

'Well, that's good. But it's not just the pregnancy thing. It's the heartbreak thing.' She didn't hold me back, just let me breeze out of the room with a 'good point' hanging in the air, but she was right. No matter how many packets of Durex you have, the heartbreak thing can still get you.

Number one taught me a lot. Other than how to shag, and how to stop asking him for a shag when he was knackered, he taught me that I wasn't going to die alone. This was comforting, as I'd spent the previous year chasing plaintively after First Love and staring into the mirror wondering what, exactly, was so horribly wrong with me that my love was destined to be unrequited. I'd begun to wonder if perhaps the reason First Love wouldn't fuck me was because I was just fundamentally unfuckable. Glasses, bushy hair, puppy fat and a tendency to correct people's grammar did not really work to my advantage when trying to convince anyone I was a sex kitten. But although First Love remained resolute in his decision to Just Be Friends, number one seemed to like whatever limited charms I had to offer.

And, curiously, as soon as number one started liking me, other boys did too. It began gradually. Those boys who'd previously laughed at me started to simply ignore me, and those who'd ignored me gave the occasional 'hello'. It probably helped that, in my relentless quest to make number one have sex with me as often as was biologically possible, I'd taken to wearing clothes that showed off my obvious bits: out went the baggy shirts and jumpers, in came skintight, low-cut tops, and skirts in which I was—for very good reason—nervous to bend over. And it wasn't just the way I dressed. I started acting more like someone who was a possibility. The guys who'd previously written me off weren't stupid—they recognised that although I was uncool, I was nevertheless getting laid, which significantly increased the possibility that I'd be willing to lay *them*. They weren't all interested— some were still far too cool to consider me. But if you throw a stone into a crowd of seventeen-year-old boys you're bound to hit a good few virgins, at least three of whom will almost certainly have an undiscerning erection.

I wanted so much to talk about fucking. I wanted to talk about it to others who'd done it, and especially to those who hadn't. Don't get me wrong—I wasn't looking for sex tips. Given my age the best I'd have got from my peers would be untried-and-untested playground shite, things that grown adults have long since realised are either faintly amusing or complete turn-offs altogether.

'Try putting a condom on with your mouth.'

'Put whipped cream on his dick then lick it off.'

'Get him to suck on an extra strong mint then stick his tongue in your fanny.' (This last one, attempted by at least four of my close friends at the time, only ever resulted in either 'ow's, 'euggh's or 'meh's.)

I didn't want to talk to people to get their advice; I just wanted to hear them talk about fucking. I wanted to know how they felt about it—what they liked and didn't, what they'd tried and hadn't. I'd listen to my friends telling stories in voices that sounded much more confident than they were, and I'd imagine them getting hard, getting wet, frotting each other in exactly the way number one and I would. I'd store the tales up for later when I was sucking number one's cock. Who needs porn when you've a headful of teenage orgies and a nice, solid prick in your mouth?

I don't know if they thought the same about me. I'd like to think so. And I certainly told my fair share of stories. Even if the guys I was talking to weren't specifically interested in me, they were certainly interested in genuine, honest-to-goodness real-life accounts of sex. This was evidenced by erections they thought I wouldn't notice pushing visibly at the fabric of their jeans. Or t-shirts swiftly and casually draped so that they covered a guy's crotch. Alongside those I've mentioned already, there was one guy on whom they had an especially satisfying effect: First Love.

We were still speaking to each other on the phone. Once a week he'd call me, or I'd call him, and we'd spend hours lounging around chatting. We'd talk about anything that was happening in his life and, on account of our mutual interests, everything that was happening in my life that had anything to do with sex. I relayed tales of my latest fuck, my worries about number one's sex drive, my guilty lust for other boys who'd stare openly at my newly displayed tits. And I'd hear him at the other end of the phone getting–if not necessarily hard–interested.

'What's it like being on top?'

'It's fun, I guess. It depends on what he's doing.'

'What do you mean?'

'Well, if he's touching my tits, it's good. If he's looking a bit bored, not so much.'

'I think when I start having sex that'll be my favourite position. Do you keep your bra on?'

'Sometimes. Most of the time, actually. I like it like that. I prefer to be a bit less than naked. It's hotter.'

And so on.

'Has he ever fucked you with your knickers on? Has he ever come on your face? Has he fucked you in the... you know?'

And on. And on. He painted the most vivid pictures for me, of things I could be doing and had done. And I felt vaguely guilty because relaying the sex I'd had seemed ever so slightly hotter than actually doing it, because I was relaying it to him. Guiltily, I'd imagine not number one's hands firmly gripping my tits while I lowered myself onto his erection, but First Love's. With his thin wrists and quick fingers and the thick black watch on his right arm. Sometimes, when I tumbled onto (always 'onto', rarely ever into) bed with number one, I'd guide his hands to the places First Love had talked about, and imagined how he'd grin at me as he got undressed.

I would have given anything to know if First Love's cock was hard while we had those conversations. I'm not an idiot—I didn't expect him to hop on a train and come all the way back to me just for the promise of me writhing around on his dick. But I wanted him to understand that he and I could work together. Not just because we were friends who were capable of holding a conversation for more than ten minutes about something more significant than A-level coursework, but because we'd fit together so well when fucking. That he was the perfect guy for me because he wanted to fuck just like I did. As much as I did. As hard as I did.

While he was chasing girls in his new hometown, playing at being cool and interesting and—I cringe to say it—'boyfriend material', all he wanted he had already: a willing, horny girl. Although I'm sure there were any number of these girls in his new town, crucially they'd be unlikely to come out of the woodwork while he was chatting them up by offering bowling, cinema trips and the aforementioned 'coursework' discussion. To me he offered filth—dribbling, throbbing, knicker-moistening filth. The fact that he could only have these chats with me made me not only willing and horny, but—to him at least— unique.

I didn't quite have the words or the confidence to say it at the time, but what I was trying to tell him, and number one as well, is that I like sex. I want sex. Women want sex. You don't need to take us bowling to distract us from realising that you find us explosively attractive. OK you might not be best off starting a date by saying 'Hey, I've got a massive erection for you right now,' but you don't need to pretend to be a sexless Ken doll. Women like sex, and we want to know that you're horny. Most of us want to feel desired and lusted after and attractive. Ultimately, of course, if we fancy you then we want to fuck you: we're not just doing it as a favour in exchange for a cinema ticket.

I was initially too busy basking in my fucklust for number one and my miserable unrequited First Love to notice number two. He wasn't exactly a friend, just a guy I happened to have a couple of classes with. But apparently he'd been noticing me. One day he passed me a note that read:

'I'm so sorry I offended you. I didn't mean to take the piss. I actually think you're amazing and was wondering if you and your mate Jenny want to come to a house party with us on Friday?'

His ability to offend me combined with his nicely worded compliment had the desired effect. Not only did I want to go to the party, I wanted to sit on his cock and fuck him until he was dry.

I'll rewind a bit. Number two had exploded into my life by not just offending me but *enraging* me. It had happened a few days earlier, when I was waiting at a bus stop with number one. I was standing up and number one was sitting on the bin just beside me. He, I think, had one hand down my top, and I was seeing if I could brush one or other of my hands over the erection he was cultivating inside his baggy jeans. I was enjoying the moment partly because of the simple, public hotness of it, and partly because we were in an excellent position for snogging, with our mouths at identical heights.

Height had always been an issue for us, because number one was short, around five foot three or four inches, and I have always been a massive girl. I stand at five foot eleven in bare feet, which means that in high-heeled boots I rock a good six feet three inches.

This didn't cause any major issues between the two of us—after all, I was more than capable of retrieving things from high shelves without assistance, so it had never occurred to me that I should limit my potential boyfriends to those who could reach a couple of inches higher than I could. But for some reason as soon as I started dating a short guy, everyone wanted to point it out.

'You're tall,' they'd say.

'Why, yes, I am,' I'd reply.

'And he's... well... he's quite short.' Usually uttered with a quizzical expression.

'So he is.' Usually uttered with an angry 'when are you going to fuck off?' expression.

'Does it make it hard when you shag?' they'd ask.

'No. But it makes it hard to avoid spanking people like you who mention it,' I'd wish I'd answered.

The average height for guys in England is around five foot nine or ten. Using this information, even the young version of me was able to deduce that if I only fucked guys who were taller than I was I'd spend most of my life alone. I decided that this was not a scenario I was particularly happy with.

Even leaving the practicalities aside—I didn't fancy carrying a measuring stick around with me and wearing a t-shirt that said 'you must be at least this tall to ride'—there is genuinely nothing wrong with a male/female coupling in which the guy is shorter. The only reason we think it's weird is because cretins point out that society has expectations about height. It's a way to make people feel self-conscious about things they have no control over—playground bullying that grown-ups should have grown out of.

Number one stood just a bit higher than my shoulder, but I got used to it after about a week. From then on the only time I noticed it was when judgemental strangers would make snide comments. 'Don't you get a sore neck?' 'Isn't it hard to fuck up against a wall?' They're not really interested. They just want to discuss it and point out how ridiculous it is that we don't conform to the exact physical expectations that they'd have regarding gender and height. Ha fucking ha.

I later learned that it wasn't just height. People feel like it's their business to comment on almost any aspect of your taste. I've lost count of the number of times I've told someone how hot I find a particular guy only to hear them reply, 'What, him?! But he's so old/fat/short/bald/pale/scruffy.'

The only possible response to these people is 'fuck you.' Whoever you choose for a partner, there'll be some weapons-grade bastard looking sideways at you with raised eyebrows, wondering what on earth it is you see in each other. If you listen to them the only people you'll end up dating are the bastards themselves, while all the nice people look on from the sidelines, far too polite to ask why you're dating someone whose idea of 'compatibility' is based on a size ratio.

Number one taught me my first lesson in ignoring the hell out of these people, and a bloody valuable one it was too.

So, back to the bus stop and the bin. Number one and I were snogging in full view of an understandably disgusted band of students. My black lipstick was smeared halfway across his face, making it look like he had a big purple bruise, and every now and then someone would mutter 'Get a room,' demonstrating how thoroughly the majority of people miss the fact that the only reason people frot in public is because they rarely have a room to go to. But neither number one nor I gave the tiniest of shits. We were young, and happy, and so horny it hurt. My cunt would twitch and I could feel the pain deep inside me as I pulled him closer, willing the bus to come quickly so we could head to his house and retire to the room our fellow students were so keen that we should get.

And then the bus drew up at the stop, and we turned around to get on. Two boys I vaguely knew were sitting on the upper deck, pointing down at us and laughing. I caught the eye of one of them, recognising number two from the classes we had together at college. As he caught my eye he laughed even louder, gesturing through the window to hammer home the point—unless it hadn't been hurtfully obvious enough—that it was my boyfriend he was laughing at.

I gave him the finger, and then took the boy back home to fuck.

The next day I tackled him head-on. I didn't mind being laughed at, but I wanted to know exactly why this borderline stranger felt he could comment on—or point mockingly at—the boyfriend I was so proud of. I confronted him in the only way that seemed fitting to a dramatic prick like me: loudly, angrily, and where I knew everyone would see. I wanted number two to feel as humiliated and pissed off as I did. I wanted him to feel sorry. I wanted him to know exactly why I was angry, and how he'd made me feel. And, because he was quite attractive and I was never one to miss an opportunity, I wanted him to get a good look at my tits.

'What the FUCK did you think you were doing yesterday?'

'I... umm... I just thought it was funny.'

'What was funny?'

'Your boyfriend.'

'What about my boyfriend?'

'He's... umm... short?'

'True. But he's also a very good fuck.'

'...'

'If you ever do that again I will tear your face off.' I don't remember my exact words, but I'm sure they were at least as obnoxious as these, if not more so. I tossed my head like an arrogant shit, put my hands on my hips, puffed my chest out just to make utterly sure that he had a good opportunity to look at my boobs, then turned on my heel and walked away.

Clearly what I deserved was to be taken down a peg or two. No matter how right I was—and I was—to tell him off, number two wouldn't have been entirely to blame if he'd never spoken to or of me again, except for perhaps the occasional mention of 'that shouty goth girl'. But he didn't: instead he sent me that note:

'I'm so sorry I offended you. I didn't mean to take the piss. I actually think you're amazing and was wondering if you and your mate Jenny want to come to a house party with us on Friday?'

Of *course* I went to the party.

Almost everything about number two reminded me of First Love. He was intelligent, he was witty, he was funny, he was more than willing to take the piss out of me. But best of all, he was a virgin. A genuine, honest-to-God, never-even-fingered-a-girl virgin.

Number two was tall—he'd have to be—and blond. He had big shoulders and thick wrists and soft, fat fingers. I was fascinated by how different he was to number one: loud and brash and extrovert, while number one hid shyly behind me. His height and bulk was a welcome change from one's lithe nimbleness. It made me feel small and delicate in a way I hadn't experienced before. I was curious about how it would feel to have him lie on top of me, pinning me down with hands that were stronger than mine. He felt different, acted different, smelled different.

Where number one had grown used to my almost constant need to fuck, number two was practically shaking with a need for it. His wide, terrified eyes pleaded not 'I can't' but 'can I?' It was desire coupled with fear—the fear that if he actually tried to fuck me we wouldn't be friends any more. He'd play the short-term game and try to cop a feel only to find that me and my tits would walk away forever. I'd look at number two and will him to make a move, and he'd look at me and will me to let him.

It was a frustrating friendship. We'd joke, and play, write filthy notes during English lessons, and brush up against each other on the bus. When we hugged I quivered at the feeling of his hard-on digging into my hips. And yet all the time he was holding back because he thought I wouldn't want him. While I'd spent my childhood being told that men always want sex, he'd had the lesson from the other side: women didn't want sex, and that was that.

These lessons are still being taught, despite the material being dramatically out of date. I've lost count of the number of times I've shocked a guy by admitting what is not exactly a revolutionary truth: I like it when guys come in my mouth. I like anal. I like that thing boys do late at night when they nudge me with their erection as a means of testing whether I fancy a shag. That it takes time for a new message—women like sex too, dickheads!—to be disseminated isn't particularly surprising, what's surprising is that the message took hold in the first place. It doesn't do us much good as a species to maintain the belief that fifty per cent of the population doesn't enjoy something that the other fifty per cent is desperate for.

As far as number two was aware, there was some magical formula that consisted of flowers, fun and flattery and if you got those things in just the right quantities then a girl would reward you with a grudging fuck.

But he was wrong.

I wanted him so badly I utterly ached. His tentative touches would leave me trembling—hot and wet and desperate for him to do more. And it's so hard to say 'do more, *please* do more' when you're seventeen and insecure and only just getting to grips with the fact that you've got boobs, and puppy fat, and legs you're apparently supposed to shave at least once a sodding week from now on. As an adult I've got over this problem, and will happily open my mouth to utter a 'please, *please* fuck me' when the situation demands it. But when I was younger I was still nervous—of rejection, of being labelled a slut. So I waited, and I writhed, and I masturbated vigorously thinking about his touches and praying that he'd become a bit bolder.

We'd spent countless nights together already, having fallen onto adjoining portions of floor when house parties wound down. Ever aware of the potential for gossip, we'd touch each other up in the dark, breathing as quietly and as infrequently as possible to avoid waking those who were sleeping nearby. I'd lie next to him panting with longing, while he tentatively ran his fingers over my nipples. He never tired of the feel of them, the miracle of keeping me on a knife-edge of desire for so long. By the early hours, when we finally managed to sleep, my nipples would be red-raw and throbbing with pain.

Eventually I realised he wasn't going to make a proper move. Having never experienced sex, he was happy to stick to whatever we were doing—touching each other gently to facilitate future wanks—until one or other of us was driven completely insane. So I got a bit bolder myself.

One night, in a bed with a few others asleep beside us, he slipped his hand tentatively into my knickers. I was slick with frustrated desire, wet as only a teenage girl can get. He was trembling with fear and so hard I worried I'd hurt him if I squeezed his dick with any kind of vigour.

When his hand reached my cunt and he realised how wet I was he couldn't keep silent—he moaned.

Just remembering number two's surprised, lustful moan is one of my hottest memories.

After hearing his stifled cry, I couldn't leave without doing something. At that point I'd have traded my money, my youth, even my as-yet-unfinished A-levels just to have him inside me. I whispered to him and grabbed his hand. We left our friends sleeping and scurried into an empty bedroom, where we fell onto the bed—me in a panting, aching heap and he in a trembling, terrified one. I kissed him; I told him I wanted him. I fluttered my seventeen-year-old eyelashes and begged him to fuck me.

But he couldn't fuck me.

He was so scared that he couldn't get hard. I sucked him gently, I told him he was hot, I told him I was desperate for it, and eventually I got him just hard enough to roll on a condom and try. I climbed on top of him, slipped him into me, and sat down slowly on his semi-hard cock. But it was clear that it just wasn't happening.

He'd lost his virginity—just. But he'd mislaid a fair portion of his dignity, too, and it broke my heart to think that instead of remembering me with a gleeful nostalgia, he'd look back on the whole thing with shame. The idea of that made me desperately sad. And, OK, the idea of not actually getting to fuck him at all made me sadder. He believed sex was a gift I was bestowing on him, to have him open it only to find the sexual equivalent of novelty socks was more than I could bear.

A couple of weeks later, at his house, he was relaxed. Not calm, as such—his cock was straining at the fabric of his jeans—but he was much readier to fuck.

'What do I do?'

'Whatever you want.'

'Can I do this?'

'Yes. Please.'

'What if I'm crap?'

'You're not.'

He ran his fingers nervously over my body, touching wherever he thought he was allowed. I pulled up my top, unhooked my bra, guided him. I wanted to show him he wasn't just allowed, he was needed. I needed his touch, needed him inside me to quell the aching hurt in my cunt. He didn't need to make me come, he just needed to be in me, to give me some release.

He struggled to take off his jeans, his hands shaking with lust and frustration. I helped him get them off, wrapped my legs around him, and held myself up, nice and wide and easy so he could slide himself in.

With his hands each side of my head, he pushed his cock into me—deep and rock hard. I felt it stretch me out, open me up, scratch the itch that he'd created during those long nights of furtively stroking my nipples. The itch he'd created with that anguished desperate moan.

The sex itself was good, but the best thing was that as I sighed with satisfaction he finally understood that I wasn't exchanging sex with him for anything: sex itself was the goal. I wasn't fucking him because he wanted it, but because I needed it. I need sex like I need music and dancing and chocolate cake. And I was no more 'letting him' have sex with me than I'd 'let' someone give me a birthday present.

I grinned as he sped up, and thrust angrily against him so he could feel every movement. As he got closer he let out a strangled cry, and I squeezed my cunt and thighs extra tight around him as I felt him come hard inside me.

It was possibly the best five seconds of my entire fucking life.

CHAPTER FOUR

LIFE WOULD BE MUCH EASIER IF WE DIDN'T HAVE ANY OF THESE PESKY 'EMOTIONS' TO CONTEND WITH

It'd be a pretty short story, and a pretty boring life, if we all lived happily ever after at this point. So, not content with just fucking each other, number one, number two and I set about breaking each other's hearts.

It makes sense, of course. I'd learned how to fuck, and how to have a relationship, how to be polite to partners' parents and avoid answering too many questions from my own. It was only logical that the next lesson I should learn would be the one I couldn't do the research for: how relationships end and why makes you feel as if the whole world has crumbled around you. Or, as my mum rather succinctly put it: the heartbreak thing.

I sound callous when I talk about number one. First Love had hooked me with his beauty and his wit and the fun we had together, but number one's main attraction was his geographical convenience and willingness to actually get naked with me. To be honest, given his willingness to lie down and let me suck him off, I'd probably have fallen for him even if he'd had three heads and a drinking problem. But although he gave me fluttery feelings and brought me toast in bed on Saturday and called me 'pretty', he was clearly never going to hold my attention when other guys showed an interest.

At school I'd looked enviously at the girls who had boyfriends. Not just mates who they flirted with, but genuine boyfriends, who'd pass them notes in class and kiss them at breaktime and admit to their friends they were 'going out' with. I'd spent most of my childhood being one of the kids whose name was frequently a punchline, the one who boys would approach, say 'will you go out with my mate?' and then run away laughing when I naïvely accepted. Having not just one but two guys who wanted me felt unusual and fragile, as if someone was playing a long-winded trick on me that would end with them both running away shouting, 'Ha! She said yes! What a loser!' I was convinced that, having been unfuckable for so long, being fuckable couldn't possibly last for long enough that I'd be forced to choose between one and two. I held on to both of them because I assumed that soon I'd have neither.

What's more, beside these immature calculations, I genuinely loved number one—his soft, shy, easy-going nature and the way he looked at me with adoring and exhausted eyes. Even as I held number two and whispered filth into his ear and gripped his cock and rubbed myself against him, I knew I loved number one. He was special to me because he was the first, the one with whom I'd learned and played and experimented and practised. He expected nothing more of me than that I just keep doing that with him. And I couldn't bear to break his heart.

I began fucking number two in more risky places. Many of my friends knew that I was cheating on number one, but none of them were quite willing to tip him off.

They were either as scared as I was of breaking his heart, or scared of the bolshy goth persona that emptily threatened to break their legs.

So, in the absence of anyone to stop me, I kept going.

One Saturday afternoon, my friends and I met at Amy's house to hang out. And by 'hang out' I mean 'pool all of our money and get as drunk as possible'. Number one came along, with a group of friends from his college—the loud, swearing kids we'd all known for years.

None of our school friends would have dared suggest that we—one of the longest-term couples in the group—got a room, so I sat comfortably curled up with number one on a sofa, sharing a bottle of something that called itself cider and occasionally leaning in for a snog. I had one of my hands flat on his stomach, feeling the smooth, hard contours that were the result of nothing more than a few sit-ups and a hell of a lot of sex.

By this time Amy was on the arm of a nineteen-year-old who looked down upon us from the lofty height of his two-year advantage. He kept touching her and getting brushed off, Amy being less convinced about the joy of sex when it was about to happen in her parents' bedroom. Number one and I, unburdened by any Oedipal disgust about Amy's parents, traded coy smiles and whispered to each other, growing hotter and more desperate to retire to the bedroom with each mouthful of sour booze that we swallowed.

Then the doorbell rang, and my desire for number one dissolved completely. At the door was Jenny, who was now so fully immersed in number two's friendship group that she'd started seeing one of his friends. She brought her current boyfriend and—in a move that both delighted and terrified me —number two himself.

As an adult I've realised that mixing friendship groups is rarely a good idea. The people you know from school are more than likely to bring up embarrassing stories about your childhood in front of your work colleagues, your work colleagues will disappoint you by being hideously dull, and everyone will be left with the vague sense that you're not quite the person they thought you were and perhaps it's best to cross you off their Christmas card list. All that's stressful enough without the added tension of knowing that at any moment you might forget which one you're legitimately fucking and stick your hand down the wrong pair of trousers.

The same rule of not mixing groups applied equally to our college-aged friends, but Jenny and I didn't have the maturity to realise it until we introduced everyone. The two gangs didn't exactly hit it off, as awkward jokes about the kids from 'the thick college' were met with an excruciating silence, a couple of multisyllable words were deemed 'wanky', and it dawned on each group that they were essentially rival factions.

The main difference, of course, wasn't one of snobbery but just understanding. The group from the vocational college had what sounded like a bewildering array of potential career paths. Future football coaches, sound engineers and electricians were met with blank looks when they tried to engage with the academic types. Those from the posh college couldn't comprehend why anyone would want to actually earn money rather than sit in seminars being a smug arsehole, while the vocational kids didn't realise that there was a formula to life that some of us were rigidly and unimaginatively following:

'What are you doing after college?'

'Well... university.' The unspoken 'of course' hanging ominously in the air.

I was definitely in the 'smug academic' camp. As far as I was aware, university wasn't even a choice, it was just what you did after college. So during our brief discussion of the merits of tertiary education, number one gripped me tighter. He was decisively on the other side of the fence.

While I snoozed through lectures, he'd complete an apprenticeship in something useful, and get a job that entailed getting off his arse rather than sitting on it. But given that no amount of regular sex with him had prevented me from handing in my UCAS application, he knew that at some point our paths would have to diverge quite drastically. Every day that passed drew us one step closer to the time when I'd pack up my bags and fuck a hell of a long way off.

This tension wasn't in any way relieved by number two–loud, brash, funny and university-bound. Like me. He was clutching a half-bottle of whisky and teasing me for drinking piss. Laughing at my flushed cheeks and wandering hands and subtly letting me know how much he disapproved of number one.

'You two look comfy.'

'We are.'

'Hey man.' A sideways look at number one. 'That's an amazing pair of jeans you've got. Did you rip them yourself or did you buy them like that?'

'I...' I stutter when I'm nervous, he should have said. But he didn't. 'I... I d-did them myself.'

But by the time he'd finished the sentence number two had turned away, trying not to notice number one's hands firmly, possessively around my waist.

As he started to roll a cigarette I pushed number one to the side, and made my way to the designated smoking area–Amy's garage.

There was a door to the garage through the kitchen. To get there, I had to walk past everyone in the lounge, cigarette packet on display to show that I was just off for a smoke. I walked quickly, willing no one else to jump up and say, 'I'll join you,' or 'Grab me a lager while you're in there.' I didn't look once at number two, steadily rolling a cigarette on the coffee table.

I settled in the garage and sparked up. With one hand I steadied myself against the workbench and with the other I clutched my cigarette between trembling fingers. I breathed deeply, knowing he was on his way. I pictured him walking in the door and grabbing hold of me in exactly the same spot number one had, pulling me towards him by the waist, pressing his instant erection hard against the crotch of my jeans.

He came in. Shaking just as much as I was, he took the cigarette from my hand and put it in the ashtray.

He grabbed me just where I wanted him to, fitting his bigger hands in the curve just above my hips. As he pulled me towards him, I could feel his dick pressed up tight against me, hear his shallow breathing and feel the rapid beat of his heart.

'Can we?' he asked, fumbling to open the zip on my jeans. I nodded, but pressed a finger to my lips. We were both scared that someone would come in, but incapable of stopping ourselves.

There wasn't much room, just a narrow corridor between shelves of paint tins and the workbench where my cigarette was still burning in the ashtray. He turned me around, placed a firm hand on the back of my neck, and bent me over the workbench. I could hear that wonderful sound—the clink as he undid his belt buckle— and I slid my jeans down until I could just feel the waistband tight against the back of my thighs. I pulled my knickers down to meet them, presenting him with my backside and my slick, naked cunt.

As he pushed himself inside me there was another of those killer lustful moans. His legs started trembling and he held tighter on to my hips to keep his balance. I gripped the workbench and pushed back and up, filling myself with his dick.

With each thrust I held my breath, bit my lip to stop myself from gasping. I could smell the smoke and his aftershave and hear the workbench rattle with every stroke of the fuck. Everything was heightened by the worry that at any minute the door could open and we'd be exposed: my knickers round my thighs and his cock jutting out of the gap in his tight black boxers.

It didn't last long—longer than the five seconds that marked our initial success, but not quite long enough for me to come around his cock. With a stifled grunt, he pushed into me one final time, and I held back a sigh of lustful satisfaction as I felt him shooting spunk hard into me.

I straightened up and turned around to see his eyes shining with satisfaction. He picked up the dying embers of my cigarette and took a final drag, barely suppressing his filthy smile.

We hadn't been caught. We were safe.

For the rest of the afternoon I sat on the sofa with number one, crossing and uncrossing my legs, jiggling my knee when I felt the crotch of my jeans rest tight up against my clit. When number two caught my eye I had to stop myself from grinning. I could feel his spunk drying on the inside of my thighs, and number one's hand resting on the back of my neck. I loved them both, and I felt lucky. And I felt invincible.

Cheating on someone is like breaking a particularly arduous diet: knowing that what you're doing is bad makes it all the more delicious. The stronger your moral feeling against it, the sexier it is to be fucked by someone who isn't your boyfriend. Of course, it doesn't help to explain this to someone whose heart you've just broken. I'm far less likely to fuck other people when I'm in an open relationship, but for some reason when I've tried to explain this to boys I love they have failed to appreciate the irony.

Fucking boys who aren't my boyfriend is hot. It doesn't always have to be a risky fuck, where I'm holding my own hand over my mouth to try and avoid moaning and giving the game away. Sometimes all it takes is the knowledge that what I'm doing is wrong.

And it *is* wrong, I know that. I'm no more going to engage in an ethical debate with a heartbroken lover than I'm going to show him framed prints of my own infidelities. Everyone knows cheating is wrong, even those of us who have done it. I could tell you that I was young and inexperienced and desperate to be loved, and none of that—despite being true—would make anything that I did OK.

Cheating is bad: you've made a promise to someone that you're not keeping. You're breaking one of the very few promises that they genuinely care if you keep. You're lying, you're sneaking around, you're potentially humiliating them: you're sipping cider and watching your secret lover roll cigarettes while your boyfriend casually fondles your arse. It's mean and it's wrong, of course, but it's also searingly, painfully, moan-out-loud hot.

Not that I think that justifies it, of course. The hotness comes by way of explanation rather than excuse. For now, the conclusion of this episode comes in the form of some restorative justice: I got my comeuppance.

It wasn't nearly as dramatic as it should have been. Number one didn't burst into the garage while two and I were fucking, or find his underwear on my bedroom floor. There were no screams or recriminations, no public shouting matches and no dramatic fist fights. There was just a text message, a brief moment of panic, and then the end of my world.

I was in number one's bedroom with him, sharing a quick catch-up and the obligatory post-college blow job before we set off for dinner. It was his eighteenth birthday, and I was excited. His family were taking us both out for a posh meal and I was excited about giving him his present. I'd bought him a Zippo, which sounds like a crap gift until you remember that:

We were just kids, who back then were still labouring under the impression that smoking was anything other than idiotic.

He'd been gagging to have a Zippo for ages, seeing it as an adult gift that marked a commitment to smoking which he thought was cool (see above).

I'd had a romantic slogan engraved on the side, designed to mitigate a little of my guilt about number two and also—hopefully—let number one know that no matter how inadequate my love for him, it was at least genuine.

Guys doing Zippo tricks are hot. Watching him slap Zippos closed with a quick flip of his fingers drew attention to his hands and made me melt. I wanted to watch him do that more often.

I was sitting on his bed, jiggling my knee with a mixture of excitement about giving him his present and residual arousal because he'd just come in my mouth. He was getting dressed for the evening. Watching guys get dressed has always been one of my favourite things. It's like a striptease in reverse, and I can take my time and drink in every inch of his body, without the pressure of having to pretend that I'm not thinking about his dick.

He'd just pulled on a shirt when my phone went. Loudly.

There was a pause as I realised that he was closer to it than I was. It should have been in my bag, stowed safely so that he wouldn't be tempted to rifle through it to read texts. It struck me as odd that it wasn't where it should be, but dumped on the floor in a pile of clothes that he'd cast aside earlier. I sprang forward quickly, aware that I was in the danger zone. The possibility that the text was, in fact, from number two had my head swimming.

I dived for the phone, only realising as I picked it up that number one had dived with me.

Nowadays we'd no more read someone else's texts than we'd rifle through their knicker drawer, but back then no one had had a mobile for long enough to build up an etiquette around them. No one we knew had yet been caught cheating because of something as modern as an SMS, so grabbing someone's phone to read them their text was as natural as letting them copy your homework. So it didn't surprise me that he'd reached for the phone, but it did surprise me that he'd done so with such speed. I wondered if he could sense why I needed it. Or, more realistically, why I needed him not to see it.

'It's OK, it's mine,' I said, probably a little too defensively. 'Yours has that stupid ringtone.'

He didn't say anything, just stared at me. My sinking feeling grew stronger as I watched all the colour drain from his face. He wasn't jealous or suspicious, he was guilty.

The phone was his.

Not just something that belonged to him, but something that was so utterly and completely his I didn't even know about it. A different phone. A different number. A text from a girl called Carly, and what felt like the end of the universe.

He looked at me with terrified eyes, mouth slightly open and straining for words. He wanted to say something—anything to stop me from understanding what was going on. But I understood. This beautiful, adoring boy who I'd spent two years taking for granted had found someone who gave him exactly that filthy, kick-in-the-gut of lust that number two had given me. Someone who was missing him and loving him and making him feel all the things I couldn't. She—this someone, this other, this girl who had the temerity to not be me—was calling him 'sexy' and asking why he hadn't been round to see her at lunchtime.

The boy who'd make me buttered toast in the mornings, who'd share cider with me on the sofa, the boy who once painted a plastic rose purple then left it on my doorstep: this boy was gone. Someone else had a phone number that he'd never given me, and when she called it, he'd go.

As I lay on my bed that night screaming thick, deep lungfuls of despair into my pillow, there was no self-pity or sense of unfairness. There was pain, an aching pain that sent spasms through my chest and introduced me forcefully to the reason they call it 'heartbreak', but it was a pain that I knew I deserved.

It's all very well saying 'cheating is bad', and understanding in the abstract just how much potential pain you're causing your partner by fucking someone else.

It's easy to admit that I'm selfish and horny and incapable of hearing 'Do you want to have sex?' without dropping my knickers before the rising inflection, but any understanding of this prior to that day was entirely abstract. Being on the receiving end of someone else's infidelity hammers the point home with much greater force than any stern lecture I could have given myself before.

Number one was never going to be forever. The chances of us clinking glasses at our fiftieth wedding anniversary were vanishingly remote. I was always going to leave town for uni, putting him more than two hours away by train at a time when neither of us were rich enough to pay for a four-hour round trip each weekend. If you'd asked me a week before how I felt about number one, I'd have given you a long-winded explanation of why we were so different and how, despite being fun, it was never going to last.

But as I lay on my bed, hiccupping irregular sobs and generally acting like the emotional wreck that exists beneath the skin of almost every teenager, I imagined things had been far better than they were because I realised that I couldn't have any of that lovely stuff any more. I remembered the wild and passionate fucks rather than the routine or incompetent ones. I focused on the songs he'd practised for weeks just because he knew I liked to sing them while he played guitar. How he'd save roast potatoes from his Sunday lunch—my family were vegetarian and therefore incapable of achieving the superior flavour of potatoes made in the meat pan—and present them to me with a flourish later in the evening. I remembered a time when he'd drunkenly, and with as serious a face as he was capable of wearing, asked me to marry him.

Number one wasn't The One. He wasn't First Love or even one of my greatest loves. But he was the first person to utterly break my heart, and leave me in the tattered, twitching, zombie-like state of the newly depressed, and that's a pretty valuable thing to be.

At the time I hated him, and wanted to rip up everything he'd ever given me, every photo he'd ever taken of us, stoned and grinning and surrounded by friends. I wanted to stamp on the cheap jewellery he'd saved his meagre allowance to buy, and cut the strings on his stupid guitar so he couldn't play any of 'our' songs to 'her'. But now, as a grown-up who can barely remember exactly which songs were 'ours' and which ones just remind me of fumbling shed-based sex, I'm grateful. Because number one gave me a taste of misery and made me a bit more understanding. It's not as if I lacked empathy before my heart broke, but I certainly couldn't see, with such visceral clarity, exactly how hard my own actions could come back on other people. Empathy is important. It stops us rutting each other willy-nilly and killing our enemies on the street. It's the thin line between telling someone they're wrong and telling them they're a stupid and disgraceful waste of brain cells.

I stand by what I said before: cheating is hot, even if it's also immoral and cruel. The fact that crack is illegal, doesn't mean it makes you any less high. However, like most things that give you an adrenaline rush or slick knickers, there's a certain amount of risk involved. The hot, angry tears that wrecked me that night were shed in the knowledge that it could easily have been me who was found out. It could have been my phone, my text, and his shuddering sobs.

Number one's cheating didn't detract from the fact that, when I was huddled in the garage with two, the feeling was exciting and sexy and dangerous. But what it did show me was that the danger wasn't as simple as just 'getting caught'—a phrase that sounds giggling and insignificant. I'd imagined the naughtiness of 'getting into trouble' or the childish 'getting dumped'. I'd thought that number one would be a combination of angry and upset, but I hadn't pictured anything that came close to this level of despair.

So although cheating is hot, and the burning lust is, in some situations, worth taking a certain amount of risk for, the level of risk it stands up to is almost vanishingly small when you know exactly how much it hurts. If you're offered something from someone new, it's tempting to weigh it up against the surface-level consequences: your partner's tears, their rage or what they'll say if they burst in on you, writhing naked with your bit-on-the-side. But when you have to imagine what they'll actually *feel*: the wrenching, pulsing agony of betrayal? Suddenly the risk seems so much greater.

My mum declared him a bastard and wouldn't have him in the house. My stepdad, never usually one for dramatic emotional outbursts, told me he was a 'little shit' and that I deserved someone more faithful.

I didn't correct them, because I couldn't see any way of defending his honour without admitting the truth:

'Yeah, he's a dick but I'm not exactly Julie Andrews myself, Mum. Did I tell you about the time I fucked someone else while he was in the next room? Then later I fucked *him*, so I could feel two boys' spunk mix together inside me. Shall I put the kettle on?'

So I let them continue to slander a guy who barely deserved it and instead sought advice from people who knew me a bit better. My friends, knowing that I was at least seven shades of bastard myself, refrained from telling me what 'all men' were like and instead focused on advising me on how to go about taking my mind off him. Their unanimous conclusion was that I should go and get spectacularly laid, so that is exactly what I did.

Like most good things, sex is best had in abundance. This is my way of saying that numbers three, four and five happened at the same time.

It was summer, just a week before I was due to leave town for university. I'd like to say that one thing led to another but actually, having a three- or—in this case— foursome takes a lot of effort, determination, and some seriously liberated friends.

It started, as most groupfucks tend to, with a very small amount of flirting and suggestion in just the right places. Very rarely does one head out for the night expecting to end it shagging three of your friends into collective exhaustion. It starts, as everything does, with flirting.

I'd already told Kate that I fancied Andy. In fact, I'd fancied Andy even while numbers one and two had held the majority of my attention. He was tall, dark, and so ordinary-looking that it took a good few glances before you noticed the charms he did have: broad shoulders and huge hands, beautiful scruffy hair, which he didn't slick back with the expensive goo that most boys his age felt was compulsory. He wore his jeans hanging just a little way off his hips so you could see the angles of his hipbones, and he smiled like the virgins used to back when they were in the majority. Although not a virgin himself, he was clearly horny enough to do a passable impression of one—he used to hug me tightly so my boobs would squash satisfyingly against his chest.

Imaginative members of our group of friends called him 'spunk arm' because, during a drunken fumble with my friend Jenny a year earlier, he'd spunked up her arm. But he'd also shown that he wasn't particularly shy. While he was busy pumping teaspoons of jizz into the sleeve of her pyjamas, there'd been six other people in the room giggling at the rustling noises and the sound of his laboured breathing.

I had my eye on Andy.

Kate was different—a much closer friend who I'd got to know during countless nights spent spinning and giggling after necking plastic tumblers full of vodka and Coke. Our friendship was cemented one dramatic evening when I emptied at least three pints' worth of the sickly substance out of my stomach, through her window, and down the side of her otherwise pristine house. Kate was like me: loud, brash and confident, with a similar gothy look and penchant for squashing her tits into the nearest eager-looking guy. I told her that I fancied Andy and she confessed to a similar infatuation with Si.

It was short for Simon, but Simon was not a name that fitted this guy at all. Skinny, troublingly pale, Si looked like he'd been raised in a cupboard with no light, oxygen or fun. His dark hair and bright blue eyes would probably have served him well in the Twilight generation, but when I was a teenager that only drew odd stares in the street and the occasional ministrations of an equally pale gothic girl.

Kate was just one of those gothic girls.

Si's house was immaculate, a shrine to minimalism and money. No one we knew had white carpets or a glass coffee table, because most of our friends' parents recognised that there is a direct correlation between how much something costs and how likely it is that your children will destroy it.

So: shoes off, sober faces on, Si, Kate, Andy and I tiptoed into the lounge. Beers were placed carefully on coasters on the coffee table as he did a quick tour to establish that his parents were not only out but, having taken their overnight suitcase, likely to remain so until we'd cleaned up the remnants of our intimate party the next morning.

Formalities thus observed, we settled into the leather sofas and began to earnestly and conspicuously not talk about sex.

As adults, if a threesome is on the cards, I like to think that we'd be mature enough to be able to discuss it beforehand—not only to establish what people didn't like, but ideally to ascertain what they do. After all, if you've never spoken to someone about sex, you have very little idea what will send them into violent fits of ecstasy.

But sadly this kind of communication frequently stumps even the most liberal of adults. When trying to start a threesome, my adult self has been disappointed to find that the scenario hasn't changed much since I was a teenager:

Step 1: Someone mentions something slightly sexy, as a prelude to some discussion of sex in a general sense: 'You know that so-and-so and such-and-such are fucking? I'd never have thought it. She does have a lovely arse, though. I'm jealous.'

Step 2: Obligatory awkward silence.

Step 3: Eventually someone leaps on the comment and tries to expand the discussion to include more specific tales or boasts: 'I fucked her once. It was amazing.'

Step 4: Repeat Step 2.

Step 5: The bravest of you will endeavour to bring the sexy chat closer to home, by complimenting someone who is actually in the room: 'You know, Trina, you've got a lovely arse as well.'

Step 6: The complimentee accepts the compliment, and raises the game by introducing a practical element: 'Thanks. Would you like to give it a bit of a squeeze?'

Step 7: If you're lucky, others will join in with compliments and playful flirting. But here's the crucial bit: in order to make that gargantuan leap from flirting to fucking, one of you has to be brave enough to voice the make-or-break suggestion. 'Shall we move into the bedroom?' or 'How about you lick my nipples?' or 'Why don't you get your dick out and let me suck it?' have all worked for me in the past. But it takes a hell of a lot of courage to make those suggestions, so if you're the one that wants the threesome, that courage has to come from you.

With Andy, Kate and Si, it was inevitably my courage that won out. The general chatter had been about one of our friends who had recently come out. Kate moved neatly on to how hot it was watching two guys get off with each other, then told Si how hot he looked on that particular evening. Eventually I took the bull by the horns and asked Andy and Si to kiss.

They did not kiss.

Disappointing, but understandable: straight gentlemen are less inclined to kiss each other to turn me on than my girlfriends are to kiss me for similar reasons. It's possible, of course, that I've just met fewer bi-curious men than women. But, more realistically, I suspect the reason guys are nervous about tongue-fucking each other in front of me is because society still has a childish, disgusted squeamishness about gay guys. Lesbians are, of course, fine. Two pairs of tits rubbing together or a pair of ladies connected at the face is something to be pored over, admired, filmed in black and white and used to sell perfume. But hot, stubbly man kisses are far less common. This is a shame, because two guys kissing is beautiful. I'd like to see more of it—hurried goodbye snogs at airports, deep, lusty snogs in bars, and nervous, dribbly snogs at school discos. Sadly I suspect we're a few years off this yet, because although two women kissing might raise an eyebrow or an erection, two guys pulling each other with testosterone-fuelled enthusiasm still has people either apoplectic with bigoted rage or pursing their lips disapprovingly and whispering: 'Euggh. Bumming.'

But I digress. There are certainly far more important things for the gay rights movement to do than hear about my desire for more snogging. The upshot of society's hatred for the thing I find most beautiful is that in order to persuade the boys to kiss—unnatural, sick, dirty boylust—I had to first agree to have sex with Kate—hooray! Lesbians!

So I did.

Kate, sitting next to me on the sofa, smelt intriguingly and disturbingly feminine. She was so like me that I was surprised when her neck smelt different. We started with a kiss—a deep, long, slow kiss to give the boys time to shift position and get the best view. Si on the adjacent sofa, leaning forward to get as close as possible without spoiling the magic, and Andy on the armchair opposite, getting comfortable like he was in a particularly dirty cinema.

Kate sighed a little as I pulled off her top. I planted a series of kisses from her jawline right down her neck and across her collarbone, ending just where her bra started. It was ill fitting, with her tits spilling slightly over the edge, and, as I unhooked it, I remember feeling a shivery sense of dread, not because I didn't want to fuck her, but because I didn't know how. Although all guys are different, I at least knew the basic things I could do to make them happy, and to eventually make them come. But beautiful and full though they were, I had no idea what to do with Kate's tits whatsoever.

I needn't have worried. A bit of hesitant kissing showed me that I was at least on the right track, as her nipples stood out stiff and dark against her pale skin. I put one in my mouth, and pressed my face hard into her, enjoying the feeling of softness around my mouth. I slid off the sofa and onto the floor, kneeling in front of her to give me easier access to the parts I felt I should touch. I bit her gently, then continued my way down her body, kissing the underside of her breasts, then running my hands down her hips, and below, to lift the hem of her skirt.

It was summer—there were no tights to worry about, just a dark, lacy pair of knickers. I put my face between her legs and breathed in the smell of her—tangy, rich, less sweet than my own smell. I'm not sure why I was surprised, but I was. I'd expected that she and I would be almost identical, and was taken aback by the differences between us: her skin was softer, her tits were larger and squashed much more easily beneath my fingers. I was so desperate to find similarities that when I put my face in her cunt and made the first tentative licks, I expected to feel a corresponding surge of pleasure on my own clit.

The boys looked on with growing delight as we messed around. I don't want to say 'fucked'; it was far less competent than that. I licked at her while she ran her fingers through my hair, sighing either with pleasure or— more likely—frustration that I was doing things so horribly wrong.

After a while, I figured we should get our end of the bargain, and see what the boys could do. I stood up and walked over to Andy, almost frozen to his chair in disbelief. I sat down on his lap, and kissed him, rubbing my salty, Kate-flavoured tongue up against his own.

I could feel how hard he was through his jeans, and I squirmed up against him. Part of me still wanted to watch him kiss Si, to see the two of them nervously lapping at each other like I'd lapped at Kate. But things had gone past that point. As Andy pushed my knickers aside and slid his fingers inside me, Kate and Si were fumbling with a condom on the other sofa. I lay my head on Andy's shoulder and turned towards the other couple so that we could both watch them as he fingered me. Si's trousers were now halfway down his legs as he thrust eagerly at Kate, his twitching dick lubed with a mixture of my saliva and her tangy, rich-smelling come.

Andy led me to their sofa and bent me over, so my face was close to Kate's tits. Understanding, I started licking her, feeling her jiggle against me as she was fucked. Andy pulled my jeans down and rolled a condom onto his cock, with practised speed and an urgent need to get inside me.

He fucked me hard from behind, with a power that felt deliciously angry. He was bigger than both number one and number two, and I felt aching thuds deep inside me as he forced his dick all the way in. I backed eagerly onto him, rocking down to meet him with each thrust, then forward again to push my face into Kate.

Si was nearly done. I could hear him in my ear, making louder noises than any of the boys I'd fucked before, a higher-pitched moaning to complement Andy's occasional guttural grunts. The noise made me hurt with lust, wishing I could time each spike of pleasure with one or other of the cries from the boys.

Si sped up, edging closer to orgasm, causing Kate to pant faster in time with him. He grabbed the back of my head, pushing me forward to meet Kate's mouth, and I felt his hand twitch as our tongues met. He came while I was kissing her, letting out one final moan and shudder that caused Andy to speed up in response. Seeing the three of us sandwiched together gave him that final kick. He gave one last hard thrust and uttered a deep, satisfying 'ungh', as I felt his dick twitch inside me.

Later that evening we moved to—as was traditional—Si's parents bedroom, where the whole thing happened again. A few different combinations in quick succession: Si fucking me, me sucking Si while Kate played with me and Andy looked on. Andy fucking me as I lay on top of Kate, Si alternating between us by lazily dipping his cock into each mouth in turn.

We didn't get the boys to kiss in the end, so it wasn't as perfect as it could have been, but as far as Saturday nights in go, it certainly beat nursing a broken heart.

CHAPTER FIVE

How Do You Solve A Problem Like A Guy Who's Not That Bothered About Fucking You?

What turns you on? There can be few questions with such a range of varied and interesting answers. Beautiful hands, a good sense of humour, trousers that hang perfectly off chiselled, narrow hips—just a tiny scratch on the surface of what my own answer would be.

There are some things I like that are pretty common. Who, for example, would turn down a guy so witty that his off-the-cuff jokes have you doubled over with laughter? Pretty much everyone wants a good sense of humour, and it's rare that you'll hear someone saying, 'Nah, I want my partner to be quite boring, actually. Rambling stories with no punchlines and anecdotes about traffic jams, that sort of thing.'

At the opposite end of the spectrum there are those whose turn-ons are so heartbreakingly rare that they struggle to find anyone who might even vaguely resemble their 'ideal' partner. Foot fetishists, furries, and friggers of all tastes wander mournfully through the loneliest corridors of the internet, hoping they'll eventually run into someone who is turned on by the same weird and wonderful things.

Wherever you sit on this spectrum—and I'm lucky enough to straddle a fairly large section of it, being horny enough that anything with even the vaguest whiff of semen will probably have me clicking curiously on a banner ad— it's unlikely that any specific turn-on of yours will press identical buttons for everyone else.

I like boys who are skinny-ish, wiry but not muscular— imagine a slightly malnourished ageing skateboarder. If someone's really muscular it says to me not 'I go to the gym' but 'I will expect you to go to the gym', and the tiny part of my brain that is responsible for rational future planning anticipates that I might not want to hop on that particular treadmill, so it shuts down my sexual interest. But the part of my brain that's still a sixteen-year-old goth lusts after the eyeliner-wearing skinny emo boys, and anticipates long, stoned afternoons followed by lazy fucking to a pop-punk soundtrack. So while other girls are getting melty over muscled men in the gym, I'm drooling over the boys who wouldn't be seen dead in one.

This is as it should be. Becoming muscular takes a hell of a lot of work, so why would anyone bother to do that if it didn't appeal to people who were their type? Muscular people are more likely to hit it off with other gym-bunnies simply because their rippling fitness is a visible demonstration of just what they have in common. The guys with biceps and triceps and six-packs aren't missing out on much by not attracting my attention. The closest I ever get to a gym is when I take a brisk hike swiftly past it in the direction of the nearest pub.

What I'm perhaps tortuously getting at is this: almost nothing is a universal turn-on. What makes me go 'mmm' might make you go 'euggh', and vice versa.

But is there anything that's *nearly* universal? Any one quality that, if everyone had it, would make us all instantly a bit more attractive to potential partners? Something we could all do to make ourselves just a bit sexier? After all, if it could be scientifically proven that blondes actually did have more fun, I'd be reaching for the bleach before you could say, 'Hang on a second, won't it look weird with your massive black eyebrows?'

Number six taught me exactly what that universal thing might be—not by having it, but by lacking it. Number six taught me the importance of enthusiasm.

The first term of university was eye opening only in that I had never believed that an experience could so wholeheartedly live up to every preconceived notion I had about it. From the moment I arrived in my student room—single bed: check, grimy sink in the corner: check, shared with a friendly, chain-smoking northerner: check—to the day I headed home for Christmas—exhausted from all the drinking: check, having failed to produce anything resembling academic thought: check, carrying a bagful of suspiciously stained laundry: check—I lived every single cliché I'd heard about.

During the first term of university I didn't so much get in with the wrong crowd as fail to get in with a crowd at all. The friends I made were a mishmash of people from my course, some I'd met in halls, and others who just happened to wander by at a point where I was sober enough to chat without instantly vomiting.

I'd been drinking with some of these almost-friends from approximately 11 a.m. until about 4 p.m., at which point I wobbled home to grab a well-earned nap before the evening. Or, as my flatmates and I called it, 'basically the morning'.

Having set the scene so far, I'm sure you'll understand me when I describe Rena as the least responsible person in our flat. Don't get well acquainted, she doesn't play a huge part in this story. She breezed into my life with a headful of house music and a bagful of energy, then dropped out of university some time into the second term. In the few months between arriving and leaving she set about taking All the Drugs in the City, setting fire to at least two things in her bedroom and maintaining a series of round-the-clock Loud Sex Marathons with her worryingly malnourished boyfriend.

The night I met number six had been masterminded by Rena. The plan was as follows:

Head to pub.

Drink everything we can find.

Head to club.

Repeat step 2.

The plan was going well—by around midnight we were bouncing happily away in a cheap nightclub that played a bizarre mix of terrifying angry metal and hilarious eighties cheese. The friendly staff dished out lurid cocktails, which hadn't been shaken or stirred so much as 'fished out of a large dustbin'.

I was sampling one of these cocktails, waiting for Rena to finish vomiting up her share, when I spotted a boy on the dance floor. He was hot—baggy jeans draped nicely over his hips, wide shoulders pushing out a tight-ish t-shirt. His head was completely shaved, but he had a goatee that served the twin purpose of giving his face a bit of shape and making me think that he was far older than he actually was. But most fascinating of all, he was alone. Weirdly, unusually, attention-grabbingly alone.

I watched him for a while, intrigued. I couldn't quite grasp the concept of dancing when you weren't doing it with someone, but he ploughed on regardless, bouncing through the room, flailing at the right places, bobbing his head at others. I got a bit breathless from the sheer confidence of it. This man, this hot man, this man that I desperately wanted to lick, this man was *dancing on his own*.

The next few hours get a bit blurry, but I can tell you that I was far too shy to actually approach this guy, so Rena staggered over and introduced us both. There was dancing, more dancing, a vague attempt to sober up, then finally a walk back to our student halls accompanied by some relatively awkward conversation. As soon as we were back, Rena bopped gaily around the kitchen before stumbling into her bedroom with a slurry 'havalovlyevening' and number six and I were left alone.

He was even hotter in the strip-lights of the kitchen than he was in the club. He leant against the fridge-freezer, broad-shouldered and nonchalant, almost challenging me to make a proper move.

So I moved.

He kissed slowly, with the casual confidence of someone who wouldn't be rushed. He put one arm around my waist, resting his palm on the small of my back to pull me in closer, but he kept the other hand in his pocket.

It had been more than a month since my night of victory with Kate, Andy and Si—a month which felt, if not exactly lonely, at least like it was missing something. Wanking was all well and good, but I was aching to have something to wrap my thighs around, to squeeze, to fill me up.

Consequently, I was overjoyed to discover that number six was huge, almost freakishly so. As I dragged him out of the kitchen and into the hallway, I ran my hand down the front of his jeans and let out a muffled 'oh' of surprise.

This was a cock that had weight and heft. A dick that was intimidating. If I could barely get my hand round it, what the hell would it do to my cunt?

The answer, disappointingly, was 'not much'. I dragged my mattress out into the hallway, anticipating sex so loud and dirty that it would wake my sleeping roommate, and number six and I got down to it.

Scratch that—*I* got down to it. I took off my shirt and bra, lay down on the mattress, and pulled him close to me. I kissed him, I squeezed him tight so my tits flattened out against his chest, I wrapped my legs around him and pulled him up against me, so I could feel his big, solid dick pushing against my crotch. I stroked him, I grabbed him, I shoved both my hands down the back of his boxers so I could squeeze his arse and pull him even tighter up against me. I moaned when I felt his dick press against my clit. I wriggled to get him in just the right position. I sighed, I writhed, I all but ripped off the rest of our clothes in a bid to induce some kind of passion.

But the man remained cold. He was hard, of course, and he gave the impression that he'd quite like to put his dick in me. But the key words here are 'quite like'—it was something he could take or leave, like a biscuit to accompany a cup of tea. He was horny enough to fuck me, but far too cool to show that he wanted to. I got the clear impression that he was doing me a favour, like letting me copy his homework. He was hot, of course, so perhaps he thought that giving me the gift of his massive prick was something for which I should either fork out some money or build him a shrine. Given that all I wanted to do was hump him tipsily in a corridor, I can see why he might have been a bit disappointed.

But for the sake of my fragile ego, he didn't have to make it so bloody obvious. Although it's always nice to fuck someone who wouldn't look out of place in a fashion shoot, I'd prefer to go with someone who is actually enjoying it. You can have a face like a plate of minced beef and still be an excellent shag, as long as you have the right attitude. Put your back into it, sure, but more importantly, put your fucking *heart* into it.

A few perfunctory squeezes of my tits later, he was sliding on a condom, his face set in a stoic expression that said, 'OK, if I really must,' and when he finally lay down and slid into me, I swear I actually heard him sigh. Not, as I'm sure you've gathered, a sexy sigh. It was a sigh that says 'mine's a hard life' and 'let's get this over with' and 'whatever you like, darling'. I hadn't experienced such crushing reluctance since number one submitting, for the fourth time in one evening, to my relentlessly amateur blow jobs.

He came, I think. After a few minutes of his slowly rhythmic humping, my overenthusiastic moans and wriggles, and a disappointing lack of his-mouth-to-my-tits contact, he came. Or maybe he didn't. I was so nonplussed with the whole situation that I'm not convinced I cared by that point.

I lay awake for an hour afterwards, wishing he'd gone home and trying to shake the gruesome feeling that I'd just been pity-fucked.

Enthusiasm: it's not just hot, it's vital. It might not be enough to guarantee a first-class shag, but it'll certainly help you pass the boundary of 'mediocre' and into 'that was fun maybe we should try it again the other way up' territory.

It's surprising how often people fall into the trap of trying to hide their enthusiasm. You don't want to look desperate, of course, but there's a hell of a lot you can do with enthusiasm before you look wretched. For instance:

'Oh God, I want to fuck you so hard.'—Enthusiastic.

'Pleeeeeeeeease?'—Desperate.

'See how hard my cock is? Put it in your mouth.'—Enthusiastic.

'Come on, it *is* my birthday.'—Desperate.

Number six, if I'd had to place him somewhere on the spectrum between 'desperate' and 'running for the hills', would hover somewhere near 'I'll fuck you if I have to but I'd rather read a book'.

Clearly what I should have done is stopped having sex with him. In my experience, the thing most likely to make someone want to fuck you is to stop trying to fuck them. Suddenly, what was a toy they were relatively bored of playing with becomes an invaluable prize that they must win at all costs. As an adult I am more discerning about these things, and am able to stop mid-fuck if it's turning into something more akin to a game of Scrabble than a night of wild abandon. But I was young, naïive and insanely horny, so I fucked him anyway.

Lesson duly learned.

Number seven was beautiful—wiry and pale, with catlike eyes and jet-black hair. He was tall and slim, full of nervous energy. He had a habit of picking everything up, playing with it in his hands, then putting it back down again, as if he wanted to touch everything in the room. Lighters, glasses, boxes of matches, beer mats—he'd reach for it, turn it over and over in his hands, then put it down and pick up another. Most of the time he wasn't even aware he was doing it.

His energy was exciting. The first time I met him he was working behind a bar, and I was fascinated by the speed at which he'd serve people. He'd whip a bottle out of the fridge, click the cap off and slam it on the bar with a flourish in one smooth movement. I took to drinking Smirnoff Ice just for the pleasure of watching him do it—one, two, three, whip, click, slam.

He had a dangerous smile to go with his catlike eyes—lopsided and sarcastic. He'd grin at me as he placed my bottle on the bar, cocking that smile at me, and I melted. Everything about him told me that he was new, different and exciting. This was a man who would never have a headache, never sigh in resignation, never refuse a blow job. Above all, this was a man who would never *ever* meet my mother.

'You drinking after work?'

'Sure. Want to stay while I lock up?' He could have asked if I'd like to crawl across broken glass to get his dick in my mouth. Yes. Yes, I did want to stay. And I wanted him to give me the fuck that his smile was promising: an aggressive, passionate, angry shag.

I didn't know him for long, a few weeks at best. After our initial meeting we fell into a late-night routine—meeting late, drinking together, then dragging each other into alleyways and grabbing crotches as we made our way back to his house, and nights of rough, hectic sex that left me sore. He liked me best from behind, where he could grip my hips and shove himself in with force, pulling me back onto his dick with quick, hard strokes.

But not all nights were that fun. On some nights he'd drink. When I got pissed I got obnoxious and horny. I'd announce in a too-loud voice that I wanted to sit on him, then I'd paw at his arse and kiss his neck and squeeze his dick on the night bus home. He, on the other hand, got angry. He'd punch trees and bus stops until his fists were bloody and shout non-sequiturs at inanimate objects.

'What the FUCK. What the fucking FUCK. Prick. PRICK.'

I'd never heard the menace in swearwords before, and I was worried for him.

Number seven was an angry guy—not angry with me, but angry at the world. He'd be mad with rage and self-pity and vodka, and the only thing that would calm him was for me to hold him as he rocked back and forth on the floor, in a ball of sobbing self-hate.

One night he got a bit too drunk. He lashed out at people on the way home, spitting spite and fury— 'What the FUCK are you looking at?'—and I'd had to work extra hard to cool him down. We got home and by the time I'd helped him sober up I was exhausted. Too much time spent placating this wild, angry boy meant I just wanted to go to bed. To sleep. I fell exhausted under the covers while he stayed awake to smoke a joint. I lay alone, feeling warm and comfortable, and waiting for him to return, spent and calm if not actually happy. He'd apologise, for the seven hundredth time, and tell me, for the seven thousandth time, that vodka did bad things.

He crept into the bedroom and took off his clothes. Swaying slightly, he stood next to the bed in his underwear and I could see the thick outline of his dick against the tight grey fabric. Sleepily, lazily, I smiled. He was still beautiful, despite his red-rimmed eyes and blank frown. Still hard, still passionate, and still someone capable of making my stomach tense with lust. He slipped off his pants, climbed into bed beside me and grabbed a handful of my arse.

'I want to fuck you now.'

I wriggled against him as he said it, and sighed sleepily. I liked that he wanted me, and just that feeling of being wanted woke me up. His enthusiasm had me wet despite my exhaustion.

'Why are you wearing your knickers?'

'I'm tired.'

He bit my neck. His dick pressed against one of my thighs. I rolled over to face him and could see the need in his eyes. He ran his hand up my body and roughly grabbed at one of my tits. He gripped my nipple between his fingers and squeezed—hard.

'You're not that tired. Your nipples are solid like ice.' He played with me some more, pinching at me, squeezing me, and eventually pushing harder into me, to try and shove away my reluctance. He rolled on top of me and I almost opened my legs, imagining his moan of satisfaction. It was tempting to hear that moan, to feel him shudder with relief as he slid into me. I just couldn't quite bring myself to hear it now.

'I want to fuck you too. But I'm so tired. We can fuck tomorrow.' I was hovering between lust and sleep, but the ache in my limbs and slight spinning in my still-drunk head told me that sex wasn't a good idea. I put my hands on his hips and pushed him gently away. He raised himself by the elbows, so his face loomed high above mine. He wasn't smiling, but his eyes were a window onto his pure desire.

'No. I want to fuck you now.'

And at that I decided that I definitely didn't want to fuck him. His tone had changed from growlingly seductive to the whining of a petulant child. The drawn-out 'nooow' made me feel like a mean, spiteful playmate who was taking his toys away. It would have been easy enough for me to say yes, but I didn't. So I told him no. I said 'tomorrow'. I said 'I'm tired' and I said 'but you're hot' and I said 'I'll be more fun tomorrow', and I sighed with happiness that he was calm and hot and he wanted me, and I told him I needed to sleep, and I just couldn't have sex right now.

And then he punched me in the face.

Not a full-on punch, there was no meaty sound as his fist connected. It was more of a lazy thump, the kind you'd give to a stereo that was skipping or a TV with a slightly fuzzy picture. I was broken, I wasn't working, and he was just giving me a thump to change the channel. I don't remember the pain, I just remember the shock, and the fear, and the thin trickle of blood that dripped from my nose to the bedsheets as I flipped over, closed my eyes and let him fuck me.

I almost didn't include this story in the book. I could have told you other stories about number seven: how he'd let me beat him at games of pool because he liked seeing me jump up and down in delight, how he'd talk to me for hours about his different types of weed then wrap them in cling-film, with adorable precision, before he put them away. How we drifted apart after a few weeks of sex and I haven't seen him since.

But I didn't. I wanted to tell this story because there's a moral in it somewhere. Seven was sorry after what happened, of course he was. He apologised briefly in the morning, cringing with a crippling sense of guilt, and I stroked his hair, and neither of us mentioned it again.

There's enthusiastic sex, there's desperate sex, then there's something so far removed from either of these things that it stops being sex altogether. His initial enthusiasm had spilled over into something darker and much worse: weakness, ineptitude, callousness. A cold, selfish cruelty.

I've told people this story since then and they've asked if it means anything, if it's significant. Did what happened with number seven put me off control? Put me off the dominance and power that I'd been eagerly frigging myself to before?

No. Because what seven did was neither powerful nor controlling, it was weak and inept. From the pirates of my tentative teenage wanks to the men you'll meet later in this book, a guy who is genuinely in control makes me catch my breath. It's sexy. A robust statement that I'm his, and he can do what he likes with me.

If seven had been powerful he could have had me eating out of the palm of his hand. He'd have rolled over and gone to sleep, secure in the knowledge that I'd want him all the more tomorrow. He could have planned how to tease me the next morning, mocking me for denying him a fuck then making me spend the next hour begging him for release. If he really wanted something that night, he could have held me as I tried and failed to drift off to sleep. As evidenced by my previous behaviour, I'll usually decide about five minutes into a good cuddle-from-behind that I quite fancy a shag.

That wasn't what number seven did. He wasn't powerful or controlling, he was weak and cruel. It had no effect on my dreams of pirates and perverts. Power is hot, and will always be hot. But you don't get to *take* that power, I give it to you.

CHAPTER SIX

You Rarely Hear About How The Star Cross'd Lovers Fucked Loudly In The Toilets

Let's rewind a few months. Because by the point at which I met numbers six and seven I was already in love. Not the childlike 'I'm in such awe that you're willing to be with me' love that I'd felt for number one, or the naive, unrequited lust-from-a-distance that I felt for First Love. This was true love—Romeo and Juliet stuff. Comparing thee to a summer's day stuff. Holding a stereo above your head in the street outside their bedroom window and sobbing loudly into the night stuff.

True love.

I met him at the very first lecture on the very first day of university. Groups of philosophy students gathered in the corridor outside the theatre, competing to see who could throw in the most casual mention of the most obscure philosopher that they'd read about somewhere. I missed out on the one-upmanship not because I lacked the arrogance, but because I lacked the knowledge. I was only vaguely aware of what the first lecture would be about, and desperately hoping that no one would clock the dark circles under my eyes and faint whiff of vodka Red Bull on my breath.

I was unenthusiastic about studying, far more excited about what Being A Student entailed—carrying books to and from the library, having debates in seminars, joining ridiculous drinking societies and eating cold baked beans straight from the can while my flatmates had a row about the washing up. But the main reason I was excited was because of the opportunity to meet men. Clever, well-spoken men. Men who knew who Nietzsche was—and who could, hopefully, tell me—who could talk more than I could and beat me in a debate. Guys who'd tell hilarious, witty, highbrow jokes that I didn't understand, then explain them to me so I could tell them to someone else and pretend to be more intelligent than I was.

Shamelessly, I wanted to find lots of student versions of the boys I liked before: I wanted First Love's filthy friendship, number two's intelligence and wit, and, crucially, number one's willingness to fuck me. There were surely any number of boys around the university who'd tick these boxes, and I wanted to be the one to collect them all.

I was still smarting from number one. He'd loved me desperately, and I'd loved him. We'd shared everything for two years, got on well, fell in love and fucked like dynamite yet still everything went to shit. I was disgusted at how easily I'd managed to take something so comfortable and break it. Love was bloody great while I was building it and making it and writing wanky teenaged poetry about it, but I was horrified to find that I was able to discard it so easily. Of course the breakage wasn't solely my fault, number one had rolled his sleeves up and given it a good couple of cracks himself. But this didn't make me feel any better: my treatment of him was bad enough that him seeking comfort from a girl who wouldn't ignore his opinions or laugh at his earnest guitar serenading seemed almost inevitable. What's more, because we'd both been unfaithful the whole thing ended with a depressing inevitability, a sort of 'fuck that then' that was clearly far less dramatic than the relationship deserved. It made our time together feel insignificant, and I suspect both of us would have felt happier if we'd at least smashed a few plates or had a passionate post-break-up spitefuck.

There was no denying it: sex had been brilliant, but love hadn't quite made my world go round in the way that I'd expected. It was definitely something to be avoided, at least until I'd managed to get my high hopes in check.

So I picked my way nervously into the first lecture of the academic year, caring less about the course material than about who might be in the room. I didn't doubt that there'd be some witty, intelligent boys in polo-necks who I could drunkenly throw myself at. I'd heard they were ten-a-penny at university. I just needed to decide in which order I would fuck them and how best to detach myself from them when they inevitably fell deeply in love with me and insisted on dragging me into a relationship that I was far too cool and carefree to tie myself to.

Talking to any of the boys directly was not an option, of course. Their searing intelligence and knowledge of who or what Wittgenstein was meant that I couldn't approach them in case they realised that I knew nothing at all, and had probably got into university via some administrative fluke. Any approach I made would have to be facilitated by alcohol, meaning that although I'd be at my most pissed and obnoxious, hopefully they'd be drunk enough to give me their phone number rather than test my academic knowledge.

I entered the theatre and sat next to a girl—a tall, horsy-looking type who was more than happy to engage me in traditional first-year chit-chat. I remember thinking that we got on quite well. She wasn't the most exciting of people, but she hadn't terrified me with mentions of obscure philosophers, nor had she told me to sod off. I was halfway through a daydream in which we became the best of friends, when He walked in.

Number eight.

Tall, skinny, almost gothically pale, with carefully messy dark hair and big brown Disneyesque eyes. He hovered at the entrance, scanning the hall to try and choose a seat. His nervousness implied a charming modesty that didn't fit with the indisputable fact that he was hotter than the fucking sun. A vision. His slightly scruffy look echoed the outfit worn by one of the many men of my dreams, but he had a slightly effeminate quality and a charming clumsiness that I hadn't had the imagination to be dreaming about.

For what seemed like a thousand years, he deliberated over where to sit. As he looked up and down the room I saw him in profile from both sides. I looked him up and down, noting the long dark coat hanging perfectly from his slim shoulders and the frayed jeans beneath. I saw us walking to lectures together, laughing in the pub, sitting in silence in the library. In the moment it took him to choose a seat I'd imagined how I'd introduce him to my parents. I saw the first sordid fuck I hoped we'd have, a semi-clothed desperate coupling on the stairs outside the lecture theatre.

Horsy girl was still speaking, and I nodded and smiled at what I think were the right places, but by this point my mind was elsewhere—I was watching number eight, willing him to get closer, and willing him to choose the empty seat right next to me.

He was making his way down the row of seats that I was sitting on, tripping over a few students as he picked his way towards me. I decided that if he spoke to me it was a sign. This man, this beautiful man, this vision: this was the man I would marry.

'Sorry, do you mind if I sit here?'

I don't even remember the girl's name.

Why are we expected to place friendship over love? Don't get me wrong, friendship is awesome. Having people who are willing to stand by you through thick and thin, stop you making mistakes, and hold your hair back while you're vomiting up the mistakes you *have* made is utterly crucial.

I'd no more tell my friends to fuck off than I'd cut off one of my arms, but all the same, no friend will ever take precedence over a lover. Why do we ever expect them to?

Say what you like: 'friends come first', 'men come and go but your friends will be there forever' or even—if you're an unforgivable cunt—'bros before hos'. But ultimately if you fall in love with someone the chances of you sacking them off because one of your mates doesn't think they're good enough for you are low indeed.

It's not your fault. No matter how much you love your friends your body is hard wired to seek out certain things: food, shelter, comfort, and sweaty wriggling with someone who makes you hurt with joy. People do the oddest things in the name of love: they give up dream jobs, ditch families, move halfway across the world. You rarely see people leaping over barriers at airports to prevent loved ones leaving these days, but that's not because we're lacking in passion, we're just more cautious about terrorists. Love is still one of the greatest motivators, and makes us act like what we are: one of the stupidest breeds of monkey.

No one should feel bad for putting love, or even sex, above friendship—I certainly don't. Don't beat yourself up about the times you've blown off trips to the pub with your mates in favour of staying at home cementing your shiny new relationship with lots of delicious getting-to-know-you shagging. As the saying goes: your friends will be there no matter what. You might only have one chance to grab the guy or girl of your dreams, and if it all goes pear-shaped your friends will be there to pick up the pieces, pass you the tissues, and repeatedly call you a dickhead until you feel much better about the whole thing.

This is all by way of explaining that when I met number eight everything else fell away. I'd made some tentative friendships during Freshers' Week, by getting lots of rounds in and pretending to be interested in other people's degree subjects. But most of these friendships faded into the background as soon as he appeared. My roommate and I were still close, on account of the fact that we shared a room so we'd bloody well better be. Rena—for the first two terms at least—was still an excellent person to get into trouble with every now and then. But when number eight was with me, all my friends became neatly irrelevant.

Pub trips, club nights, lunches in the Union—these things were only interesting to me if they included him. If he wasn't there I'd make polite small talk, craning my neck to look over other people's shoulders to see if he was about to walk into the room. In lectures I'd seek him out and in seminars I'd disagree with him. Not always because I thought he was wrong, although I frequently did, but because I just loved hearing him debate me. I'd steer my flatmates towards the clubs that he'd be at and invite him to anything that could even vaguely be described as a social event. It's lucky he was on a philosophy course and not something more hands-on—if he was a chemist or an engineer I'd have followed him into the lab in a mooning, lovesick daze and ended up setting fire to half the university.

But this would be a pretty shit love story if everything ended there—me lusting helplessly after a boy I couldn't have, and wanking myself into a froth every evening while imagining him taking me roughly up against a bookcase in the Ethics section of the library.

Long story short: he liked me too. I say 'liked' rather than 'loved', because it took him a while to decide he actually loved me. He's long been forgiven for that. If everyone were as decisive—no, not impulsive, *decisive*—as I am then we'd never get any interesting emotional build up. Love stories would last for three pages:

Page one: Girl meets boy

Page two: Girl sucks boy's dick

Page three: Girl meets a new boy, and the whole charade begins again.

But number eight *liked* me.

He liked me enough to seek me out and sit next to me on the first day. By week two he liked me enough to meet me before each lecture, and invite me for drinks afterwards. We started sharing ideas before seminars, notes during classes, and giggles together in the back row. Eventually we graduated to sharing stories, jokes and hugs that lasted ever-so-slightly too long.

There's nothing quite like the thrill of realising that someone important likes you. Unrequited love has its advantages. The object of your slavish devotion can remain pristine on their pedestal, never having the chance to sully themselves by utterly disappointing you. But it doesn't come within a thousand miles of the real deal—someone who, knowing you've put them up there, invites you onto the pedestal to join them. And then snogs you. And then continues to balance precariously with you on the pedestal while you examine each other suspiciously for flaws before realising that neither of you can see them.

I don't want you to picture a cheesy cinematic montage, in which eight and I gradually learn more about each other and squeal with delight each time we discover a new nugget of commonality. We just spent time hanging out, pretending we were cool, making mistakes that showed how we were actually idiots, then delightedly realising that the other person liked us even more for our idiocy.

Case in point: one afternoon in the students' union, we sat with a group of friends discussing the article we'd been assigned to read for our latest seminar. In between bites of lunch we took it in turns to compete over how much of the actual text we'd absorbed, and how many of the words we understood. Eight, who had that magical combination of intelligence combined with a willingness to actually read the relevant course material, turned to me and said:

'So. What do you think of the method he puts forward to explain the difference between qualitative and quantitative identity?'

To which I suavely replied, 'ARGH, fuck,' and then dribbled too-hot lasagne down my chin.

He laughed, and his eyes lit up: he was the bumbling fool who'd found someone even more bumbling and foolish to join forces with.

On a different occasion, walking to a lecture, I noticed his shoelaces were undone.

'Your shoes are undone,' I opined, wittily.

'It's fine,' he replied. 'These ones always come undone. It won't be a...' I think you can guess what happened next. I reached out to catch him as he tripped over his laces and hurtled into a doorframe, spilling books and papers and dignity on his way down.

Eight and I weren't love's young dream, but we were a matched pair of losers. Trying desperately to live up to the aloof images we tried to project to win friends, we were both amazed to learn that the one person we each wanted to be friends with was interested in even the shitty parts. We didn't so much grow together as stick together, like complementary pieces of awkwardly cut Velcro.

In the evenings we'd get drunk then collapse beside each other, not quite touching. He had a girlfriend at a university in another city who he was determined to make a show of being faithful to. Consequently the very first touches I remember were tentative. He'd brush my arm, or I'd lean on his shoulder. We'd lie next to each other, barely breathing, just waiting for the other one to reach out and give the first shivering touch.

In public we were friends, but in private we were driving each other insane. Sleeping fell to the bottom of my priority list. The nights I spent with number eight were the only time we could really be close, and I'd lie awake feeling him next to me, going slowly mad himself.

Our flirting got less playful and more desperate. My vague attempts at seduction—'How about a fuck?'—were rejected with awkward laughs or trembling sighs. While his—Oh, God. His occasional drunken declarations of lust gave me pangs of longing that squeezed my chest and made me hurt for him.

'You know, when you were wearing those tight trousers I looked at your arse and wanted to *bite* it.'

'I saw your knickers when you bent over in the pub. I want to put my fucking *face* in them.'

'You can't wear that top tonight. I'll fuck you. I'll *have to fuck you.*'

So I wore the top, and I wore the tight trousers, and I drank and danced and flirted and hoped until eventually, one day, he fucked me.

He was almost fully clothed; I was in a dressing gown. We'd touched and sighed and failed to sleep for two nights in a row. Delirious with exhaustion and lust, I rolled a condom onto him, wrapped my legs around his waist, and just looked at him with pleading eyes. He stared stoically at the wall and bit his lip as he thrust at me, willing himself not to come too soon. The waves of orgasm gave way neatly to waves of guilt as we lay next to each other and knew that this was not the last time we'd lose control.

Despite telling ourselves on a thrice-daily basis that we wouldn't fuck again, we did. Whenever we could be alone we'd make a show of sleeping separately, or keeping our trousers on, or even pretending that, despite it being three o'clock in the morning, one or other of us would leave soon, putting distance between us to ensure we'd stay chaste.

But eventually it became clear to both of us—and anyone at university who'd had the misfortune to share our bedrooms—that we wouldn't. Persuasion turned to pleading turned to mutual obsession, as we'd fuck and touch when we hoped no one was looking. Sometimes they were looking, but I don't think we really cared.

His friends played gigs in crappy dive pubs in my hometown, and one weekend we made the six-hour round trip to see them hammer out some songs. They performed punk-pop covers as we drank lager and Smirnoff Ice and groped each other in the crowd. When the songs were over we made out on a sofa that smelt like roll-up fags and sour sick, and we watched the door of the gents to check when they were empty.

When the coast was clear he rushed in, with me sauntering casually behind him as if punky girls pissing in the gents is completely normal—which, to be fair, it is. I followed him in and we locked the door, pulling at each other's clothes and kissing the way that kids do, all tongues and spit and desperation.

I pulled his trousers down to his ankles and he sat on the lowered seat of the toilet. He gripped his cock and grinned as I hiked up my skirt, pulled my knickers to one side, and sat down hard onto him. My boots were slipping on the wet floor, so I held on to the walls of the cubicle to get purchase. He put his hand over my mouth to keep me quiet as I fucked him—quick, hard strokes, squeezing my cunt tight to make him gasp, jerking sharply up and down so he could watch my tits jiggle in a tight, punky corset top.

He shuddered as he came inside me, and I squeezed tighter to better feel his dick pumping the last few squirts nice and deep.

As we left one of my friends came in to use the loo. Noting my filthy grin he gave a cheeky salute.

Number eight closed the door behind him and followed me out, shouting after him: 'I wouldn't use that one, mate—the seat's broken.'

In the car on the way back to university, I placed my hand firmly on his crotch and kept him hard for the whole three-hour drive. Although he wasn't my boyfriend, that trip made me feel as if, one day, he might be.

Occasional mentions of his girlfriend still hovered in the air to remind me that, despite the crushing weight of our mutual affection, I was still just a fuck. I'd never seen her and barely knew anything about her. He wouldn't show me pictures or talk to me about her or give me any hint as to whether their relationship—adoring though it was—had any semblance of the passion that had the two of us driving each other cross-eyed with lust. But during that trip he opened up a little, and gave me a taste of how we'd be if she weren't around. He might not be my boyfriend, but he'd introduced me to his friends—his friends who knew her—and he hadn't been nervous or scared. Even when they'd greeted us with raised eyebrows and innuendo, he'd shrugged and laughed and kissed me.

All I wanted was for him to do that every single day for the rest of my life.

I was well into my twenties before I heard the term 'Madonna/Whore complex'. Back then I'd have said that there were certain boys who were just bastards: those who wanted the filthy sex with some girls, but wouldn't do anything more than make love to the women they were betting their future on. I've been surprised at the number of guys I meet in real life who think like this: you can fuck a dirty girl any which way, but a wife is someone who must remain 'unspoiled'.

There were their girlfriends, there were lovers, there were wives, and then somewhere in the seediest corners of their life lurked the dirty girls: the ones who'd fuck you in toilets and take it up the arse. I was, still am, and always will be the latter. But there's no earthly reason why I can't also be the former.

It's rarely as transparent as that, of course. Few men would ever say, 'I couldn't possibly go out with you after all those times I've jizzed in the crack of your ass.' Or 'I'm going to marry Julie, because she's more wholesome. She'd be in the kitchen baking while you're bent over the counter getting spanked with a wooden spoon.' But there's a pattern, and it was number eight who introduced me to it.

As he gradually opened up, and introduced me to his friends, I found out more about his girlfriend. She was pretty, fun, polite, and not like me at all. If I made a crap joke he'd call me a dick and playfully punch me on the arm. If she made a crap joke he'd laugh politely to show he was listening. She was a nice girl with whom he had missionary-style, roses-on-Valentine's-Day sex. With me he had 'drink all the vodka then fuck me in the arse' sex. Not that I'm criticising his style—I *like* the 'drink all the vodka then fuck me in the arse' sex—I just couldn't see why he couldn't combine the two, and get himself a girlfriend—me, please please me—who'd be equally delighted by both roses and filth.

But at no point did he say to me, 'Hey, you know all that amazing sex we've been having? Why don't we make that an official thing and do it every day for as long as is humanly possible until we inevitably get utterly sick of the sight of each other?' He'd umm, and err, and equivocate about whether we should actually be 'girlfriend and boyfriend', then late at night he'd act exactly as I'd want any boyfriend to act: by rubbing his prick up against me, pinching my nipples, and growling that I was a dirty girl.

Hence the Madonna/whore thing. The Madonnas were the good girls: the ones who passed their exams and were polite to your parents and would make excellent wives and caring mothers. The whores? Girls like me who drank and smoked and partied, and fucked and fucked and fucked. The girls who took it rough and hard, and moaned with pleasure throughout. The girls who sucked your dick with sloppy enthusiasm and a finger up your arse. The girls who'd touch your cock in public and beg you to fuck them and swallow your come.

I'm not blaming him for how he felt at the time, and I won't be screaming in the faces of any other men who have this complex. They're wrong, and they're possibly a little unimaginative, but can we really blame them for thinking like this? After all, when was the last time you saw a proper, full-on love story that managed to combine filthy sex with romantic, Romeo-and-Juliet-style love without implying that either of the protagonists was in some way fucked up?

Have you ever seen a movie in which the hero fucks a girl from behind then marries her at the end? Rarely. If a guy fucks a girl doggy style, she's a slut. The shagging's a dramatic ruse to show his character is tortured and horny early on in the film. If he fucks her up against a wall she might be a slightly deeper character but is still ultimately expendable. She'll be killed, dumped or betrayed shortly after the camera's panned away. But missionary? Ah, this girl's The One. The One our hero will end up with, the love of his life. The one whose name will be top of the credits list, and who'll parade with him up the red carpet at the premiere. She's our Madonna.

Real life, of course, isn't anything remotely like that, and the idea that women can be divided into these two camps is laughable. There are around three and a half billion women on the planet, to imagine that they're one or the other is as idiotic as saying that men can't iron and women can't read maps. Men can't 'spot' a certain type of woman any more than women can decide to *be* one. We don't ponder, as we reach sexual maturity, whether we'll be either virtuous or slutty, good or bad. We make decisions as life goes along that in this particular moment we'll be coy, in that moment charming, in the next we'll whip our knickers off and hump someone silly. And these decisions no more make us a certain 'type' of woman than our decision to wear a tiara to a fancy dress party makes us an actual princess.

More importantly, some of us make the decision that we don't want a husband who can't cope with our desire. Female desire is so much more than a need for occasional cunnilingus and languid, insipid missionary-style sex. Some of us want husbands who treat us like fucktoys— whose eyes cloud over with desire when they see us lounging on the sofa in an old t-shirt. Some of us want husbands who are willing to watch us fuck other men, directing the scene from the corner of the room and masturbating frantically while we get nailed. Some of us want husbands with whom we can watch gangbang porn and wank lazily on the sofa. Some of us don't want husbands at all.

Eventually and inevitably, after hundreds of nights of hot, angry fucking, I called number eight on this bullshit. It's just shy of midnight on a street somewhere near my student halls. He's wobbling and drunk, as am I. He's got that look—the one I need to bite my lip to resist—his face is dark and his hands are trembling and I know that the blood's flowing quickly to his dick. He asks the next question with the confidence of a man expecting a 'yes':

'Will there be a quiet place for me to fuck you when we get back to yours?'

'No.'

'What about the kitchen?'

'No, not "no, there's nowhere". No, we can't fuck.'

'Why?'

'Because I'm sick of this.'

'What?'

'This.'

'Of fucking me?'

'Of being fucked over.'

He nodded. He knew most of what I meant. I'd moaned and I'd whined and I'd shouted and I'd sobbed into countless glasses of wine in front of him before. He knew what I meant. I wasn't sick of the fucking, but of all the things that happened in between fucks. When he'd talk about his girlfriend, when he'd refuse to bring me to breakfast in his student halls, when he'd hide me from people he wasn't ready for me to know. When, on the rare occasions he did introduce me, he'd called me his 'err... friend'.

'So, you don't want to hang out with me unless you can be my girlfriend?'

'Sort of. But it's more than that.' Deep breath, count to ten. You're an idiot. You're about to throw away the hottest thing that's ever breezed nonchalantly into your life. 'I don't mind not being your girlfriend, but I won't be the up-the-arse girl.'

'So we can have normal sex?'

'No. We can't have *any* sex. Because what I want is to have filthy sex with you. I want to fuck in toilets and corridors. I want to fuck with the lights on. I want to make you come just with my fingers. I want to watch disgusting, degrading porn with you and then have you recreate it all over my fucking face. But I also love you, and want to do the "going out" and "meeting each other's friends" stuff. And you won't let me do all of these things at once.'

'So you just want to stop?'

'I can't stop tearing myself to shreds over you. But I *can* stop fucking you. So I have to do that.'

'What if we just fucked a few times more?'

'What if you just have a wank?'

'OK. Do you want to watch?'

'Do you understand what I'm saying?'

He paused, and we kept walking. He knew what I meant but didn't want to admit it, because by accepting it he was resigning himself to making a choice that he'd been dodging since the first day we met.

'You're saying you like it when I fuck you in the arse, but you don't just want to be the "up the arse" girl?'

'Yes.'

'And you don't want to be the "sucks me off in the kitchen" girl tonight?'

I looked at him. He was grinning and his eyebrows were raised to show that he was half joking. Expecting a no, hoping for a yes.

'No.'

A nod. A sigh. Not acceptance, but an admission that I'd won this round.

'How about the "touches my dick a bit in the street right now" girl?' Definitely hoping for a yes.

'No.'

'OK. I'm sorry. OK.'

A week later he broke up with his girlfriend.

CHAPTER SEVEN

WHY DO ALL THE RORSCHACH INK BLOTS LOOK LIKE SEXY PIRATES WITH ERECTIONS?

Fetish is a weird word. When you say 'fetish' most people think of bondage, spanking, chains and submission—tall, angry women in big black leather boots stomping on someone's balls for money. Or timid, *Fifty Shades* nymphettes being brutalised by rich old men.

But fetish doesn't always have to be terrifying, and it certainly doesn't have to kick off with £200 corsets and trips to seedy nightclubs. Like many couples, number eight and I began with a bit of playful spanking.

Thwack.

'Count 'em.'

'I... Really?'

Thwack.

It wasn't a paddle or a belt, or the whip of my pirate-themed teenage wanks, just his bare hand on my naked arse. I was bent over a chair in his living room, skirt hitched up around my waist, shirt open and bra pulled down so my tits jiggled every time he struck me.

'Really. Count 'em.'

Thwack.

'Three.'

'No, one.'

Thwack.

'Two.'

'No, one.'

Thwack.

'One.'

'Good girl.'

I did not like counting. I gripped the legs of the chair until my knuckles went white, desperate for a fuck but gritting my teeth and biting my tongue to avoid talking back. I wanted him to spank me, wanted to feel his hand slapping hard—satisfying, loud strokes across both of my cheeks. But I did not—*not*—want to count them.

Thwack.

'Two.'

Something about this spanking-and-counting thing was funny. Not hilarious, or even giggle-in-the-back-row funny, but odd. Number eight, having heard about my desire to be used and abused, had thrown himself head first into the role of a teacher/mentor/sexy pirate, and yet for some reason I was wary of doing all the things he asked. I liked most of the things he commanded me to do when he put on his faux-angry face: 'suck my cock', 'get down on your knees', 'bend over, hold this in your cunt, and wait right here until I get back', but actually counting the number of times he spanked me just felt a bit too much. Too obvious. Too trite. Like I wasn't doing it because it was hot but because that was just how people did spanking.

So why did I feel so horny? Why was it that bending over the back of a chair shouting 'onetwothreefourfivesix' should make my cunt slick, and my nipples ache with a need to be touched?

Thwack.

'Three.'

We'd read a lot of porn together. Erotic stories, blogs, forums; if the back of a cereal packet had had descriptions of sexual beatings we'd have pored over it together while we frigged ourselves off. The stories were hot, the spanking was hot. The pain, dominance and power were all hot. And we'd live the scenes we'd read about in the ways we'd seen them described. With frequent slaps, slick knickers, and, inevitably, counting.

Thwack.

'Ow! Four.'

There was no getting around it, it wasn't just the counting: I didn't like the *pain* either. I liked being spanked—the nakedness and the vulnerability both ticked boxes that made my gut wrench. But the actual pain? Not so much. Being an imaginative pair of perverts, we'd played not just with the traditional items—belts, whips, canes—but some less traditional ones too—wooden spoons, books, laptop charger cables. If it looked like it'd make a satisfying slapping sound when brought swiftly into contact with someone's arse, chances are I'd been hit with it. And although I relished the moment when number eight's eyes would alight on something new with which to hit me, I couldn't help recoiling from the stinging slap itself.

Thwack.

'No, seriously, ow. Five.'

'Can you take one more?'

But despite my dislike of counting, and the fact that most of our spankings were punctuated with cries of 'ouch, dickhead, stop it now', something drew us both back. When he kissed me, touched me, or grabbed me with any degree of fervour, all I wanted was to bend over the nearest solid bit of furniture so he could beat me into shuddering sobs. It was miserably painful, but I didn't want it to stop.

A pause. A kind word. A quick rub with his hands to feel the glowing warmth of my backside.

'One more?'

'Oh, go on then.'

Thwack.

There's a wide, deep, stormy ocean of difference between something that's sexy and something that's hot. *Hot* hot. It's the difference between something that makes you go 'ooh', and something that makes you go 'unnngh'.

If a guy grabs me around the waist and pulls me towards him gently, there'll be a tingling sensation in my limbs, something that says, 'Hey, this is interesting. Pay attention.' That's an 'ooh' moment, and it's sexy as hell. But if that same guy puts the same hands firmly around my waist and spins me around before pulling me towards him, pushing his swollen cock firmly up against my arse so I can feel it rubbing against me? That's 'unnngh'. I feel a kick, deep in my stomach, as my whole body responds. I have no control over it. I don't need to pay attention, it happens automatically. My muscles tense, my cunt starts to get slick, and waves of longing shoot up and down my arms.

That feeling? That's the feeling spanking gives me. Not for the whole session—I'm not overcome by gut-punching lust throughout. There's a 'pay attention' atmosphere as I'm lying, or kneeling, or sitting semi-naked and waiting for the first thwack. But then, inevitably, something will happen that brings that *hot* hot feeling to the fore.

The first slap. Unnngh.

A whispered 'Pull down your fucking knickers.' Argh.

The sound of a belt being pulled through the loops of his trousers. Oh God.

It's those things I'm chasing, not the pain. The pain is a sideshow. The pain is an accessory. The pain is not the point.

So what *is* the point? Is it the talking and the role-play? Maybe. Dirty talk can press the hot buttons, especially if growled at exactly the right point mid-fuck. It can also be a rather excellent way to ensure that the fuck happens in the first place, something I'd been vaguely aware of when exchanging sexual boasts with friends as a teenager. Dirty talk makes people pay attention.

Case in point: there is a new(ish) porn phenomenon that involves ladies of varying descriptions giving guys detailed instructions on how to wank. They're sexily dressed, but rarely naked, and occasionally you can see nothing of them other than an extreme close-up of their faces as they describe, with delicious embellishment, exactly how they want the guy to get off. They use dirty, sexy, husky voices, and even I—who lacks the equipment with which to follow their instruction— find it hard to avoid paying attention.

There should definitely be a similar thing for girls, or at least some sort of dirty-talk manual that partners can read to get a few ideas on how best to call someone a filthy girl. I've met any number of guys who'd willingly fumble half-heartedly at my clit to turn me on, but few who'd whisper something filthy in my ear—an altogether more efficient turn-on for me than any amount of genital rummaging.

Perhaps that's why the counting thing puts me off. When I'm pre-fuck horny and dripping with desire, there are far hotter things I could hear than 'one, two, three'. You telling me to pull down my knickers? Yes. You growling that I'm a filthy little slut? Hell yes. But you running me through the six-times table? Nah. You might as well be reciting the alphabet.

Words are beautiful. Talking is beautiful. But the talking has to be a bit more complex than just a count, or basic instructions. Crucially, if you want what you say to strike that 'unnngh' chord it has to be something more than just a phrase you remember from a hot sex blog, or an erotic book— something that actually turns *you* on. If it turns you on, it probably works for me.

Did you just tell me about a time when you fucked your girlfriend up against a wall? I am probably wet. Did you whisper in my ear that you're hard under the table and you want me to sit on it? Likewise.

When I talk dirty to a guy, I'm not reciting lines, I genuinely mean it, and that's what I want him to do for me. I want him to say 'hold my dick' and 'that's it' and 'keep going'. I want him to say:

Come here. Touch it. Fucking touch it. Yeah, that's it. Wrap your hands right round it you filthy bitch.

Squeeze.

Yeah, that's it. That's good. Good girl. Can you feel how hard I am? You did that to me you slut. Keep going. Did I ask you to stop? Fucking touch it, you slut.

Now take off your pants. That's it, take them off and let me see you. Take all of it off. Now get down on your fucking knees. I want you to suck nice and hard on my cock.

That's it—suck it. Good girl. Right to the back of your throat. Come on. Take it. Oh fuck that's good. Spit on it. Squeeze harder. Well done.

Stand up, turn round, bend over. All the way. Grip your ankles.

You know what I'm going to do now, right? I'm going to fuck you. Ask me to fuck you. Go on, beg me to fuck you. You want this? You want this, you dirty bitch. Ah, you do want it, you're so wet

Oh, fuck that's good. You feel so good. You're so wet. I'm going to fuck you nice and hard and you're going to stay quiet. Shut up. Hold your ankles, don't straighten up. Oh fuck, that's good.

I'm going to fuck you hard and then I'm going to come inside you. No, you don't get to come. God, that's good.

Oh.

Fuck.

Can you feel that? Do you like that? You like my cock nice and hard inside you? Yeah? Oh God, I'm going to come. I'm going to come right inside you. You. You. Dirty.

Filthy.

Little.

Bitch.

...

Good girl.

Number eight and I talked dirty—not just while we were fucking, but at any point when something hot struck us.

The question: 'How do you feel about [insert whatever depraved fetish one of us had recently read about]?' was common, and decisions on whether we should have a go at something were based mainly on the look in the other's eyes when the idea was floated.

In real life people rarely sit down with a checklist of every sexual possibility, and compare the boxes they've personally ticked. Apart from anything else, the conversation would be excruciating: 'I've said "yes" to fisting but only "maybe" to anal fisting, sweetheart, how about you?'

'Well, I've said I'm willing to fist you, but I'd prefer to watch someone else do it just because I've got quite big hands and I'm not convinced as to the practicalities. What have you put for piss-play?'

Far sexier, then, to tell each other stories and watch for the telltale signs that someone's interested. I was amazed at the range of things he'd come out with that I'd never thought about before. Most of us have a reasonably narrow view of what we might or might not want to do, but I was delighted to discover that my own list was much more flexible than I'd imagined.

Part of this was because I was in love with eight. I'd have considered almost anything he suggested just to see his cock twitch while I mulled it over. Things that I'd previously have shied away from became fun. Occasionally he was so confident that I'd enjoy something—'That wine bottle on the side table looks like it'd fit rigidly in her cunt'—that he'd surprise me with it while we were fucking, an urgent 'I'm going to do this now' that gave me simultaneous permission to say no and a desperate curiosity to say yes, to see what it would feel like.

Not that everything was perfect, you understand. I'd be horrified if you put this book down with the impression that I am anything other than a ridiculous fuck-up. In between the dirty talk and the frantic sex and the long mornings spent lying in a painfully narrow student bed dreaming up new and disgusting things to do to each other, there were a hell of a lot of fights. Many of these fights were innocuous: rows about which film we'd watch or why I'd somehow managed to cover his bedlinen in hair dye for the seventy-sixth time. But the majority of the fights centred on my inability to control my jealousy. When he'd mention other girls, or go out without me, I'd be instantly reminded of all the times he'd left me for the weekend to visit his girlfriend, and worry that sooner or later I'd be pushed back to where I'd been before: the 'up the arse' girl, who wasn't suitable for anything significant.

Still, apart from throwing the occasional glass of wine over him when my insecurity overwhelmed me (white wine, not red – I'm not a *complete* bastard), I did pretty well at making the most of the phenomenal luck that had brought us together in the first place. I wanted to come up with new ideas, to be the one to playfully suggest things that later became a common element of our sex. But unfortunately for eight, my imagination was too busy focusing on the one thing I wanted most of all.

'I keep thinking about you getting fucked by other men,' I whisper in his ear as we're lying in bed. I'm behind him, with my crotch up tight against his arse, running my hand up and down his body, from the top of his thigh to the curve of his waist.

'Really? Describe it.'

'Well, I'm sucking your dick, and two other guys are watching, just touching themselves and looking at your cock sliding in and out of my mouth—spit-lubed and rigid."

'Uh huh.' His mouth's getting dry, and he swallows.

I pull him in a bit closer, his naked arse up tight against my crotch. 'When you're trembling and nervous and on the edge, I step back out of the way and the guys step forward. You're shy but keen. Not enthusiastic, just curious. Your dick's still really hard, and you roll over so you're face down on the bed, the head of it rubbing uncomfortably on the fabric.'

By this point I've got his dick in my hand, and I'm gently rubbing the head with my thumb. He whimpers.

'One of the guys holds you down. He's stroking your hair with one hand and his prick with the other, while the second guy covers his in lube. It's wet and slick and you're a bit scared. You can hear the squelch as he makes himself ready to fuck you.'

'And does he fuck me?'

'Oh yeah.' A pause, and I feel his dick twitch in my hand as I squeeze it. 'He fucks you hard. There's no gentleness or concern that he'll hurt you—he just shoves himself in, nice and quick. You're moaning a bit, but you push your arse up against him...' He pushes his arse up against me... '... and feel every stroke of him like a smack. His dick's so deep inside you that you're scared. But the other guy holds you, and strokes your hair, and keeps you calm.' By now I'm lazily stroking number eight, feeling him wriggle and twitch in the hope that I'll go faster. I don't go faster.

'Do you like that story?'

'Unngh. Yeah.'

'Do you want to get fucked?'

'Yeah.'

I speed up. There's another whimper and then a groan as he orgasms, and I squeeze the end of his dick to feel the pressure as his come shoots all over the tips of my fingers.

I'd like to report that this incident led to an immediate trawl of the internet for hot young gay guys willing to fuck number eight while I masturbated furiously in the corner of the room, but these things take time. He was hot for the idea, but nervous, so I was happy to let it sit with him, burning holes in the erotic part of his brain, until he was ready to take things a step further.

He starts the conversation: 'I want to get fucked.'

'What, here in the beer garden?' It's summertime, shortly before our end of year exams, so of *course* we're in a pub garden. I'm sitting at a picnic table peeling the labels off bottles of cider and he's lying with his head in my lap. I stub out my cigarette and look down at him. His t-shirt has ridden up so I can see the smooth flatness of his stomach, and a hint of the dark hair at the waistband of his jeans.

He frowns. 'Not here. But I do want to get fucked.' The way he phrased it made me wet. He didn't want to fuck, he wanted to *get* fucked. To my mind, this conversation was only heading in one direction—straight home to my place where we'd hunt for lithe, horny guys who'd be willing to shag my boy into a quivering mass of sexual ecstasy. But I was wrong.

'Can I choose you a boy?'

'How about *you* be the boy?'

'I... err... what?'

There's something magical about the prostate. It is the sexual holy grail, the ark of the covenant, the key to the lost city of Atlantis. And like all the greatest and most valuable treasures, it's hidden in a place where not everyone is comfortable venturing. This is unfortunate for squeamish types who—for reasons of hygiene or simply disgust—are unwilling to shove their fingers into a guy's ass. However, for those who might be tempted to have a go, allow me to offer the following by way of gentle persuasion.

Like most girls of my generation, my first introduction to the possibilities of prostate massage came via the educational cinematic masterpiece *American Pie*, in which a college-aged Seann William Scott is encouraged into producing a semen donation by a vampy nurse with a rubber glove and bottle of lubricant. He bends over a table, as per her instructions, and she shoves a finger inside him, no doubt applying a medically safe degree of pressure in exactly the right place. Seann William Scott makes 'ooh' and 'aah' faces for about ten seconds or so, then jizzes into a plastic cup.

I, and no doubt quite a few other people who have played with prostates, was delighted to discover that—barring the inclusion of a plastic cup—this is a pretty accurate depiction of how prostate massage usually goes down.

One of the appeals of this type of activity is that it's such an easy win. When you make a guy come with your hands you're competing not just with all of his previous lovers, who may have been better than you at applying pressure to the right places or maintaining a consistent speed, you're competing with the world champion—him. There's any number of different ways that a wank can be disappointing. Just as your partner will never be able to rub you off in the same way you do, you'll find it impossible to make him come with anything like the degree of efficiency that he can achieve himself. Giving a hand job is like making a cup of tea: it's nice if someone does it for you, but you always do it better yourself.

Not so with prostate massage. Although most guys are capable of doing this themselves, you're given a head start in this particular race because you're better placed to do it: it's easier to finger someone else's ass than it is to finger your own.

I'd tried this with number eight before in the way most people do: an exploratory finger while I was giving him head. It was amazing. I didn't expect the speed with which he responded—an aching moan, a quick twitch, then his ass tensing around my fingers in spasms as he not just squirted but *pumped* spunk into my mouth. Like a firehose. Like champagne. Like a fucking good time.

So his request that I 'be the boy' was a logical next step. Prostate massage plus naked girl plus the feeling of being dominated: all of these hit his 'unnngh' buttons, and his eyes shone so much at the thought of it that I expected them to start watering.

Two hours later, after a brief stop at our friendly neighbourhood sex shop, we were back in my bedroom with a bottle of lube and something large, black and strap-on-able.

'Take off your pants.'

He lay on his back on the bed, naked from the waist down, and I could see how much he was looking forward to this. His cock stood straight up in the air, solid and thick and glistening at the tip. I pushed his knees up towards his shoulders, knelt on the bed between his splayed legs, then wet the tips of my fingers and traced them around and around the head of his cock.

'Do you want me to fuck you?'

He nodded.

'Tell me. Tell me you want me to fuck you.'

'I want you to fuck me.'

'Say please.' I reached for the lube as he babbled, desperately.

'Please fuck me. Oh please fuck me. I just want to feel you in me, I need to come.'

I had one hand on his dick while my other hand squeezed the best part of half a tube of lube onto my own.

Although it wasn't something I'd fantasised about, something intangible about this situation made me tingle with arousal. There was no pain, no spanking. I wasn't being submissive. I was just kneeling between the boy's legs, pressing the tip of my fake dick right up against his ass, and yet something was giving me that lustful kick.

'Touch your dick.'

He obeyed immediately. Quivering with lust and nervous about being fucked for the first time, he stroked himself slowly, not wanting to come before I'd had him.

He was close enough to coming just from the anticipation of what we were doing, so when I slid first one then two fingers inside him he tensed up.

'Ah, no, please.'

I stroked his prostate, very gently, and felt every muscle in his body tense as he tried not to come. I'd never been so powerful. 'You're going to come when I fuck you.'

'Yeah.' He nodded a few times, more a reflex twitch than a nod of agreement. He stared at me with wide eyes and bit his lip, as I used my lubed-up hand to guide my dick into him. He groaned.

'Does it hurt?'

'Yes. But it's good.'

'How good?' I tentatively slid it back out, then in again, a bit further this time. Another groan. A twitch.

'Good.'

And I knelt up, put a hand on each of his raised knees, and pushed them backwards, opening him up and pushing him back, as I slid in and out of him. His face was tight in an expression of both pain and ecstasy, knit with concentration in an effort not to come. But I wanted him to come. I knew that the build up and the nervousness and the panic and the joy of being fucked in a whole new way would lead to an orgasm that shot from deep inside him, spraying mouthfuls of spunk over and across his whole body.

I fucked him harder, and I grabbed his dick, and it happened exactly as I'd hoped: he shot ropes of spunk that hit not just his chest and face but the wall beyond his head. He moaned and cried out, his stomach tensing as he did and he raised himself up slightly towards me. I felt a slight movement on my dick as his ass tensed with the impact of the orgasm, and his own cock jerked violently in my hand.

The word is 'pegging', invented by sex advice columnist Dan Savage. It might not be a regular weapon in the average person's sexual arsenal, but it's perhaps more common than you think. What's more, for some people it's a fetish in the truest sense of the word: they can't come without it.

Although that wasn't the case for either eight or—clearly—me, there was certainly something about it that hit the right buttons. It wasn't the domination. I'm a reluctant dominant at the best of times, unable to fully embrace the mentality of a gleeful sadist because I'm worrying about how crap my knots are and whether my arse looks fat in this strap-on. It wasn't the physical sensations either; although the feeling of penetrating someone is intriguingly different, it's essentially just a bit of rubber occasionally bumping up against your crotch.

But, as with all of the new things we were doing, something about it was hot. I just couldn't quite pinpoint what it was.

I have a theory that no matter where you live, you're never more than a couple of hours' drive from something that will help you fulfil your sexual fantasies. Not just because humans are generally a bunch of perverts, but because sex is a multi-million pound industry. Whether your fantasy involves being spanked, tied up, pissed on or infantilised, there'll be someone somewhere willing to take your money in exchange for a product or service to fulfil it.

And so with courage in one hand and the dregs of our student loans in another, number eight and I set off to a fetish market. A fetish market, for those who haven't yet had the pleasure, does almost exactly what it says on the tin: it's a collection of stalls laid out by the aforementioned sex industry pioneers selling riding crops, saddles and everything in between. The one we went to was held in a nightclub, so that in the evening it could be turned into a dungeon and the paddles, ropes, corsets and nipple clamps that eager perverts had purchased at the market could be given their first airing.

We wandered through the stalls, unsure exactly how much of our meagre student funds could legitimately be spent on things we'd inevitably end up getting covered in spunk. We bought a few things, out of a combination of curiosity and politeness, but shopping wasn't the main aim of the day. We were there to see if, as we'd assumed from our pre-fetish club reading on blogs and forums, beating the shit out of each other in a place like this would give us just the sort of 'unngh' kick we were chasing.

Let's start by busting a common myth: not everyone in fetish clubs is either old, fat or ugly. In fact, fetish clubs are one of the few places where you can confidently walk into a room and know you'll feel neither over nor underdressed, neither fat nor thin, old nor young. Why? Because we perverts are a diverse bunch.

The fetish club in which eight and I made our debut was about as varied as they get. At twenty, we were the youngest couple there, but not quite the youngest overall: a trembling eighteen-year-old boy introduced himself as a submissive and chatted to me in reverential tones, assuming, because of my height, that I was there to spank rather than be spanked. He introduced us to an older couple who seemed to know everyone in the place. The woman, in collar, corset and not much else, shied away from conversation while her dominant held forth— introducing people, quizzing them on their likes and dislikes, and doing his best to appear the generous host. A woman aged about forty, with a cherry-coloured fascinator and beautifully toned biceps, introduced herself as the house domme, and offered to give us a tour of the club.

We'd been there before for dancing, but the place had been transformed. Where previously there'd been gangs of students moshing to whatever the latest metal track was, now there were crucifixes and frames. In the area usually reserved for chilling out there were now spanking horses and what looked to me like massage tables, but turned out to be almost the exact opposite. Later that evening a man in tight PVC knickers was lying face down on one of these tables, receiving the most thorough and painful beating I'd ever seen.

The domme showed us around every piece of equipment, explaining what they were for and—for the ones that weren't occupied—how to use them. Everything felt close and hot. A few couples had started playing already, and eight and I joined the groups of people watching from a respectful distance. We were mesmerised by the force and anger behind the beatings that were taking place. By the skill with which the dominants wielded whips, tawses, riding crops, and the stamina of the submissives who could grit their teeth through onslaughts that lasted for what seemed like hours. It made us feel like our previous attempts had been not just amateur but childish—we'd been playing doctors and nurses while these guys were performing brain surgery.

There was a pattern emerging around the club. Some couples would play quietly in a corner, avoiding the crowds, and the voyeurs would move between the couples, or sometimes groups, who were putting on the best show. It didn't feel wholly competitive, but the couples with the largest audience did seem to be quite proud of it— submissive women with mesmerising arses would stick them further out, dominants would lean back to put their full weight behind the slaps, and occasionally turn to the crowd to grin or offer the chance to join in.

'She loves it when you watch. Do you want to come a bit closer?'

'Hold this. Now hit her with it. Come on, harder than that.'

It was against the rules to join in without being invited, but I could see that some of the watchers were itching to get involved—to pick up a crop or a whip and take it out on one of the exhibitionists. And some people, like myself, were envious of the people tied to stocks, frames and horses, being beaten and appraised by a gang of eager sadists.

Number eight ran his hands over my shoulders, stroking the skin that was exposed by my corset. He stood right behind me, and I could feel his arousal pressing up against my arse.

'Do you want to do this?'

'Yes. But I'm nervous.'

I felt intimidated by the other players—harder and stronger than I was, and able to take far more pain. The thwacks I could hear ringing off the walls in the sweaty club were so much louder, so much scarier than the pathetic slapping noises I'd heard at home. I was worried not that eight would hit me harder, but that he wouldn't, and the gathering throng would wander off, bored and faintly disgusted by my weakness.

Then the domme stepped in.

'Seeing as it's my club, do you want me to give you a proper introduction?'

Eight's eyes lit up.

'You want to spank her?'

'I want to *belt* her. Are you happy for me to show you?'

He nodded so hard he nearly snapped his neck, placing my hand firmly in hers so that she could lead me to one of the less intimidating bits of equipment. It was a plain-looking bench, similar to the ones we'd used in gym class at school, except it was covered in shiny red leather. At her instruction I bent over it and hitched up my skirt, revealing knickers that—now that they were on display— felt six times thinner and more see-through than they actually were. I flushed and she leant down to whisper in my ear:

'Red means stop.'

OK, got it. Red meant stop. So all I had to do to avoid detection, avoid the crowd knowing that I was a loser, was avoid saying the word 'red'. Perhaps not the effect that the domme was aiming to have, but nevertheless I bit my lip and prepared to power through an onslaught of slaps, whips and searing agony.

'This one looks really nervous,' she announced to the stragglers who were gathering to watch.

'I *am* nervous,' I said, forgetting that in order to let my submissive side out I had to keep a lid on the side that was a babbling chatterbox.

Thwack.

'When you're spoken to.'

Thwack.

The belt felt warm and strong. There was a thick heft to it and the sound was louder than I expected. The strokes hurt—a lot—and I burned with shame. I wasn't worried that people were watching but that they weren't. That they'd glance over briefly, judge me to be insufficient, then move on. Two of the women being beaten nearby were fully naked. You could see the whips cutting bright red stripes into their arses, while *I* still had my knickers on. Amateur. I wanted to feel the 'unngh', the kick that made it all worthwhile, but despite a general tingling of arousal, I knew this wasn't quite what I was chasing.

Thwack.

Number eight stood by my head, one hand placed gently on the back of my neck, restraining me if I twitched upwards at a particularly painful stroke.

Thwack. Thwack. She rained down more and more slaps, some striking right in the middle of one cheek, others slicing across the softer, more sensitive skin at the top of my thighs. I bit my lip and waited for the kick, the moment that told me 'you're enjoying this'. But it still didn't come.

Eight now had both of his hands on my neck, standing directly in front of me so that even with lowered eyes I could see his crotch. I made out the shape of his growing erection, pushed tight down against one leg by the seam. And just as I spotted it, he whispered to me:

'They can all see you. How do you feel?'

And *then* it came. I felt... unnngh. My stomach contracted and my arms went weak, and I pushed my head up and back against number eight, feeling the warmth of his hands and the strength with which he was holding me down.

My worries about being judged and humiliated vanished straight away as I realised, finally, what it was about all of this that I liked. It wasn't the pain, or the counting, or the power play: I liked the erections. It wasn't what was happening that made me hot, it was the fact that *he* liked it. His solid dick pressing against the seam of his crotch, the thought of more men in the audience looking on and growing hard in exactly the same way—that's what I was there for.

Everything eight and I had been chasing together—that kick, that lust, that 'unngh'—for me was caused by how other people reacted to sexual things. If he, or any of the gathering guys, had been standing at a distance, bored and nonchalant, like number six leaning casually against the fridge in my kitchen, that kick would never have come.

Do I like fucking guys in the arse? Not particularly. Do I like pain? Hell no. But do I like what happens to guys when these things happen? Yes. It's not unusual, it's not weird, but it took me a while to realise it: my fetish was for giving guys erections. I wanted, more than anything, to be sexually objectified.

I know what you're probably thinking: that's a bit creepy, no? It's a bit weird. It certainly not very *feminist*, is it? People have said this to me before, and given me well-meaning lectures about having strength and power and not giving up your freedom and independence to some bloody *man* who'll use you for sexual kicks and then discard you. And I agree wholeheartedly—to give everything to a partner just for their sexual pleasure is a horrible thing to do, and for them to take it, use it, and do things you don't want is unconscionable. But I have never understood why this should apply to *me*, because—and let's be crystal clear about it—that is not what is happening here.

The difference, as ever, is in the context. And the context here is that I actively want a partner to do this. Not because I think I'm a bad girl and need to be punished, because I have low self-esteem or Daddy issues. I want him to do these things to me because—and this is going to sound so simple it's positively crude—they make my cunt wet. It's not as interesting an explanation as any of the more psychological hypotheses, but it's the closest I can come to the honest-to-goodness truth. I want to be used more than I want to be stroked and gentled. Fulfilling my genuine sexual fantasies doesn't make my partner an abuser, it makes him a sex god.

What's more, just because guys do these things to me when I'm horny that doesn't mean they're doing them all the time. I want guys to beat me, spit on me, call me a whore and then respect my opinions on sexual politics. These things aren't mutually exclusive as long as you understand the context in which you're doing them. Call me a whore in the bedroom and I'll moan. Call me a whore in the pub and I'll tell you to piss off and get your round in. Beat me when I ask you to and I'll love you forever. Beat me when I don't and I'll call the police.

I'm not actually giving up any power by getting spanked, or being called a whore. I don't necessarily want to claim it's empowering—it's no more empowering than any other sexual act. I tend to feel more empowered by delivering a good speech or writing a decent argument than I do by writhing around until I reach a gurning, sweaty orgasm. But still, the key thing is that I'm not being *dis*empowered.

I'd be giving up far more by refusing to listen to my actual brain when it tells me 'you like it when guys spit in your mouth' and instead pretended that by insisting on a cleaner, sanitised, *egalitarian* fuck I was somehow being truer to myself. All else being equal, the sexual act itself is irrelevant to whether you're being oppressed or used. You can give up your power in the missionary position: someone can take advantage of you while they're gently stroking your hair and calling you 'princess'. What matters isn't what you do, it's how you—and the person you're fucking—*feel*.

Sure, if I met a complete twat who believed that it was a woman's job to please a man in bed, and he tried to fuck me in the arse, I would hurl him out of my bedroom before you can say, 'Take your battered copy of *The Game* with you, you misogynist prick.' However, with other guys it is more than possible for me to enjoy him fucking me in the arse, calling me a whore/slut/wench/bitch/cunt then jizzing on my face, spitting on me and then rolling over to go to sleep. Why? Because sex isn't a university debate. When you shag you're not championing a particular cause, or stating your opinion on the way the world should be, you're doing things that make you hot. And this guy, the face-jizzing spitter, just happens to make me hotter than anyone else.

To say that what eight and I did in the bedroom was significant in terms of a power exchange in the relationship is to misunderstand the nature of relationships. Power is about so much more than sex. And sex is about far more than power. I'd be doing eight—and thousands of other feminist, sensitive, dominant guys—a huge disservice if I implied that by getting beaten I was handing them my freedom on a platter. Do we honestly, truly believe that men are so bloody stupid as to think that the way they treat women in the bedroom necessarily has to be the way they treat them outside it? I hope not. I've never met a man who thinks that because I submit to him in the bedroom I'll be anything other than my usual feisty, argumentative self in the pub. Let's not patronise men by assuming that they are one-dimensional creatures who can't understand the difference between rough sex for mutual pleasure and manipulative, power-hungry borderline rape.

I know what I like: reading books, watching incomprehensibly long US drama series, cider, cheese, that satisfying sound when you pop the lid on a new jar of coffee, and sex that makes the guy I'm with diamond hard and trembling with desire. To read more into what I do in bed implies that I'm doing it for reasons other than because I like it. What better way to remove my sexual agency and make my choices insignificant?

Fair enough, a girl getting spat on might not strike you as a particularly feminist image. We're certainly not going to be marching the streets holding banners with pictures of girls in hog-tie being spunked on by throbbing men. But burying what I want sexually because the physical acts seem a bit tasteless doesn't strike me as particularly feminist either. I'm not saying we should all burn our knickers and take it up the arse, I'm saying that if I enjoy it and you enjoy it, let's do it. You can come all over my face, rub it in and make me eat it while crooning that I'm a filthy fucking slut who totally deserves it. You can squeeze my tits so hard it hurts and tell me I'll take it because it's what you want to do. But that doesn't mean you're going to do any of this in the street, a business meeting, or a situation other than the bedroom. Just because I squeezed number eight's balls until he winced then forced butt-plugs into his lubed-up ass didn't mean that I didn't also respect his views on the economy. Likewise, I can whimper girlishly and do what you say in bed without implying that I should also do the hoovering, bear your children, earn less money than you and be denied my right to vote.

We can discuss the philosophical ramifications of our dirty shag over a pint in the pub afterwards, when your respect for me hasn't waned one iota because I get turned on to see you being dominant. Just give me a second to grab my wallet and wash all this jizz off my face.

CHAPTER EIGHT

Being A Cultural Ambassador Is, Like Most Things In Life, More Fun With Your Knickers Off

'Would it be *san*?'

'Nah, I'm pretty sure it's *sama*—more polite.'

'Really?'

'Yeah, *sama* is the most polite one.'

'We should probably check on the internet.'

We were on our way to a fetish bar, trying to answer one of the questions I never thought I'd need to ask: what is the correct way in which to address a Japanese dominatrix?

Number eight and I, due to a few administrative fuck-ups and eventually a decision to avoid getting Real Jobs after university, had somehow ended up in Japan. We swapped books and lessons for... well... more books and lessons, because it turns out that if you have a degree, a nice smile, and an ability to speak English very slowly and clearly, in Japan you can get a job as a teacher. A job where to my delight, despite my bumbling idiocy and fear of the vast majority of my co-workers, my students were obliged to call me *sensei*.

There are a thousand different aspects to Japan. It's a fascinating country. Depending on how much you've heard or read about it, you'll probably think it famous for geisha, sushi, or well-behaved schoolchildren. I saw almost no evidence for the latter, and there's clearly more to commend the nation than raw fish and white-faced entertainers.

Let's take a tiny break here to explain what Japan both is and isn't. When I've spoken to kinky people—or, indeed, people who are simply fascinated by kink yet faintly squeamish about the idea of actually doing it—they've all made comments along the lines of 'Well, Japan's the kinkiest place of all.' In the minds of almost everyone I know who has access to the internet, Japan is a pervert's Mecca: the home of spanking, bondage, piss-play, bukkake, and shoving live eels into one's vagina. If you judged a country purely by the porn it exports, you might imagine that Japanese people spend at least fifty per cent of their spare time finding larger, squirmier, and more unusual things to insert into their sexy orifices. But that's clearly not true. Just as sushi is more interesting than chicken curry and geisha are more interesting than supermarket cashiers, we'll be more likely to hear about Japan's knicker vending machines than it's everyday, routine sex.

The word '*hentai*', usually attributed to a certain type of animated pornography, in Japanese literally means 'pervert' or 'perverted'. But what exactly counts as perverted? It all depends on what we're used to seeing. If I asked a nun to watch what you get up to, she'd probably label you a pervert for some of the milder acts you take part in. Yet if I asked a pornographer to do the same, she'd probably be unimpressed at the lack of anything particularly marketable about your humdrum humping.

I like the word 'pervert' purely because of this ambiguity. When someone calls me a pervert, usually all they mean is 'you've done things that I haven't'. If I've given head to a guy under the desk while he chairs a serious meeting—sadly something that will probably remain a fantasy—and you haven't, then it's easier to call me a pervert than if I'm admitting to something you're used to.

I've been called a pervert for looking just a couple of seconds too long at the hot scruffy-looking guy at the bar in a tight t-shirt and jeans that have slipped down to reveal his boxers. For confessing to friends that not only did I fuck a certain guy, but that he spat in my mouth and I liked it. For admitting that I am so in love with a particular celebrity that I'd willingly lie beneath his feet and let him pee on my face. Perverts are usually just people who like filth but have the outrageous cheek to not be ashamed of it.

OK, maybe my last example was a little bit niche. Still, I'm always surprised at how easily some people brand things pervy or weird for no better reason than that they, personally, haven't done them. If you admit to enjoying something a bit odd, you're suddenly a pervert—a member of a club so diverse that no two members will ever agree on why they joined. Some trawl the internet to find men who might be willing to fuck them while their boyfriend watches. Others prefer hosting tea parties for unrealistic sex dolls. Still more are donning nappies, bursting balloons in their trousers, dressing up as foxes or drinking urine like it's vintage champagne.

Just the one word isn't really good enough to encompass the realms of what we use it for: a pervert is just someone who has fucked in ways that you haven't.

In Japan, number eight and I set out to fuck in ways we previously hadn't. I was constantly amazed by his willingness to embrace the darker things I thought about, and his uncanny ability to find new things that'd make me go 'unnngh'. He, more than anyone else I knew over there, wanted to embrace everything about Japan. Not just the karaoke bars, in which we spent countless evenings caterwauling eighties pop hits, but the less obvious things. He'd drag me along to tiny hole-in-the-wall restaurants, and enthuse about food I'd never heard of. He'd look up unusual festivals and traditions, then cross-reference train timetables so we could go along to witness them.

I loved him for his enthusiastic ability to make me get off my arse. Number eight stopped me sitting in front of a computer, wishing we could be the adventurous ones, and made plans that allowed us to do the adventurous things I'd been wishing for. He knew what I wanted, and he made it happen. Close to the top of his list: love hotels.

For those who aren't familiar with them, a love hotel is aimed purely at the market of 'people who need to fuck'. While horny English people looking for a shag might settle for a discount night in a Travelodge, the Japanese have a selection of unique hotel rooms aimed purely at the 'randy couples' market, which can be rented by the hour. They're often used by young couples, who can't shag in their parents' houses for fear of being heard, but they're also handy if you're a boss looking to shag your secretary, a pair of secret star-crossed lovers, or an older married couple looking for a filthy thrill.

Most of the rooms are hired anonymously—you don't book in advance, you just nip in through the small entrance and walk into a deserted lobby. There'll usually be a bank of pictures on a wall, or a board in the centre of the lobby, with prices listed next to each room. The plainest rooms are the cheapest, but they're by no means actually plain. Bed, chairs and en suite bathrooms come as standard, but so do sex toy vending machines and huge TVs with a selection of porn channels. If you want something a bit fancier you can pick a room with added extras: stocks at the end of the bed, walk-in wet rooms with pornographic murals picked out in tiny mosaics, carousel horses, cinema seats, crucifixes, train carriages, school desks and almost anything else you could imagine. On one memorable occasion the room I'd selected came with a special plastic mat, an industrial-sized bottle of baby oil, and a video instructing you how to use these items to wriggle your partner to a sticky orgasm on the bathroom floor.

Despite it not being our first love hotel visit, number eight and I are nervous, as we always are when we place ourselves into situations where there's a possibility that we'll have to speak more than basic Japanese. As is standard, both of us know the Japanese word for 'dick'—*chinko*, if you're curious—and cunt—*manko*, although I don't recommend you crack that one out in polite conversation—but there's always the possibility that a new situation will throw up a sentence babbled so quickly we won't understand it. The chance that someone will hurriedly tell us 'You may not copulate in this room lest you incur the wrath of the Emperor,' then we blithely misunderstand and amble ignorantly into the place we're not supposed to go, is a constant source of worry.

We've been to love hotels before, and some of them are anonymous enough that we'll never need to expose our crap Japanese speaking skills. We just walk in, press a button, put money in a slot and get a room key from a tray. We enter the room, fuck, sleep, and leave with the slightly eerie impression that the building itself is serving us.

But on some occasions, as with this one, we have to go through the terrifying ordeal of actually speaking to someone. The 'someone' in this case is hidden behind a blacked-out screen in the lobby, just a pair of hands visible to take our money. We choose our room and wander over, placing the correct amount through the slot.

'Number twelve, please.'

A mid-range room. No stocks or crucifixes—they're too expensive—but a promising array of interesting things to explore.

The person behind the desk doesn't say a word, just hands us our key and points in the direction of the lift, which is now flashing to indicate that we can enter. We shuffle quickly across the lobby and step into the corridor. Clearly we've made our first mistake: the woman behind the glass comes hurtling out from her anonymous booth.

'No, no, what are you doing?'

Red faces, embarrassment, a panic as neither of us remember the most linguistically deferential way to apologise for whatever slight we've committed.

'Umm... sorry?' And I really am sorry—what have we done? We've heard stories about foreigners being turned away from love hotels before, and we're worried that the cashier thinks we might be the wrong kind of customer.

'Your shoes. Your shoes! Take them off.'

And she points at the corridor entrance, where there's a neat frame containing rows and rows of slippers. We definitely should have spotted this, and as we cram our far-too-big feet into the delicate slippers, we giggle with embarrassment.

Suitably shod, we get into the lift, which automatically breezes up a few floors and deposits us at just the right one for our room. A quick fumble with the key and we're in: the bright lights showing up everything the room has to offer.

At the centre is a massive bed with a panel of switches that control everything, including a giant TV on one of the walls connected not just to a PlayStation but a karaoke machine. There's a 'welcome basket' on a coffee table filled with sachets of lube, condoms and packets of Bourbon biscuits. A vending machine selling cheap-looking jelly objects in a variety of different sizes from 'embarrassingly tiny' to 'holy Jesus you're not putting that anywhere near my cunt'. The bathroom is more of a wet room, tiled from floor to ceiling with three different shower heads and a gigantic bath in one corner and with another TV right next to it, presumably to facilitate luxuriously soapy porn viewings.

Faced with such a dazzling number of sexual toys to play with, number eight and I did what any reasonable couple would do: we bounced on the bed. We ate all the biscuits. We ran a massive bath, using all of the bubbles we could find in the room. We played PlayStation and sang karaoke and watched as much porn as we could before the 'free time' ran out and the TV started asking us, in the politest language possible, to stop being tight and put some fucking money in. We had the least sexy, most childish fun we could possibly have had to make sure we'd got our money's worth.

I'm not one for mixing comedy and sex—tits don't make 'honk honk' noises when you squeeze them, and you don't hang towels off a rock-hard dick. Sex is supposed to be something that makes you groan with ecstasy rather than giggle with shame. But that doesn't mean that it can't be playful. In Japan, number eight and I were playful. That goes for the sex as well as the bed-bouncing.

Later that night I knelt on the floor of the wet room and slipped his spit-lubed dick into my mouth. He pulled my hair back and gripped his cock with the other hand, whispering:

'Are you ready? I'm going to piss on you.'

'I... yes. OK.' I closed my eyes and fought to suppress a childish smirk. This felt like a game, albeit one for which I had no idea what the rules were. I just wanted to play because he'd invited me to.

'Open your eyes.'

I opened them. And he was looking down at me, meeting my playfulness with a similar look of his own. I wasn't quite sure he'd do it, until his expression changed— the smirk replaced quickly with a cross between pain and arousal as he forced himself, through a rock solid erection, to let out a thin stream of piss all over my chest.

And it wiped the playful grin straight off my face. It was amazing–disgusting. I had never felt so used before, so surprised at myself, so utterly at his mercy. The stream got stronger, and he played it further up my body, over my neck, into my hair, and, as I closed my eyes again, right onto my face.

He made me kneel up–despite the heated floor of the bathroom I was shivering. I felt exposed and humiliated and in serious need of sex. I wanted him to fuck me right on the floor, to hold me close and show me how turned on he was. I wanted him to lick my neck and tell me it tasted good, tell me I tasted good. But he didn't.

'Your turn.' He lay on the floor, his head directly in front of my knees, and closed his eyes, a flicker of amusement creeping back onto his face.

'You've got to be joking.' I wasn't averse to the idea, I just couldn't cope with such a quick switch— one minute I'm kneeling in front of him while he pisses on me, the next he's lying with his head buried in my crotch, willing me to do the same to him. It had the opposite effect to the one he'd intended: he wanted to give me the power back, to make me dominant and strong, so I could better get revenge on him for humiliating me. But instead I felt like the world's worst comedian when confronted by a witty heckler.

'Go on, what are you waiting for?' He was open-mouthed, eager, and all but tapping his foot in anticipation. But all I could do was strain and panic. None of my muscles worked, at least none of the ones that mattered at that point in time. Kneeling over him, my thighs were clenched and my face screwed up in exertion, pushing with all the force I could muster and just willing myself to do it.

I felt like an arse. How was it possible that I'd actually *forgotten* how to piss? Something I'd done four or five times a day for around twenty-two years suddenly seemed like the most difficult thing in the world. I'd have felt less uncomfortable if he'd stood over me while I tried to solve a quadratic equation.

Please oh please oh please, just a dribble?

He'd only been lying there for three minutes, but it felt to me like the whole evening. I was regretting all the time we'd spent mucking around in the bedroom when I should have been drinking glass after glass of water in anticipation of this moment.

I shouldn't have prayed for a dribble, really, because eventually a dribble came out. A tiny, less-than-thimbleful of piss trickled slowly onto his waiting face, and he grinned.

'Is that it?'

I wanted the ground to open up, swallow me, and then send vengeful demons out to punch him in his smug, not-quite-piss-covered face.

Later on as we were showering he pulled me towards him, and put his lips right next to my ear. Expecting words of comfort, I held him closer, thinking he'd make some joke about earlier to make me feel less upset, less inadequate, less impotent.

'That's one—nil to me, dickhead,' he said. I threw the soap at him.

I told you that story not because of what happened in the middle—there are probably many of you for whom the idea of a man pissing on my face is about as distasteful as... well... getting piss in your face. But I tell it for the beginning and the end. These bits are missing from almost every porn film and erotic story since the beginning of time. OK, there's the beginning where they fall in love, or meet in an elevator, or one comes to fix the other one's fridge. But where's the beginning where they get hammered in the pub and one teases the other about his haircut and then he playfully slaps her on the arm? Where's the beginning where he takes a picture of his cock on her mobile phone then jokingly threatens to send it to her mum? Where, if you'll forgive the absurdly cheesy cliché, is the *love*?

Sex isn't about comedy, but it's a hell of a lot better with someone who'll laugh it off if you can't tie knots properly, if you try something a bit extreme, or fail to muster enough piss to cover their expectant, loving face.

Pervery doesn't always have to be done with a totally stiff upper lip. Although power play requires a bit of concentration, one of the main things I've learned by playing is that we're all fallible humans deep down. It's not always sexy, but it is often very comforting.

'Breathe deeply, put your face in the pillow.' A phrase that usually gets me wriggling with anticipation: something good and domly is about to happen. He'll spank me, lube me up, and fuck me in the arse: I'm excited.

'I'm going to do something I've never done before.' Oh boy, even better. He's got something horrible in his sick and twisted head, and he's going to violate me in ways I never thought possible.

'Ready?'

'Oh yes... definite—ARGH WHAT THE FUCK IS THAT?' A searing, burning pain deep inside me. I gripped the bedsheets and screamed.

'It's ginger.' I turned round and looked into his face, pale with worry. 'I read about it on the internet.'

'I don't care where you read about it, get it THE FUCK out of my ARSE.'

When he'd calmed me down by removing the evil root, he made it up to me by fucking me hard enough in the cunt that I forgot about the pain in my ass, then cooking me a delicious stir fry.

One all, I think.

Spicy sex toys didn't work, so eight went for something at the other end of the spectrum.

'Breathe deeply, put your face in the pillow.' Similar wriggling and excitement, in anticipation of more domly magic.

'I'm going to do something I've never done before.' OK, brilliant, I thought. Definitely not ginger then.

'Ready?'

'Ye—ARGH WHAT THE HELL IS IT THIS TIME?'

'Ice. Sorry.' He fumbled to try and get rid of it as I did more dramatic writhing and squealing.

'Does it hurt?' he asked, redundantly.

'YES. YES IT HURTS VERY MUCH.'

'Sorry. Is it cold?'

'It's cold, sure, but I can live with that. Why is it so FUCKING SPIKY?'

It turns out that ice cubes, like most cubes, have corners. I don't think either of us won that one.

'OK, this time you're going to do something scary for me. Are you ready?'

I was ready, but I wasn't scared. This was eight, the guy who'd push me just far enough that I'd scream and bollock him for putting alien objects in my arse, but who'd always pull back if he thought he'd fucked up.

We'd planned this evening specially—cleared our schedules for three hours so that we could spend as much time as possible doing new and horrible things to each other. It had started as soon as I'd arrived at his flat— fishnet tights, a tiny skirt, a top that my tits were struggling to squeeze out of and knickers slick from the long train journey, anticipating all of the ways in which the boy might terrorise me. I was definitely ready for something scary.

He made me kneel on the floor with my back to him, then he pushed me forwards until my face was on the floor, cheek firmly squashed onto the polished wood and arse sticking up in the air. He lifted my skirt to expose me then slowly peeled down my tights and my knickers.

I heard the sound of lube coming out of the bottle, then immediately that slick, cold sensation as he slathered it over and into my ass. Cool, but not freezing. Scary, but not new.

Gently, slowly, he pushed a butt-plug inside me. It was small enough that I didn't cry out, but large enough that I felt stretched. I was aware of it without being hurt by it, aroused but not afraid. He pulled up my knickers and tights, smoothed my skirt back down and told me to stand up.

I wobbled slightly as I stood, then turned around to look at him. His eyes were smiling, but he kept his composure as he told me I was a slut. A bad slut. A filthy slut. *His* slut.

'And because you're mine, you're going to do something for me.'

I nodded. I wasn't entirely sure what this thing would be but I was very much hoping it would involve, at some point, his dick going into my mouth.

'Whatever you want,' I said, dipping down slightly in anticipation of the order that I really wanted.

'I want some ice cream. Go to the shop and get me some.'

Bastard.

'You're a bastard.'

'I know. Here's a thousand yen. Get some ice cream. Now.' And he opened the door.

Ten steps, eleven steps, twelve steps... I wobbled uncertainly towards the shop. I'd guessed it was about a hundred steps away, down the corridor, out into the street, sharp turn to the left then round the corner. I got to twenty-five steps and the sign was in sight—7-Eleven. A big, flashing neon finish line. Thirty steps... thirty-one... I could feel the plug slipping inside me, I was aware of no sensation other than the stretching, and the tension in my ass as I tried my hardest to clamp down on it, to keep it in. Thirty-five steps, thirty-six... It slipped. It was a small movement at first, then a sudden whoosh as my muscle tension worked against me and the whole thing slid out and into my knickers. I froze.

A young couple—no more than eighteen—walked past me, casting occasional glances at the weird girl who'd stopped in the middle of the pavement. I waited until they'd passed, then hobbled back to the boy's flat, thanking whoever invented fishnets for their net-like, butt-plug-catching nature.

I got back to the flat and he beat me for failing him. Then he made me dinner, sans ice cream, and we laughed.

'You'll get me back for that, won't you?' he asked, with barely disguised glee.

'Oh yeah.'

We weren't constantly giggling or taking the piss out of each other. If the whole thing had been a joke neither of us would have had the confidence to get naked, let alone utter potentially cringe-worthy things like 'sit on my dick, bitch' during lustful moments. But it wasn't wholly straight-faced either. BDSM doesn't require a permanent sexy frown. You don't need to worry about getting things wrong. And you certainly shouldn't worry if you do something to your partner that in the cold light of day seems ridiculous: if number eight and I hadn't been able to have fun, we'd never have got past having sex in a t-shirt with the lights off.

Some people are capable of separating power-play from actual sex, but the vast majority of people who do it are doing it with someone they'll have to cook dinner for later. Someone who they'll buy comedy Christmas presents for, and tease about their ragged sweat pants. Number eight was one minute my dominant, the next my best friend, then later he'd be the guy who held my hair back while I puked into the toilet.

Back to the bar, then, where our sexual appetites have taken a back seat in the face of our worry that we'd be unable to correctly address a Japanese dominatrix. In Japanese, you add a different suffix onto people's names depending on your relationship with them. Your teacher would be Matsumoto-sensei to you, but Matsumoto-san to his bank manager, Matsumoto-sama if he were the boss of a large company, and Matsumoto-chan if he were either a child or a pet.

But what do you call a dominatrix? 'Sama' is the most respectful, and might seem obvious, but in a language where there can be five different ways of saying thank you, depending on who you want to thank, number eight and I were both a bit worried that there might be another as yet undiscovered form of honorific Japanese designed to give the appropriate degree of respect to a woman who'd accept payment in exchange for stamping on one's balls.

When we entered the bar, we both went a little weak at the knees. The mistress was stunning: tall and dark and dressed head-to-toe in latex. We plumped for sama, which, given her giggles, was clearly not offensive and yet still not quite right. As she poured us drinks and we ran through the few phrases we'd practised to help us ascertain what the deal was—in case you're interested, the deal was: women get in for free and can drink anything they like, men pay through the nose and get to drink watered-down shōchū, no one's allowed to fuck on the sofas. But what I hadn't anticipated was her first question. Pouring a dark shot of whisky into my glass, she turned her beautiful, intimidating dark eyes on me:

'What are you?'

'I'm...' I'm a girl? I'm English? I'm a teacher? I couldn't understand what she was looking for. I settled on 'I'm... sorry, I don't understand.'

'Domme, sub, switch, what are you?'

Ah, got it. She wanted to know what I was so she could work out whether to offer me a beating, or offer me the opportunity to beat one of the men sitting in their pants and worshipping her from across the bar. Domme? Sub? I'm a bit of both. I'm certainly not averse to doing either as long as there's a guy sitting nearby with a rock-on. But I don't think I'm a switch—that implies there's an equal amount of pleasure in both S and M, and I felt like that would be dishonest. Besides, it was all getting far too BDSM-y: I didn't want to give myself any particular label in case it refused to come unstuck and number eight and I got caught in a trap of being unable to have sex unless one or other of us was squealing in agony.

But if I'm not domme, sub or switch, just what, exactly, am I?

'*Wakarimasen.*' I don't really know.

She repeated the three categories: domme, sub, switch. 'What are you?'

And suddenly it came: '*Hentai desu.*'

I'm a pervert.

CHAPTER NINE

WHATEVER IT IS THAT WOMEN WANT, I'M CERTAIN IT'S SOMETHING MORE COMPETENT THAN THIS

'She fancies you.'

'No she doesn't.'

'She does.'

'She definitely doesn't.'

'You should fuck her.'

'But I'm not even bi.'

'But you fancy her.'

'…'

'Fuck her.'

Whispered challenges at 3 a.m are not usually the start of a beautiful thing. But in this case the boy was right—she did fancy me. I knew it, and it made me tremble. It made me horny. It made me arrogant. It made me feel like that one creepy guy who stares sleazily at girls as they hang off the bar.

She was smaller than me, and that made me feel powerful. I wanted to wrap my arms around her and protect her and carry her like she was mine. And she was so curvy, with an arse that would ripple if you smacked it and tits you could bury your face in. They jiggled when she laughed, trapped in bras that were slightly too small, and tops that stretched thin over them.

After a drunken night out, during which I'd accidentally brushed her boobs with my elbow as I poured drinks for others at our table, she invited us back to crash at her flat.

Number eight and I lay in her bed while she settled down on the sofa in the next room.

'You could fuck her.'

'I couldn't.'

'She wants you to.'

He stroked me roughly under the duvet as I listened to her moving around in the next room, turning off lights, lying down, getting up again for a drink, shuffling papers as she rolled a joint. The boy put his face right next to mine and looked at me with challenging eyes. He touched me and felt how wet I was at the thought of holding her, sliding my hand down her pants to see if she wanted it too.

I left the room and stood in the lounge—knickers and a t-shirt and a challenging smile. She smiled back, jerked her head in the direction of the bedroom, wondering after eight. I mimed 'asleep' then went to get water.

She stood up as I came back into the room. Black dress, too small, far too small, hugging her curves, stretching tight across her chest, bra straps digging into shoulders. I downed my water and turned to her casually. Testing, hesitantly, I pulled her towards me and leant down. I put my face right in front of hers, and waited for her to eat me up.

She did.

She was soft, but so forceful. She kissed like a guy, but everything about her was girly—her smell, her softness, her small hands and hard nipples. I couldn't help but put my own hands all over her, feeling beneath her dress for where her bra began, the ridges I'd seen where the straps dug into her back.

I lifted her skirt up so I could feel the line of her lacy girlish knickers.

I tried to drag her back into the room with him and she shook her head, suddenly scared that he'd be jealous and angry. Still holding my face in her hands, she walked backwards to the sofa. Raised her skirt up over her head and took her dress off. She was stunning—curvy and pale, with long honey-blonde hair. I bent my face to her neck and kissed.

I'll admit it—I still didn't have a clue how to fuck girls. I could remember what I'd done with Kate, but only with the hindsight that it probably didn't rock her world. Number nine knew more than I did, but I didn't want to just lie back while she fucked me. She was different to Kate because, to put it bluntly, I fancied her. This revelation would have probably helped me no end when I was eighteen. Fun and beautiful though Kate was, my gaze didn't follow her across the room as it had with number nine. Kate and I were nervous and awkward because we wanted to impress the boys. I was awkward with nine because I wanted to impress *her*.

So I tried to imagine what the boy would do, what number eight would want to do if he were here on the sofa beside her. So I kissed her neck, I stroked her, I pulled down her bra so she spilled out of the top. I ran my tongue over her nipples, and felt their cold hardness in my mouth. I ran my hands all over her—her hips, her stomach, her ass—and I squeezed. I tasted her sweat and her perfume and played my fingertips gently over her nipples.

And when I could think of nothing else to do I put my face in her crotch, buried my mouth in the warm wetness of her knickers and breathed in.

Holy Christ she smelt good. Her scent, like Kate's, was different to mine—sour and hot and warm. I hooked my hands under the waistband and pulled her knickers down, leaving them dangling from one ankle so I could spread her legs wide and kneel between them. She threw her head back over one arm of the sofa, and I kept my hands firmly on her ass as I buried my face in her cunt.

She was wet. It was too easy. She trembled on first contact and, as I ran my tongue harder over her clit, her thighs twitched.

She put her hand over her mouth to stifle her panting; she didn't want the boy to hear next door. Her other hand fluttered, looking for purchase on something, settling on my hair.

As she moved faster, grinding her cunt onto my face, I ran my hands up onto her tits. I took one nipple in each hand and tugged them gently. She let out soft moans, and bucked her hips as I licked her.

Despite trying to be quiet, she let out a few very soft, strangled noises as she came. Not spectacularly, not gushingly—she just came. Her legs jerked, she let go of my hair, her stomach tensed, and she looked up. She grinned to see me—chin drenched in her come, sticking my tongue out like I'd done something bad.

I kissed her goodnight and went back into the bedroom where the boy was waiting. He lay staring at the ceiling with sparkling eyes, breathing heavily as I entered.

I slid into bed and sat astride him, felt his rock solid cock twitching beneath me. I sat on it, just enough for the tip to rest inside me. He thrust his hips up, desperate to push it all the way in—harder than he'd ever been before. I pulled away slightly, keeping him at a measured distance, and put my mouth next to his ear. He sighed. I whispered a quick account of what had happened, and asked him if he'd heard. He moaned softly—yes. I sat down, sliding right onto him until his cock was deep inside my cunt, and I felt him shudder and come as I spat the taste of her into his mouth.

I didn't just love number nine, I idolised her. She was everything I'd imagined the perfect woman to be—every good quality that I'd not quite acquired, she had in bucketloads. She was funny as well as fun, tripping through life with a joke for everyone who looked sad, and a few sharp words for those who'd made them so. When she was in the room everyone's eyes were on her, but she was independent and feisty, as ready with a 'fuck you' as a 'fuck me'. She gave just enough of herself that you were always left wanting more. One more kiss, another dance, five more minutes drinking tea and chattering while I soak up your infectious laughter.

She was ours—not mine, *ours*. The boy fell almost as heavily for her as I did, not just entranced by the idea of hot lesbians but the thought of two girls who were into each other and into him. She wasn't there to spice up any element of our life, to tick our threesome box: she was a gift given to both of us, which we lost no time in unwrapping. If we'd known who to send a thank you letter to, it would have run to over a hundred pages.

That first night led to more nights, in which eight was not just a bystander. The girl and I would take turns to play with him, sharing gleeful grins as we passed his dick between our mouths. She'd let me stroke and play with her while she held his cock, and she'd lie on top of me as he rolled on a condom.

I was nervous the first time he fucked her. Not just nervous, terrified. Of all the ups and downs that the boy and I had shared, jealousy was the most significant. It's safe to say that most of the downs were my fault—a result of my terror that one day he'd find a girl who was better than me, kinder than me, hotter than me. Or, at the very least, one who was less prone to crying when drunk.

No one's perfect, and relationships are way more imperfect than the sum of the people in them. Peering into the cracks between the dirty sex sessions and the teasing and our mutual desire to take over the world, you could just about spot the flashes of imperfection and anger that kept us awake at night.

People are many things, of which 'flawed' and 'stupid' are certainly two, but top of the list is 'bastards'. Number eight and I had problems because we were frequently horrible to each other, for no reason other than that we couldn't successfully not be. I've never ascribed to the 'all men are bastards' school of relationship counselling. Sure, all men are bastards of some description—those who cheat and lie, those who refuse to contribute to the housework, those who don't treat their partners properly and commit the heinous crime of forgetting anniversaries. But that's not because they're men, it's because they're *people*. They mess up and they're cruel and they're unthinking and destructive. I say 'they', but of course I mean 'we'. We are bastards, all of us.

Over the course of my relationship with eight I forgot every single one of our anniversaries. I laughed at him in front of our friends. I got upset with him for being late, even if his excuses were cast-iron. He made mistakes too, of which being late for no apparent reason was a frequent one. He laughed at me in front of our friends. He told me harsh truths about myself and acted surprised when I cried. And bastardly though these things are they're not even a tenth as bad as the other things we did: lying to each other, telling the other one that perhaps our lives would have been better if we'd never met, refusing to commit to each other just in case some dream partner came along the next day.

All these things and more: we made mistakes, and we fucked up. Every. Single. Day.

For my part, the biggest mistake I made was to assume that he wasn't happy. I'd watch with suspicion as his eyes followed another woman across the room. I ruined nights out with catty comments that he wasn't paying me enough attention. I cross-examined him about his female friends. I even—and my blood runs cold just to write this down—read his emails.

He wasn't cheating on me, of course. It would take a few major tantrums and a serious talking-to before I'd accept that, yes, he did love me. And no, he wasn't planning on canning our relationship any time soon. But the problem with jealousy is that it is irrational. If eight had snogged someone else at a party I'd have been justified in screaming and wailing at him: he'd have broken a promise to me, a promise not to get drunk and snog some random twat at a party. But my jealousy wasn't prompted by anything rational at all. Wholly innocent events—the receipt of a flirty text, a look I'd interpreted as meaningful, a few too many mentions of a specific girl's name—would have my inner Iago rearing his ugly head and shouting, 'I like not that!'

I used to dream, at least once a week, that he found another girl to replace me. The heartbreaking thing about these dreams wasn't the fact that he'd gone, but that in the dream I didn't even know he'd left. I'd spot him with his arms, legs, or tongue around another girl, and I'd stride up in full Othello mode and ask what the hell he thought he was playing at. Every single time I had this dream I expected a different outcome: for him to break down and apologise and tell me he loved me and beg me back. But he never did. Instead, with a casual nonchalance he'd reply:

'Oh, I'm with *her* now. We're over.'

He'd go back to kissing this other woman while I looked on in shock, waves of heartbreak running from my neck right down to my feet, asking him over and over again:

'Why? What did I do?'

So the first time we fucked number nine I was terrified. Amazing though this was in theory, I didn't want the reality of it to rip open one of these jealous cracks that eight and I were working hard at trying to ignore. I was worried that, when push came to shove, I'd push and shove her out of the way, defending the private, precious bubble that eight and I lived in. What's more, I had to not only be 'OK' with it but actively aroused. Getting turned on by something I'd only seen in my nightmares seemed about as likely as me masturbating over pictures of my parents.

But as she kissed my neck and my nipples, and he hovered, condom-clad and nervous, behind her, he made just the move that was guaranteed to calm me down. He paused, with his hands on her backside to make sure she didn't turn and face him, then he looked directly into my eyes. It was a determined, focused trick designed to hold my attention—he looked steadily at me, raised his eyebrows, and mouthed: *Is this OK?*

And suddenly it was. Number nine was no more of a threat to us than anyone else we'd met. Not only had the boy asked if it was OK, he genuinely cared about the answer. If I'd said no he'd have pulled back, put his trousers on, and retired to another room. That vaporised any worries I'd had before. Whatever nightmares I'd have in the future, when I dreamed about this I'd wake up smiling.

After that first time we couldn't help but chase her. Each night we went out excited, hoping that she'd be there too. I snatched kisses with her in toilets and at parties, and he'd exchange meaningful looks with both of us as we ran our hands over his crotch when no one was looking. Number eight and I were on the pull, desperate to impress the woman who'd made such an impression on us.

And she made me hot. She made me wet. She made me sit up and pay attention. But I didn't get that kick-in-the-gut, not when it was just the two of us. Her curves, squeezed tight into whatever dress she'd chosen, made me horny and gave me shivers of need. I wanted to grab the neckline and pull it down, hard, watching her spill out and into my face. But without number eight it all seemed theoretical, like talking about a chemistry experiment. The practical session: the sparks and colours and reactions, came much more easily when he was there.

I'm pretty sure that the reason I missed that final spark was because, although she had everything I could reasonably want in a woman, she was ultimately still a woman.

She did all the good things I could reasonably expect from her: she put her face in my cunt and licked me and tongued me and kissed me. It felt good, in a warm and tingly sense, but it didn't feel hot, because it was still just oral sex, as opposed to the *sex* sex that I'd always craved. It sounds like heresy to dismiss it. After all, what better way for someone to express their physical affection for you than to bury their face in your crotch until you shout 'Oh God if you ever stop doing this I will DIE'? But it's just not for me.

Don't get me wrong, I don't actively dislike it, and if you want me to sit on your face I will no doubt have quite a pleasant time. Ultimately what you're doing is tonguing my clit, which is better than a kick in the teeth. But there's something missing: a cock. It doesn't have to be huge, it doesn't even have to make me come, it just has to be there—in me.

It's never been a huge problem when I've been with guys, they just think I'm a little odd. Although some women like it, some love it and others literally cannot come without it, I've always been able to take it or leave it. More often than not I'd choose to leave it. I'm not disgusted or horrified by it, and I'm more than happy to do it to someone else. But in a contest between two otherwise equal lovers, one of whom was offering to tongue me until I saw stars, and the other offering to fuck my mouth and then push me out of a window, I'd go for the latter in a heartbeat.

And so with number nine I was far happier kissing her clit while the boy fucked me from behind than squirming under her mouth and pretending I could see what the fuss was about.

However all good rules have an exception, and the rule that you should never give me head and expect me to do more than thank you politely has one too. There was one guy, once, who taught me what the fuss was about.

Number ten was short and stocky with large, soft hands and a habit of putting his head to one side then asking me disarming questions.

'Are you *always* like this?'

'Given that your life is worryingly finite, do you think you're doing a good job of it?'

'Are you actually happy with your boyfriend?'

He was cool, in a way that scared me a little. He cared about art and music. Scratch that—the scary thing was that he even *knew* about art and music. He'd listen to incomprehensible electronic noise, then recommend me tunes that sounded like keyboard demos. He'd show me blocks of colour, ask me what I thought, then look at me with a penetrating gaze that made me suspect the right answer wasn't 'That's pretty.'

What's more, he knew that eight and I weren't happy. I shouldn't have spoken to him about it. When you're not happy in a relationship the last person you should confide in is one who's got a vested interest in you splitting up. The comforting 'you're hot, you'll find someone else straight away' is easily translated into the 'I want to fuck you' that can be enough to tip you over the edge.

I hadn't stopped loving number eight. I hadn't even stopped fancying him. He still loved me, and I physically hurt for him. I couldn't hold his hand without fighting back the urge to guide it down my knickers. We'd spent years together by now, and should logically be not just bored of the other's company but ready to run for the nearest exit screaming 'I just cannot cope with one more fight about the same fucking thing!'

My conviction that he didn't love me was making me wary. We'd done well with number nine. We all enjoyed our time together and I'd managed to dodge all of the traps that would have had me slurring 'Whyyoulovehermorethanme' at 2 a.m. every single morning until he went mad. But despite me trusting him to shag nine without leaving, I couldn't shake the fact that there were countless other girls, and countless other opportunities for him to pack up his charm and his wit and his energy and his beautiful hands and his satisfying dick and swan off into the sunset with someone else. Every time he went silent, or was late, or told me he was too tired for sex, I'd sink into fearful sleep and have that dream again. I had no tangible reason to believe he'd go, but my perverse-and-not-in-a-good-way logic ran the same tired course as it has for all jealous partners since the start of time:

I love this man, he is amazing. And he's with me despite my flaws.

If he is amazing then chances are others will think so too.

If others think so too, why would he stay with someone as flawed as I am?

Every time I told him that I loved him, the heartbeat of silence before his reply nudged my inner Iago again: 'How long do you think you've got before this perfect boy fucks off? A month? A year?'

Until eventually I couldn't cope with the nudging any more, and felt I should nudge things myself.

'Shall we have a break?' I offered.

'From... us?'

Well, what else? What else *was* there? Number eight was my whole life—my best friend and my lover and my rival and my personal chef. He was my nagging mother and my teasing mate. He was almost all of my fantasies. I'd lie naked next to him at night, listening to his heavy breathing and growing wet with the desire to touch him. It was beautiful, and it was just the kind of passion that poetry had promised me: a rolling, dramatic passion that was love one minute and hate the next. But it was exhausting. Not just being tortured with lust whenever his t-shirt rode up to show his hipbones, but trying to control that lust and concentrate on the sensible things, the grown-up things. Fucking like you want to eat each other is all well and good, but you have to wake up in the morning and make breakfast without jizzing all over the coffee table. You have to be able to have conversations with meaningful endings, and recognise that a blow job isn't a meaningful ending. I was exhausted of trying to keep up with the things we did that weren't sex: conversations about the future, about what we'd do when we left Japan. Whether we'd live together and whether we'd grow old together and how we'd cope at playing grown-ups when I wouldn't stay sober and he wouldn't tell me he loved me.

And while I was growing tired of fighting this, he was growing tired too. The pauses in our conversations got longer, until it was time for bed and neither of us had found a way to finish the row. His reassurances that this was good grew more hesitant. His kisses grew less frequent.

He was exhausted.

'Yeah. From us.'

'OK.'

The nightmares didn't stop. And nor did the jealousy. Nor, in fact, did I manage to push him out of my mind for more than about fifteen waking minutes before I was either choking back sobs or crossing my legs to soak up the arousal as I remembered something filthy he'd done to me. But as number eight and I took some time apart to try and remember why we'd been together, number ten blazed into my life.

It was a scorching hot summer, and the brief whirlwind of torrid fucklust that ten and I shared stands out mainly because of the smell.

Smell's pretty nostalgic, right? Certain aftershaves remind you of particular people, the washing powder your mum still uses will always smell like home. And to this day when I'm sweating in a dripping summer's heat, I think of the sweltering sex I had with number ten.

I'd sit for two hours on a jam-packed bullet train then arrive at his house sopping wet and desperate for relief. I'd slug down two pints of water, stand for a blissful minute or two under his air conditioning unit, then focus on squishing myself up against his equally damp self.

We were slow together—long, languid afternoon fucks with short breaks to towel ourselves down between orgasms. Why is it that sex sweat smells deeply hot, whereas the sweat a guy leaks throughout an average day can have me gagging if I accidentally sit too close to him? I wouldn't volunteer to lick clean any bicycle seats at the gym, but I'll happily bury my face in a guy's armpit post-fuck to breathe in the scent of the sweat he's worked up on me.

As well as letting me play with him for hours, number ten was obsessed with giving me head. Not the head I'd had before, from well-meaning guys and an eager, giggling number nine, but head that made me drool and writhe and moan and whimper and squirm and sigh and come.

Giving me head was never—for him a token gesture. He wasn't bending down and licking as a short prelude to sex, a 'do I have to do this?' reciprocation of the head I'd given him. Regardless of whether I'd given him the same, he'd lie eagerly between my legs, get himself comfy, and then settle the fuck down.

The settling down thing is key. Head I'd had before had often felt a bit cursory. It wasn't sex, it was something that had to happen *before* sex. Like chatting someone up or offering them a coffee, it was a necessary step for guys to take before they got their dick wet. In settling down and making it clear he was going nowhere, number ten was telling me that this wasn't foreplay, it was the main event.

But there was more to it than that—something he was doing actually *felt* different. Previous partners had licked gently, as if I was a particularly fragile stamp, whereas number ten massaged my clit with forceful, liquid strokes that made me feel as if I was being pushed to orgasm, as opposed to coaxed towards it.

'How are you so good at that?'

'Flatterer.'

'No, I'm actually serious. What is it you do that other people don't?'

'Well, that's a tricky question,' he said, and he had a point. 'I've never seen anyone else do it, except in porn, and in porn it's always done for visual rather than cuntal effect.'

'That's not a real word.'

'I know. But honestly, I'm not sure. I guess I give my best head when I'm really turned on, and it's largely intuitive at that point.'

'Because you can feel me react?'

'A bit. But mainly because if I want to stay hard for any length of time when I'm doing it, I need something to stimulate my cock. And if I'm lying down, with my weight on my cock, I can move a bit and feel what I think you'll feel when my tongue's on your clit.'

'So you... rub your cock against the bedsheets?'

'Sort of, yeah.'

They don't give you tips like that in *Cosmo*. If they did, I suspect you'd see more women crossing their legs as they flick through the magazine in the hairdresser's. Something about the idea was so viscerally horny that I couldn't shake it from my mind. I imagined his face buried in my cunt and his buttocks tensing with each change of sequence, making small movements to grind himself into the duvet. On the bullet train home I took a quick trip to the toilets when the thought of it got too much. After sliding my jeans down to my knees, I pictured the movements his tongue had made, and the matching feeling in the head of his cock, and I leant against the wall and frigged myself to a parallel, leg-trembling climax.

Number ten never came while he was giving me head. He preferred to save that for when I was calm and sated, dripping with sweat and come and ready to take him fully into my mouth. But feeling his lips on my clit, and knowing that he was feeling similar things as he ground the head of his cock into the bedsheets?

I'll just file that away in the 'unngh' pile.

CHAPTER TEN

A Brief Interlude In Which I Discover That I Am Not Exactly A Talented Seductress

Number ten was a trip I was happy to take away from number eight. Number eleven most definitely wasn't.

A gathering of friends, a nostalgia for the country I'd soon be leaving, a heart still cracking under the weight of how much I missed eight and a hefty helping of far too much cheap booze—all of these things conspired to lead my already frazzled brain into making a poor decision.

I decided to fuck another girl.

I didn't set out to fuck her experimentally, I didn't wonder, Hey, maybe I'm a bit gay. I was pretty sure I wasn't—the 'cock fetish' thing, remember? Even before I fucked her I knew that her distinct lack of a penis would be a tricky hurdle to overcome if the sex we were to have would be anything other than a distracting, interesting way to pass the evening. I didn't decide to fuck her because she was a girl, I decided to fuck her *despite* her being a girl.

She was tall and wiry—a direct contrast to the delicate curvaceousness of number nine. She had the same confidence but it was matched with a brash, arrogant attitude that reminded me of First Love, number two, and all the domineering, egotistical famous people who strut regularly through my wank bank. From behind she looked deliciously ambiguous—feminine hips but a tight, square set in her shoulders that could easily have made her a boy. She had short, spiked hair, and she wore vest tops with no bra. When she barked raucous laughter into the night I wasn't the only person whose head was turned—we listened because of the laughter, but were looking at her nipples, which stood out hard and dark against the thin white cotton of her vest.

Number eleven swigged beer and preened, challenging people to quick-fire drinking matches that ended with lager sprays and piss-taking. I accepted her challenges a couple of times, swigging bitter fizziness to try and impress her. I was intrigued by her power. I wanted to know how it would feel to be owned by her, conquered in the same way that number eight had conquered me—with whispered commands, twinkling eyes and filthy suggestions that I carried out because I wanted to please.

I wanted to feel her hands all over me, pinching and pulling at my nipples before she flipped me over, parted my thighs, and ran her fingers over and into me.

But life, as we are constantly reminded, is a bitch. A cold-hearted bitch who point-blank refuses to deliver the exact fantasies that play out inside our heads. Whether it's birthday parties that end in bitter fights, dream holidays that end in a roach-infested hostel or, in my case, hot girlsex that ends in one of you having to escape from a tent at four in the morning swearing you'll never drink again.

The first warning sign, and the point at which I should have bowed out of the evening, happened just after I kissed her—tentatively at first. When she responded with enthusiasm I pushed back, grabbing the back of her head with my hands and pushing my chest into hers.

At that point she pulled away, sat down, and sighed mournfully. I, assuming I'd clumsily misread the situation, panicked.

'Oh, shit. What's up? I'm sorry. I'm really sorry. What did I do?'

'It's just... everyone thinks I'm a lesbian.'

Ah. Fuck. To be fair, I *had* thought she was a lesbian. But only because earlier in the evening she'd said to me, 'I'm a lesbian.'

'I'm not even really sure if I *am* gay.' She stared into the distance with a meaningful sense of angst. I, being an emotionless shitbag, could think of little more to say than:

'That's OK, let's just go and have a drink instead.'

Empathy was probably more in order. A hug, perhaps. But being a selfish arsehole who is terrified of emotional contact with strangers, I could think only of the quickest exit from the conversation. It's not a deliberate tactic: I'd give anything to be a bit better at the emotional thing. Generally I avoid telling anyone I love them, hoping instead that they'll recognise my use of the word 'dickhead' and playful teasing for the gestures of affection they so clearly are. They certainly come more easily to me than hugs. I barely ever hug my *friends*, let alone people I have only just met. I can't say 'I love you' without making vomiting noises, and if you give me a compliment I am as likely to twat you as thank you.

As number eleven sat miserably, in the throes of what was probably quite a serious contemplation of her sexuality, all I could think was, Oh God, oh God, she's going to want me to hug her, isn't she?

At that point I should definitely have given up on the idea of sex, and steered her instead back to the party for some more lager to take her mind off it. But I was stumped as to what to say. Eventually, after an awkward silence that I couldn't help but feel was entirely my fault, she wiped her eyes, smiled at me and said:

'No, no. It's OK. I probably *am* a lesbian. I do really fancy you.'

'OK. Are you sure you don't just want to think about it a bit more?'

She thought about it a bit more.

'Nope. I'm pretty sure now, I think.' As she stood up she grinned, seemingly cured of whatever temporary uncertainty had gripped her, and she steered me away from the party.

The second warning sign came on the way to her tent. We were waylaid by a group of her friends who were keen to not only chat but encourage both of us further down the road towards 'Incredibly Fucking Drunktown'. I was already wobbling slightly, but she seemed solid. Clearly she'd had more practice than I, and she proceeded to down a few more lagers, bray a few more harsh laughs, and pretend not to notice that her friends were staring at her nipples too. Eventually, after a couple of not unreasonable nudge-nudge-wink-winks about where we were off to, we left the group. And I promptly fell over.

Not a stumble or a trip, but the kind of genuine head-over-heels, arse-in-the-air fall that only comes when you've had far too much to drink and should just call it quits and head on home to bed. My linen trousers were covered with mud, and spotted slightly with blood from where my knee had hit a particularly spiky tree stump.

Eleven was concerned. At least, I think what she was displaying was concern, it might also have been stifled laughter, as she helped me up and half carried me across the field. At no point did my brain say, 'Hey, you know what? If you're too pissed to walk, you're probably not going to be brilliant at fucking.' It didn't say that, because my brain likes to screw me over sometimes, but it should have done.

Warning three came when we'd walked a bit further away from the party. It was late—well past midnight—and the only light was the faint glow coming from the campfire of the group we'd just left. She picked her way carefully between the tents, and I limped behind her. I recognised the same arrogant strut that had attracted me to her earlier: she strode with a sense of confidence and purpose, finally bending down and unzipping her tent with a triumphant flourish.

'Here we are... wait... I... What? Someone's nicked my stuff!'

'Oh my God, that's awful! What's gone missing?'

She rummaged briefly then replied: 'Ah, it's OK. This isn't my tent.' She zipped it back up and strode off again. Hobbling along behind her, I watched her eye up other potential candidates.

'Do you remember what your tent looks like?' I offered, idiotically.

'Oh yes. It's blue.'

'But it's quite dark, they all look the same. Do you remember what shape it is?'

'Yep.' She looked around before confidently asserting, 'It's sort of dome-shaped.'

And it was at that point, as we scanned the assembly of universally dome-shaped tents, that I realised she was utterly, irretrievably pissed. She hadn't fallen over, perhaps because it turns out that not all humans are as clumsy and uncoordinated as I am. But she was certainly drunk enough that she couldn't be entirely confident she'd put up a tent in the first place.

I'm normally more than happy to get a bit pissed and fuck. In fact, if I'm doing something really filthy, or someone new who might be horrified by my wobbliest bits, a bit of Dutch courage is borderline medicinal. But with both of us so utterly wrecked, I should have anticipated that any shag would be liable to end in, at best, massive disappointment and, at worst, mutual injury and a sleeping bag full of vomit.

Number eleven eventually found what was 'almost definitely' her tent, and we crept inside. There wasn't room for any fancy manoeuvres—it was a fucking *tent*, after all—so we lay side by side snogging each other partly in triumph—we found the tent!—and partly out of a bemused and exhausted resignationI guess we'd better, seeing as we've come all this way.

She squirmed one of her hands into my knickers and began frigging me—so hammered that I'm pretty sure what she was doing was down to muscle-memory rather than a genuine desire to see me come. At one point I moaned. It probably wasn't a sexual moan.

I pulled her vest off and she sat on top of me. Her tits were far too beautiful for my spinning head to appreciate, so I steadied myself as I licked her nipples, figuring that even if I couldn't fully enjoy them, at the very least I wouldn't throw up on them.

Eventually, after about ten minutes of fumbling and frigging and rustling around in the tent, number eleven sat up.

'This is seriously hot and all,' she lied, flatteringly, 'but I really need a piss.'

She left the tent, and I sat alone for the next ten minutes wondering whether she'd fallen asleep in a bush or—probably more likely—in someone else's tent. I gave it a few minutes longer, listening out for any telltale sounds to indicate that she might be coming back. Eventually I unzipped the tent and poked my head out.

At which point I realised two things:

Firstly, it was much, much later than I thought. So late, in fact, that the growing light inside the tent wasn't just my eyes becoming accustomed to the darkness, it was the dawn. Birds weren't exactly singing, but I could now make out the colours of the tents around me. And secondly, eleven clearly did have quite good coordination. Because as I looked out of the tent I could see her naked arse lit softly by the dawn light as she squatted in a nearby clearing.

Should I stay? Should I go? I was a bit worried that the whole thing had taken her a full ten minutes, and didn't really want to be the one who'd taken advantage of her when she was so pissed she could hardly piss.

Luckily one of her friends made the call for me by choosing that moment to stagger away from the party and in her direction, shouting, 'All right? Where's your girlfriend?'

To which she replied: '*That* girl? I dunno.'

I didn't see number eleven again, which was probably luckier for her than it was for me. I was quite keen to apologise for doing a shamefaced runner as she cackled with her friend, and I suspect she'd have preferred not to have to shuffle uncomfortably around the subject or—worse—tell me there was no harm done and make apologies of her own.

It did, however, annoyingly cement in my mind the fact that I was clearly more uncomfortable having sex with women than men. If it had been a hot guy having a piss mid-shag, I would have been as unlikely to leave the tent as voluntarily set fire to it. Drunk or not, I'd be happier to ride out any potential mishaps if I would be rewarded with cock at the end of the evening.

Ever since my first tentative attempts at ladysex with Kate, people have told me that I'm bisexual. I get more than a little bit annoyed by this, almost as annoyed as I get at the rather odd statement— which I've heard on numerous occasions—that 'all women are a bit bi really'.

This is clearly bullshit, but it can sometimes be hard to articulate exactly why. The main reason it's bullshit is, of course, because it writes off people's sexual feelings as things that can be easily dismissed rather than things that can shape someone's entire life. No matter what you believe about sexuality, I'd hope everyone can see why this is the sort of thing that only a total arsehole would do.

However, more subtly, it's bullshit because it assumes that it is easy for us to put ourselves in someone else's position and make judgements about what floats their boat.

At university, while I was making my first tentative steps towards pretending to understand philosophy, I read a paper by a rather excellent dude called Thomas Nagel, called 'What is it like to be a bat?'. In it, he explains that we can know that bats 'see' using sonar, and we can—if we're willing to visit a different section of the library— understand exactly how they do that. But the problem is that no matter how detailed any individual's studies they'll never be able to experience the feeling of what it is like to actually *be* that thing.

For my bi-or-not-bi purposes, it'd work like this: picture something sexual. A slim guy being bear-hug-fucked by a much larger guy, for example. You've got an image in your head now, right?

I can look at a number of physical things to try and work out what's going on—I can see if you're turned on, I can measure your erection/wetness, and if I have kickass equipment I can even see exactly which parts of your brain are active, the synapses that are firing.

But no matter how much I study I will never be able to fully experience the feeling that you have. I won't see the same image, nor understand exactly how you feel about this particular instance of guy-on-guy action.

People have physical reactions to sexual things, which we can measure and replicate. They're deliciously and delightfully scientific, which is why scientists love them. If you want to find out what someone likes, the simplest way to measure it is to show it to them and see if they get hard.

But the problem with people is that they also have opinions and emotions which, to be frank, are a pain in the arse to measure. So what's the best way, in day-to-day life, to establish what someone likes? Well, we fucking ask them.

And when we ask them, we do have to take what they say at face value. This goes for my assertion that I'm straight as well as that guy over there's assertion that he's gay. I don't know what turns you on. The only possible way I can know is for you to tell me. And you can tell me anything—you like being fucked by men, you like rubbing your cock against fully clothed women, you like rolling around in a mish-mash of people of all different sizes, shapes, colours and genders—I believe you.

Sometimes I like to fuck women, but it's quite a rare thing for me to find girls that I genuinely fancy. I have a very specific type of girl, and there are some women who make me giggle and drool and stare longingly at their tits, wishing I could pick them up, have them wrap their legs around me, and push them up against a wall while I bury my face in the smooth warmth of their cleavage. So I fuck women sometimes. But I'm not bi, I'm straight. I feel straight. I don't wake up in the night craving passionate lesbian embraces, I wake up in the night sweating and panting and reaching for the nearest cock.

Someone telling me that I'm bi is like someone claiming they know what it's like to navigate Oxford Circus using sonar. And despite my initial eagerness to have number eleven touch my softest and stickiest bits, when I woke up the next morning I understood that it wouldn't ever really have given me the same kick I got from number nine, because there were no guys around to scratch the itch that our initial fumblings had created. Fucking number eleven was something I quite fancied doing, but it wasn't ultimately what I wanted.

What *did* I want, exactly? Rather obviously, the answer to that question was the same as it had been for some time: I wanted number eight.

CHAPTER ELEVEN

Fulfilling My Fantasies Is Only Possible Because Of The Pioneering Work Of Tim Berners-Lee

Although we were apart, having spent a few months trying our best to put each other out of our minds, eight and I were inevitably drawn back together. It began with teasing emails and friendly catch-ups:

'Hey, I saw this webcomic and thought of you!'

'Thanks! That's amazing, in exchange have this amusingly captioned picture of a cat.'

These inevitably turned into lustful reminiscing and eventually tentative suggestions:

'You know, I'm still sorry that we never got to do that threesome with a guy you'd always dreamed about.'

Number eight might have had sod-all idea how to calm my jealous rages, but he knew exactly how to entice me into bed. I wasn't just after the pleasure of having two guys at once, although a buy-one-get-one-free shag which encourages you to stuff yourself full certainly has an incredible appeal. But eight knew that what I really wanted was the opportunity to watch.

I know that some of the things I've done might raise eyebrows. If you don't like getting hit I can understand why you might be surprised to discover that some people do. Likewise if you're averse to anal sex, I can understand you being slightly squeamish if a friend of yours insists on describing it in gleeful and unnecessary detail. But the thing I like that seems to be most puzzling to people is the simplest and most inoffensive of all.

I like to watch boys.

I like to watch them touch themselves. I like to see them get erections and squeeze them nice and hard. I like to see the drips of precome leaking out onto pants stretched tight over their hard-ons. I really, really like to watch boys.

How weird is this? Well, given that pornography is a multi-billion pound worldwide industry, I'd say it's not particularly weird at all. Some of my tastes would probably be dismissed as 'not even hot enough for the bargain bin in the sex shop'.

And yet, when I started a sex blog and told people they could contact me via an email address that looked a bit like 'sendmeyourdickpics' the pictures themselves were initially outnumbered by incredulous emails asking whether I was serious.

'Really? You actually want to see pictures of men's cocks?'

I don't know what to say other than 'yes'. I want to see the pictures. It breaks my heart to think that at this very minute thousands of men are beating one out yet only a very small percentage of them will be documenting the event to share with a loved one or—even better—me. It's not just hot like 'ooh, that's nice' but hot like 'I think I might have to sit down for a minute because my legs have just stopped working'.

A boy of mine once caused me to nearly faint with desire by making casual reference to the fact that sometimes, when he's cracking one off, he ties shoelaces round his cock and balls to heighten the sensation. Whether they're shoving things up their arses, squeezing their dicks nice and tight, or hollowing out a melon then fucking it like it's a long-lost lover, I love watching guys doing things with their dicks.

The issue with women wanking—or as pop culture cringingly insists on putting it, 'female masturbation', as if it's inherently weird and unusual because a girl does it— hasn't gone away. My teenaged self would be incredibly disappointed in how little ground we've gained. So little that not only do we have to lower our voices when we discuss the supposedly mysterious 'female masturbation', but that there's a sense of surprise if a woman admits to liking the look of a particularly attractive cock.

I'm surprised that anyone is surprised. We're happy to accept that straight men spend hours trawling through websites and magazines so they can see women lifting their skirts. Guys hunched over pictures of girls is so normal that we even print tits on page three of some newspapers— guys just need a boob fix, yeah? It's a bloke thing.

It shouldn't need saying but looking at hot naked people isn't just a bloke thing. It's an 'almost everyone' thing. Your taste might be different to mine: you might prefer a subtle topless shot where a guy stares sultrily down the camera lens, proudly displaying a solid, shapely chest with nice taut nipples. You might instead be a fan of the curvaceous and impressive male arse. Especially that bit just above the buttocks where, if you're lucky, there are little dimples in the flesh that are just perfect for running your fingers over. I've met quite a few women for whom the sexiest part of a guy's body is his forearms. *Forearms* for crying out loud—who *are* these perverts?

So, as far as filthy weirdness is concerned, looking at pictures of hot guys is about as depraved as fancying a nice sandwich at lunchtime. And yet for some reason when a guy asks a girl in a chat room, 'Can I c a pic of ur tits?' we roll our eyes, but when I ask men for pictures of them squeezing the head of their cock to show me how hard they are, people are surprised. I'm not the only girl who wants to see hot pictures, I'm just one of the few who is able to ask for them.

In my inbox I have hundreds of pictures of mostly faceless guys, holding themselves with one hand and using their mobile phone to take wobbly, grainy shots of themselves with the other. But some of the most prized photos of all are those I've taken myself.

Photo one: During my first year of university number eight and another boy—who never did enough to me to acquire a number—developed a petty and delicious rivalry. It wasn't that they both wanted me—this was still the period during which I was explicitly *not* number eight's girlfriend—it was that they both wanted me to want them. Exclusively.

Can you see where I'm going with this? Maybe not. I'm going to a kebab house at 3 a.m., on the evening of my nineteenth birthday. We were waiting for food and I jokingly asked them to kiss. I thought it would be one of the ultimate turn-ons: a blond I'd never fucked and a brunette whose cock I'd been sucking just a few hours earlier, choking down their disgust for one another and eating frantically at each other's faces.

'Go on,' I slurred obnoxiously, 'kiss for me.'

To my unending delight, they actually did—forcefully, passionately, and with a lust that contradicted the hatred they publicly felt for each other. Luckily I was not completely paralysed with arousal. I whipped out my camera faster than you can say 'timeless wanking classic' and took a snap.

Photo two: As I might have rather arrogantly mentioned, I get sent a lot of pictures from guys who read my blog. Barring the very odd exception—one guy sent a picture of a chicken, which, although hilarious as a play on the word 'cock', proved to be an incredibly challenging wank—these pictures are beautiful. I'm loath to do what most of the guys ask me to do and rate them, because if I rated them I'd have to admit that some were better than others, and they're all essentially excellent, but I do have my favourites.

For those who have never solicited penis pictures from internet strangers before, allow me to introduce you to the formula. Ninety-nine per cent of the pictures you're sent will be composed along these lines:

There'll be a cock in the centre of the picture, naturally, with either one hand gripped tight around the base—which, by the way, is awesome—or no hands in shot at all. One hand will be on the camera—few people go as far as to set up a tripod and a timer. In most cases the subject will not be naked, but will instead be wearing boxer shorts or trousers that have been pulled down to just below his balls. Sometimes it's a bedsheet or a carefully placed towel. Often not only will the subject of the picture be hard, you'll be able to see the odd drip or two of precome leaking onto the head of his cock. Very occasionally, if you're really lucky, the picture will have been taken just a few seconds after he's come, and both his hand and the head of his cock will be generously slicked with fresh spunk.

You would not *believe* the amount of research that has gone into that paragraph. That no one has yet offered me an honorary degree in 'cock studies' is a monumental injustice.

Anyway, the reason this particular image is my favourite is because it includes so much more than that—something you almost never see: the guy's face.

He's lying on a bed, one hand on the camera and the other hand gripping his deliciously firm cock, staring deep into the lens with big brown eyes and a face of tortured lust. The only thing hotter than seeing someone's desire confirmed by their twitching erection is seeing it reflected in their face.

Photo three: This one isn't for the faint-hearted. In fact, it's the picture most likely to be submitted as evidence when my corpse is eventually found by the police three days after I've wanked myself to death.

This picture is of a boy in the stocks.

You're probably imagining medieval stocks, but these were no such thing. In fact, they didn't even hold him in a standing position. In this picture the boy is on the floor, on his elbows and knees, with a thick iron bar running from his wrists to his ankles. His wrists are clamped into special restraints at the front and his ankles are clamped into restraints at the back.

His head is bowed, so I can only see the back, but I know his expression so well I can conjure it up without having it on film. He's looking anguished and horny and desperate to come. He's looking uncomfortable, because at the end of the stocks there's a metal clamp holding a thick rubber cock firmly in his ass. His own cock sticks out straight from between his legs, deep red and rock solid and glistening at the tip. I took the picture myself.

So when the incredulous men and women of the internet ask me if I really want to see this, the answer can be nothing but 'Hell yes!' And when eight asked me if I wanted to watch two guys fucking, my answer was the same. Perhaps with a few more exclamation marks.

Nine o'clock, a bar in the city centre. There's something quite hot about the anticipation of meeting a total stranger: sipping a beer that's gradually growing warmer and wondering whether the other party will show.

The guy we were expecting was blond. That's about as accurate a description as either of us could have given. Having seen his picture we'd both made appreciative noises. He had cheekbones and a jawline and a nose in the right place and all the things that come from being conventionally attractive. But we didn't have a copy of the photo, so we were going mainly on instinct. Our heads turned every time the door opened and we stared intently and probably quite creepily at every blond man who walked through. It was now 9.30 p.m.

'He's definitely not coming.' The boy checked his phone for the seventeen thousandth time to see whether our stranger had called or sent a text.

'I think you're right. Bollocks. He was really, seriously hot.' My disappointment was palpable.

'Still, it's not a completely wasted evening—at least there's two of us.' He put his hand on my leg under the table and instantly I melted. 'Let's get one more drink and give him till ten. He might just be shy.'

As number eight went to get the drinks another seemingly suitable candidate walked through the entrance of the bar: flustered and hot, but confident, and definitely blond. He scanned the room, settling on me and giving a small wave. My mouth dried up with nervous anticipation, but I waved back and he came over to join me.

'So, you must be...?' He tentatively offered my name.

I, panicked that number eight had chosen just that moment to step away, tried to reply as coolly as possible: 'Ungh.'

'I'm sorry, what?'

'Umm... yes. That's me. The boy's at the bar grabbing some drinks.'

'Brilliant. I'm so so sorry I'm late. I got stuck in traffic and then my phone died. I'm so glad you're still here.'

He settled into a seat, throwing off his coat to reveal a pink shirt and jeans, as well as shoulders that I wanted to sink my teeth into. It's hard to sum up how nervous I was at this point: everything about this guy seemed confident, sexy and grown up. He drove here—both grown up *and* sexy, to someone like me who is incapable of driving without bursting into fearful tears—he had booked a hotel—confident and definitely grown up; number eight and I hadn't considered the logistics—and he was looking at me with a calm smile designed to reassure me that he was neither crazy nor a time waster. In short: he was serious.

Number eight came back, introduced himself, and got our new friend a drink. Equally nervous, he babbled about how nice the pub was and sought ways to broach the topic of our imminent sex. It became apparent that, although we'd spoken to each other about this, turned the fantasy over in our heads a hundred times, neither of us knew what to say to actually make it happen.

I was confident that once we were all alone together, peeling clothes off and licking and sucking and, most importantly, watching the two guys go at it together, I'd know exactly what to say to make the good things happen. But how do you get to that point to start with? It's all very well playing the threesome rules when, as with number nine, you know someone already. It's much harder when you're constantly worried that using the wrong word or saying something too filthy might cause someone to zip up their metaphorical trousers and fuck off.

In the end we didn't need to be brave. As we should have anticipated, the stranger made the first move himself.

'So, it's getting late. Want to see how fantastic my hotel room is?'

And that was all it took to relax both of us. The stranger smiled at us and, as we walked to his hotel, he cracked jokes and messed around with us like we'd been friends for years. He'd clearly been nervous too, all three of us wondering how to break the tension. Not scared of fucking a stranger, but of asking a stranger to fuck.

We'll call him twelve.

When we entered the room there was no awkward chatter, no 'Would you like me to make you a cup of tea with this tiny hotel kettle?' or 'Oh, sorry, I appear to have accidentally brushed your tit.' We just piled together, all three of us, and got stuck in to the single most amazing night of my entire life to date.

It started not gently but passionately—a flurry of clothes and tongues and lips as we fought for each other's rapid kisses. Number twelve was equally interested in both of us, and whispered compliments and requests into number eight's ears as much as mine. We flipped quickly through as many positions as possible, understanding that we only had one night in which to do this.

I revelled in the fact that, when twelve fucked eight, he pushed eight even further into me. The boy sucked eagerly at the surprising thickness of twelve's cock, and groaned as I did the same thing to him.

When we were close to exhaustion, number twelve came on my stomach, as the boy licked droplets of our mingled sweat from my nipples.

But the best thing of all was the two boys kissing each other. From the first time I had group sex, when Si and Andy refused to snog, through all the times at university when I'd made drunken, cheeky suggestions that my boyfriends should kiss for me, and all the nights I'd spent in gay bars mesmerised by the beauty of two men frantically tonguing each other, none of this even came close to what happened that night. I lay on the bed, panting and wet and desperate with lust as number eight bent over me. The stranger knelt behind him, running his hands all over eight's naked body and making occasional horny moans. As I looked up at both of them, willing myself to fix every minute of this firmly in my mind, the stranger turned to eight and asked:

'Are you OK?'

And number eight responded with a kiss. Not just a peck-on-the-lips kiss—he turned around, put one hand on the stranger's shoulder, and pulled him forward until the pair of them were snogging with a passion that made my legs weak. I stared at them, silhouetted against the streetlight pouring in through the window, and held my breath. Just watching.

I'm a romantic at heart, you know.

The next fuck you have after a threesome is usually inspired by it. You relive the excitement of what you did, chat over the hot parts, and—in the case of number eight and I—whisper stories about what might have happened as you screw the other into a quivering wreck.

But stories, naturally, are never even close to enough. Having had what we thought was the textbook definition of 'amazing anonymous internet sex', neither of us could resist pushing things a bit further to see what else might have the same effect.

Number eight, turning his smug, cheeky smile on me in bed one morning: 'What do you want?'

Me, with a potentially worrying lack of hesitation: 'A gangbang'

'No, really, what do you want?'

'A gangbang.' Well, if you don't ask, you don't get. Sadly, I wasn't going to get.

'Let's try again. Within the realms of what I can realistically achieve in the next twenty-four hours or so, what do you want?'

'I'd like to watch another man sucking your dick.' This was something that, although the guys had done it during our threesome, still hovered in my mind as something incomplete. Sure, they'd sucked each other's cock, and the passion and enthusiasm with which they did it had me touching myself and holding my breath, desperate to come but wary of spoiling the magic. But I was still there, still involved. I was curious to see how things would feel if I wasn't involved at all, just sitting at the sidelines of my own private gay porn theatre.

There was a pause as eight looked at me, weighing up how he felt about having another guy— someone other than twelve—sucking him. I waited for his response, looking at him with a face that I hoped suggested 'you're going to love this' but in reality was probably closer to 'oh please oh please oh please'.

'...'

'...'

'I'll see what I can do.'

A few minutes on the internet and we had something—a gay guy had published a straightforward ad offering cocksucking. He just wanted to pop round someone's house, drop to his knees, suck for a while, then sod off home again. Straight guys were not only welcome, he promised, but his favourite.

An hour or so later I was sitting, tense, on the sofa, waiting for my boy to arrive. He'd gone to the station to meet our stranger, check him out and have a coffee. If all was well, he promised, they'd return together and I could watch whatever happened.

Nothing quite prepared me for the odd feeling of watching them begin. The boy sat nervously on a chair, rock solid and straining upwards, as the stranger went to work. He started by licking thickly from base to tip, smacking his lips and gripping the boy's thighs as he moistened everything. Then he took the whole cock in his mouth, and I saw the boy push himself upwards as it slipped in. Flustered though he was, he was clearly enjoying it, loving the skill with which the other guy was sucking him.

I sat in the corner on my knees, squeezing my legs together to hold in the throbbing pulse of arousal. Watching in fascination as the stranger worked my boy's dick in ways subtly different from mine. I was trying to remember, to learn, to maintain my composure. Most of all I was repeating the trick I'd used before—trying not to breathe too loudly in case it broke the spell.

It was here that we should have stopped. This was the hottest bit—the sucking, the trembling, the nervousness of the boy I knew and the casual skill of the one I didn't. Above all: the watching. If I could have paused time I'd have kept it right there, with them both solid and happy and me sitting quietly nearby, just storing everything away to recall later.

Unfortunately, it didn't stop there. There was no climactic moment as number eight came hard into the stranger's throat. My memory grows hazy halfway through this story, but at some point the boy was lying naked, face down on the bed, with number thirteen—the new stranger—poised and ready to fuck him. Ever useful, I handed them a condom then retired to my position of trembling observer, watching as they went for it.

The stranger was big, not with muscle, but with beer. The boy was lithe and skinny and almost disappeared under the mass of the other. He turned his face towards me, wincing with pain and arousal as the other guy fucked him. I clasped my hands together behind my back to try and refrain from touching myself.

And then... then things went a bit odd.

I think they felt guilty that I wasn't joining in. I think they felt bad that, although they got to rub and lick and suck and fuck each other, I was left in the corner. I think they thought I wasn't getting anything out of it.

I was summoned and, awkwardly, I went. I took off my clothes, and things suddenly turned from super-hot live-action gay porn to uncomfortable date. I didn't want to say no and look like I was rude, but saying yes meant I had to fuck someone who had been quite up front in telling us that he didn't fancy women.

Don't get me wrong, fucking two gentlemen at once is one of my favourite things, and for all the weirdness of the situation, it was still nice to be at the mercy of two naked cocks. If I'm honest, I'm frequently grateful to be in the same *time zone* as two naked cocks. But although number eight was incredibly hot for me, the other gentleman was pretty damned gay indeed. He wasn't interested in me; he was interested only in the fact that my presence kept the other guy hard.

We fucked together for a while. My boy fucked me while the stranger fucked him, and then we did it the other way around for a bit. All the while I was thinking, How can I get out of this with dignity? Watching two guys go at it makes me wet, but feeling one of them limply humping me while looking stonily into the distance, clearly thinking only of maintaining some semblance of an erection, is not exactly my cup of tea.

When it was finished I think we might actually have had a cup of tea. Just a quick one, the cup of tea that says, 'I definitely want you out of my house very soon, but I'm going to drink hot drinks with you to prove that I do not think badly of you as a person.' And, to be fair, we didn't. He was a perfectly lovely guy, and an incredibly skilled cocksucker. He was friendly and chatty and calm and experienced and easy to get on with.

He was just... you know... gay.

There are a number of morals to this story: always stick to what you agreed on the internet; don't join in sex scenes you're uncomfortable with; be honest about what you actually like, etc.

But the one I've always taken from it is that no matter how much you like someone, and how much you love fucking, sometimes not fucking is the best thing you can do. And it's not like there's any harm in watching: watching is what I do best.

CHAPTER TWELVE

No One Ever Called Christian Grey An 'Irritating Cockbag'

What's the worst thing to hear when you're having sex? 'Ouch' is probably pretty high on the list, as is the name of someone's previous girlfriend or—shudder—mum. Top of my list is cringe-making words for genitals. 'Pussy' I've already dealt with: apart from the giggling Mrs Slocombe references, it just doesn't sound like something I'd actually use to get pleasure. 'Pussies' belong to porn stars and gangsters' 'hos'—a pussy is something for a guy to fuck, not something for a girl to get genuine eye-rolling pleasure from. Coming in at a close second is words for tits that end in '-ies'. I have never had 'titties' or 'boobies', I have tits. Calling them by words that children use kills the mood quicker than a bucket of ice water or a picture of a kitten. Which leads me neatly on to the final, and most awful words to use: cute names for cock. You don't fuck someone raw with 'Barry Junior', and I certainly don't want to swallow 'Mr Winkie'. A cock is the most brilliant and powerful thing about any guy—I'm not ready for him to turn it into a fucking Disney character.

There are probably some words I've used throughout this book that give you the same shudders. 'Cock' is occasionally controversial, of course, and don't get me started on the other 'c'. If I had a pound for the number of cunts I've had to cross out, reconsider, then write back in again for want of a better word I'd have more than enough to buy a thesaurus.

But although I joke that certain words are banned from my bedroom, I don't think there's ever a wrong way and a right way to do things. Talk about your 'pussy' if that's what you prefer. You're not doing sex wrong just because you don't agree with people like me who are sitting firmly in Camp Cunt. I'm not weird because I prefer to 'fuck' than 'make love'—no weirder than anyone else, at any rate.

I love the fact that we're all so different. Whether you're aroused, amused or disgusted by any given word or act, the knowledge that everyone has a unique sexual character is both fascinating and brilliant.

Nowhere are people's differences more apparent than in a sex club.

When we returned from Japan, eight and I could cast aside worries about language and get stuck into being perverts again. Assuming that now we were in England we'd be less likely to break rules we couldn't decipher, or accidentally offend someone by using 'san' instead of 'sensei', we headed off to school.

Not a real school, of course, everyone there was over the age of eighteen, in most cases by many years. The club was laid out in a vague imitation of one, but the books and posters and facts had been replaced with canes and whips and those single-seat wooden desks that went out of fashion in the 1970s. There weren't any bells or breaktimes, and the school bullies were as likely to call you cute as kick your arse. There were no registration periods and, judging by the women walking around with ripped fishnets on display beneath ludicrously short skirts, there was probably no uniform policy either. But, like all good schools, there were rules.

On our first visit, number eight and I arrived in outfits cobbled together from whatever we could find at the back of our wardrobes that looked vaguely smart and scholarly. Rather worryingly we both looked much older than our twenty-five years. There's nothing like dressing up as a schoolgirl to highlight just how much you've aged. Shuffling uncomfortably, we presented ourselves at the entrance to the club.

'What are you here for?' barked the man at the door, who obviously hadn't read the website—'We're friendly and welcoming to new visitors!—as thoroughly as we had.

'Umm... that school night that's run by kinky people?' I offered tentatively, hoping that at no point would this man be one of my appointed teachers.

'I *know* that.' He sighed, frustrated by the fact that we were selfishly refusing to read his mind. 'What are you here *for*? To spank, to be spanked, neither, both?' He indicated a set of badges on the table nearby and explained. 'Red means you don't want to take part, you're just here to watch. Green means you're happy with people spanking you. Yellow means you're happy for some people to spank you but not others. And if you don't have a badge then that means you might spank people, but you have to ask their permission first, of course.'

We nodded, and I pointed towards a green badge.

'No, you probably don't want that. If you're new you'll want a yellow one, otherwise you might get lots of people trying to spank you.'

'Oh. But I thought that was the idea?'

He sighed again and explained that although I probably wanted to be spanked, because I hadn't been there before it'd be best if I took a yellow badge, with a green one people would be a bit more forward in their approaches.

It was my turn to sigh. I understood what he was trying to do. He saw a young(ish) girl about to enter what to him appeared to be a den of wolves, or at least a den of overexcited dominant men, and wanted to protect her.

It was understandable, of course: fetish clubs are often very intimidating places. They're essentially clubs where adults go to act out some of their more extreme and painful and extremely painful fantasies. If you're not even slightly intimidated by some of the spiky-heeled dominatrixes or bullwhip-wielding doms, you're certainly a braver person than I. The rules are there, primarily, to keep people safe. No matter how terrifying that guy in the corner with the spiky paddle is, the rules are there to reassure you that he won't hit you with it unless you want him to.

However, it's not just the potential pain that gets people nervous. Some of the most dominant people I know are intimidated by fetish clubs. Whether you're there to whip or be whipped, the nature of the club evokes the exact self-consciousness that scares the shit out of all of us: am I sexy enough? Am I scary enough? Am I doing this right? And, above all, the question that plagues almost every individual, whether they're at Mistress Vixen's Spanking Palace or the Annual Women's Institute Tea Dance—do I *fit in*?

So the rules are also there to give people a gentle nudge so that they know how to behave, and can be confident that, on the surface, at least, they fit in.

Never disturb couples who are already playing.

Never touch someone without asking.

Accept no for an answer.

If you understand the situations in which you're *not* allowed to approach someone, it becomes easier to approach them the rest of the time. Perhaps this is why more partner-swapping, play and chatting-up happens on the kink scene than in any other club I've been to: kinksters understand how not to chat someone up, so they find it easier to chat. Without these handy guidelines, fetish clubs would end up like school discos, with the submissives standing on one side of the room smiling shyly at the dominants as they work up the courage to ask someone for a dance.

So these rules are there for a reason: the badges and bells and whistles, not to mention the long list of rules on the club's website, are there so that people know what to expect. If you put on a red badge you know that no one will try to play with you, and it's your responsibility to go and proposition the face that belongs to the arse that you most want to put over your knee. If you wear a yellow badge you might have to be a bit more forward—you're submissive but you want to choose who you play with, which means you have to speak up and ask. And if you're green—well, in theory you should be fighting them off with a stick.

I should have worn green.

My problem with fetish clubs, and what those who were on it referred to as 'the scene' is that I found it incredibly difficult to get spanked. I wandered the hallowed school halls, chatting to people, batting my eyelashes at suitably angry-looking teachers and failing to get anything even remotely resembling a beating.

I was clearly doing something wrong, because no one else—even those with yellow badges that matched mine—seemed to have the same trouble. A guy dressed as a schoolgirl was being belted across a desk while reciting the six times table—which confirmed my suspicion that maths will never, ever do it for me. Two women in their early thirties, bent side-by-side over a gym horse, were being chastised by a much older guy in a headmaster's gown. A terrifying, muscular and incredibly sexy guy dressed as a school bully was strutting up and down the room swinging what looked like a policeman's night stick, occasionally obliging the blushing girls who deliberately riled him by slapping them heartily on the thighs. My arse remained depressingly un-spanked.

As a fully grown adult, with a good four years on the relative innocent I was then, I'll happily accost dominant men in these situations and say, 'Hey, I don't suppose you'd mind giving me a beating, would you?' But back then I wasn't sure. I was nervous of the rules, I didn't want to offend anyone by breaking the code that laid out how I should or shouldn't ask for it. And, above all, I was a submissive, dammit. I know plenty of women who fantasise about being tied down, beaten and fucked, but I don't know any whose fantasy starts with them having to awkwardly request it:

'Excuse me, sir. Would you be so kind as to take horrible advantage of me?'

'Well...'

'Pretty please? I just need a few slaps and for you to call me "slut". If you're feeling obliging, a quick shafting wouldn't go amiss to finish things off.'

'Oh, go on then.'

It's about as sexy as a tax return.

Of course, you can't really go to the other extreme either: just because I'm submissive it doesn't mean I'm going to submit to anyone for anything. A penchant for violent sex and humiliation is all well and good, but I don't want a stranger approaching me in a club and whipping me over a bench against my will. That behaviour moves away from the 'sex as an exciting and orgasmic mutually pleasurable game of tennis' zone into the terrifying, misogynist dystopia that people who warn me against BDSM are imagining. But no one—bar the odd genuinely evil sadist—actually wants this sort of thing to happen. The reason the rules proscribe it is because if they allowed it, no one would show up.

So what happens? We have pretty strict rules, that everyone abides by, and the results are... mixed, to say the least. Some people go home exhausted at the end of an evening, either rubbing their stinging buttocks or massaging the cramp from their whipping arm, and others, like me, often leave frustrated. At the end of our first night at school, number eight drove us home, with me bouncing in the passenger seat and begging him to speed up.

'Are we home yet? Are you going to spank me?'

As we pulled into the street: 'Seriously, I could *really* do with a spanking.' And then, as he unlocked the front door and we stepped into the living room: 'I've been such a bad g—Oh for fuck's sake, will you just fucking *hit me*?'

I was a crap submissive. But I got better.

'You, at the back. Are you talking?' The teacher was a guy I hadn't met before. Although I'd be happy to watch him beat the other girls, I didn't want to get on the wrong side of him just yet. Among the students it was common knowledge which of the teachers were slightly softer, and which of them hit hard.

This new one was an unknown quantity, but judging by the way he so clearly enjoyed swinging a thick leather tawse as he paced up and down the desks, he would definitely hit hard.

'No, Sir.' The girl in question trembled and looked back down at her book. The trembling was usually for effect, but I suspected that in this case she was nervous about her first session at the hands of this guy as well.

'Don't *ever* talk in my class.'

Crack.

I heard the tawse come down before I saw it, slapping right onto the desk in front of her. We all jumped.

'Did you hear what I said?' He knelt down, his face inches from hers.

'Yes, Sir.'

He stood up. 'Good. Because if I catch *any* of you talking in my class when you shouldn't be, you're for the belt. Do you understand?' A brief pause. 'I said *do you understand?*'

'Yes, Sir,' we chorused, obediently returning to our make-work. This was unusual—one of the most fun things about 'school' was that it gave us the opportunity to misbehave with no consequences. Having been relatively good when I was at real school, it was nice that as a grown-up child I could mess around. I enjoyed flicking the Vs behind teachers' backs and deliberately writing sarcastic answers in tests, knowing that the only punishment I'd receive would be one I wanted anyway.

But I was more obedient with this new teacher because he offered something curious and new: fear. I was scared of him in a way I hadn't been scared of anyone before.

The guys who beat me in fetish clubs would wield whips with skill and power, and I used to relish the hefty smacks they'd give me—stronger strokes than the ones number eight was comfortable dishing out. But he was still there watching out for me, stroking my hair and holding my neck like he had in the first club we'd been to. He knew all of my noises, and when I let out the right kind of sharp squeal he'd ask the dom to hold off, or he'd slow the pace by laying one of his hands on my battered arse and stroking it firmly, smoothing the pain away as I fought to regain control.

But number eight wasn't in the classroom that evening—it was only the teacher. The teacher who knew nothing about my likes and dislikes and the fact that if he used the cane on me I was liable to sob like I was having a breakdown. All he knew was that if I misbehaved he could punish me until I shouted, 'Red.'

I could feel the fear seeping through my body, out of my chest and down my arms. I could feel my pulse beat faster as the teacher strode around the desks, and I crossed my legs to hold that twitching pulse between them, beneath the crotch of my knickers, pressing deeply into my clit. I wanted to feel his hands on me, not just the painful whack of the belt or the paddle but the illicit sensation of his hands. I was dreading the pain but I wanted the touching. Teachers rarely used their hands, but I wanted his all over me—cupping the curves of my arse or pressing down on my back to keep me still, forcing me to stay there as he dealt out pain so bad that I fought to escape.

Not the giggly, exhibitionist spankings I'd received before in front of the class. I wanted something private, personal, fear-inducing. I wanted this man to really *scare* me.

So I dropped my pencil.

'Who was that?' By the time he whipped round I already had my hand up.

'It was me, Sir.'

He moved quickly; three swift paces brought him right next to my seat. He bent down and put his mouth close to my ear. Carefully enunciating every word in a growling whisper he said:

'You. Did. That. Deliberately.' I shook my head. He grabbed the back of my neck. 'Yes, you did. Say, "Yes, Sir."'

'Yes, Sir.'

He looked me in the face, his eyes blazing with rage, and did one of the sexiest things a guy can ever do: he rolled up his sleeves.

Grabbing me by the hair at the scruff of the neck, he hauled me out of my chair and dragged me into the corner of the room. He pushed my face up against the wall until my nose was touching the plaster and commanded: 'Stay there.'

He walked back down the rows, and I shivered in anticipation. He was going to get the belt. He picked it up and swung it a few times, quickly, so I could hear the 'whoosh' as it cut through the air. He walked past my desk and—thwack—brought the belt down where my hands had been.

'Lift up your skirt.' I did as I was told, exposing my bright red knickers—deliberately contravening the uniform policy to ensure I spent more time over various knees—and the sensitive, delicate area at the top of my thighs.

'Tuck your skirt in.'

Again I obeyed. I tucked the hem of my skirt into the back of my knickers so that my arse was framed for him—a pale, trembling target.

And at that point the bell rang.

There's nothing quite like waiting to get you horny. As the other girls stood up and filed out, I could feel myself burning with shame. They were giggling at me, and I didn't dare move, I just stood in the corner of the room, skirt hitched into my knickers, waiting for the first few slaps of my punishment.

I could hear the teacher pacing behind me, swinging the belt. My legs were shaking slightly, and I felt awkwardly off balance, positioned as I was almost flat up against the wall. My cunt was getting slick and wet, and I could feel the first few drops moistening my knickers. I was scared of this new teacher, but above all I was excited. This was the first time I'd been alone with someone who might hit me harder than I liked, who might push me a bit further than I'd been before. I liked that fear. It felt as if he might break the rules: swear at me, call me a slut, slip his hand into the back of my knickers to feel how wet the fear was making me.

There was no one else in the room. He'd waited for them to leave. Surely that could only mean he was planning something extra cruel, right? I shivered in anticipation as the door slammed ominously shut.

'Now,' he started.

I was feverish with excitement: Now... what? Please do something bad. Do something I'm not expecting. My foot jiggled in anticipation of what he was going to do, picturing him pulling my knickers down and slapping me with his bare hand, pushing me over one of the desks to prevent me struggling and calling me a filthy bitch. I could see him hurling the belt to one side and running his fingers against my slick cunt, unzipping his flies and fucking me with quick, sharp, functional strokes—all the things that were bad and wrong and definitely against the strict school rules.

I bit down onto my lip and held my breath. What's he going to do, this angry, terrifying man? What now?

'You're going to count these strokes.'

I got an extra six for sighing when the first thwack came.

Kinksters are, rightly, very proud of their rules. Their politeness. Their intent on making everyone feel comfortable and safe. We're only able to pretend to be schoolgirls and spend playful evenings being hit by a stranger because some early caning pioneers put together a charter that meant we could all do it safely.

Because of these no-nonsense guidelines there's a certain honesty about the kink scene that I defy anyone not to find at least a little bit charming. It's playful, it's fun, it's mostly non-judgemental. It's ultimately a bunch of grown-ups standing in a room and saying, 'Right, let's get our arses out.' And the fact that they have these rules means that you can walk into almost any reputable kink club in the country and feel that, despite the whips and spikes and terrifying heels, you're safe.

But this safety means that the things I want most desperately—a fake teacher putting his hand down my knickers and making me do something, *anything*, other than count to bloody six—often don't happen. Sometimes I wished I could stray outside the strict boundaries, just a little. I didn't just want a green badge, I wanted one that said, 'Spank me for no reason then fuck me against a wall.'

I guess that's why we develop partnerships, huh? Because a partner can be far more adept at reading the signals. Eight knew when I wanted to be spanked, and when I wanted to be left the hell alone. He could push things further with me because he was confident that he knew exactly when to stop.

I'd never been a fan of 'safe' words—the words or phrases screamed when you reach a point so painful you can't take any more. Eight and I had experimented with a few: red, stop, danger, *yamete* ('stop' in Japanese, which seems easier to say when we're in a club with other people and I don't want them to know that the clamps he's put on are about to rip my nipples off). But safe words, while handy when being spanked by someone I barely knew, made the sex I had with eight feel a bit contrived.

There's a challenge implicit in a safe word. A safe word says, 'This is the absolute limit, as much as I can take. If you do anything more I will die/call the police/punch you into the sun.' And so when I knew that there was a word I could use at any time to make it stop, all I was trying to do was prevent myself from using that word. Like the spanking I received in the first fetish club I went to, knowing that 'red' would make things stop gave me a reason to focus on not saying 'red' rather than enjoying the feeling of what was happening, and the effect it had on the rapidly stiffening guys standing around.

When eight would whisper safe words to me: 'If you say "over", it's over,' I forgot the reasons we were actually playing and instead viewed the scene as a bizarre competition, a test of stamina. I wasn't trying to come, just to prove to him how hard I could take it. If he beat me and called me a bitch, I wasn't getting wet, but celebrating my victory. Gritting my teeth and biting my tongue and hating every miserable, painful minute of it, but winning, oh boy, was I winning. I hadn't said 'red' or 'over' once, despite being desperate for it to finish. Challenge met.

But of course the challenge isn't the fun bit—the *fun* is the fun bit. Eventually eight and I realised that having a safe word which encouraged either of us to push ourselves to the point where we didn't like it was a bit pointless. We might as well call 'red' before anyone's taken their pants off, then sneak into separate rooms for a wank.

The point I'm making is that, despite the rules being necessary and important with strangers, sometimes in a relationship the rules can end up spoiling the very things that they're designed to protect. Eight and I ditched our safe words in favour of simply shouting, 'No, you fucking twat, that's really painful' if something was really painful, or 'Take that ginger out of my arse or I will force you to swallow it.' On one memorable occasion, to introduce an element of variety he shouted 'mum', which put a stop to whatever sexiness was happening pretty swiftly.

Eight and I were flexible on rules, because if we hadn't been then none of this stuff would have been sexy. If he'd beaten me until I said 'red', then most of our spanking sessions would have ended with me shouting 'red' and him quickly untying me and fetching me a mug of cocoa. As it was, the fact that there was no rule about stopping meant that he spent more time doing things that neither of us knew we liked, there being a whole world to explore between 'that's good' and 'stop doing that or I'll scream'.

The flexibility was part of the fun. At no point had we sat down with each other and ticked things off an official list: you can do this but not *that*; you can stick it here but never *there*; you can hit me with these but not those. We talked about what we liked, hinted about what we thought we might like, and kept our eyes and ears open for signs that things weren't quite hitting the mark.

We had more rigid rules elsewhere, of course. Woe betide one of us if we broke the washing-up rota, or forgot to clean the bathroom. We had evolved a complex code designed to prevent either of us from going insane, hurling the other one out onto the street and then burning their possessions in a moment of cathartic rage. But this didn't extend to sexual things: the code there was more fluid. Although technically we'd established that section four, part eleven of the code stated 'Thou shalt not sleep with other people', when I tiptoed out of the bedroom to have hot sex with number nine, the boy didn't say 'Hey, you're breaking the first rule. Please do not arouse me with your fiery lovemaking then spit girlcome into my mouth. I'm not sure we could deal with the subsequent paperwork,' he begged me to fuck her and we later added a bit of flexibility to the rule.

Yet because of the role they play in protecting people, the kink scene rules have to be more rigid than that. You don't fuck the students if you're in role as a teacher. You ask before touching someone. You take 'red' to mean 'stop'. And, unless I'm very much mistaken, when someone spanks you, you count. It's just the system.

CHAPTER THIRTEEN

There Ain't No Party Like An Awkward Sex Party

The rigidity of kink scene rules made us disillusioned with kinky clubs. We still attended the odd party, but I tried to avoid role-play scenarios that ended in my frustratedly humping a desk and wheedling 'Pleeease touch my cunt?' Humiliation's all well and good, but that wasn't exactly the kind I was after.

But there was something fantastic about playing with others that neither of us was ready to give up. For him, there was a certain kick he'd felt the first time he saw me getting fucked. When number twelve entered me and I moaned, he was gripped with a rippling wave of nausea and arousal. Something that simultaneously disgusted and intrigued him.

For my part, I enjoyed not only the obvious things—touching other guys and having them touch me, to use me in ways that made them rock solid—but the less obvious things too. I liked sleeping with men who weren't eight, not *despite* the fact that it was bad, but *because* of it. Like my encounter with the scariest teacher, some things became hot simply because eight wasn't there. Men could do things to me that he wouldn't necessarily approve of, that he wouldn't do himself. Without the boy, strange men could scare me.

Dangerous probably doesn't quite cut it. It's a different type of risk to spanking each other or being tied up, or even meeting strangers to have threesomes. In any of these situations either of us could say, 'No. Stop. I don't like this, I want out,' and the other would have moved mountains to make it happen. But when the thrill of what you're doing is based on a knowledge that what you're doing is wrong, it's hard to separate the disgust that's eating away at you from the disgust that's a necessary part of the game.

I went on dates—dinner and drinks with guys I knew, followed by sex that number eight knew we were having. I liked to come home, wet with sweat I'd worked up on someone else, and feel him trembling beneath me as I recounted what had happened, and kissed the taste of someone else onto his lips.

Number fourteen wore leather gloves and made a show of taking them off then putting them on the table beside him. He was calm, centred, well groomed and in control of everything. I'd never known him to raise his voice or get visibly excited or agitated. Number fourteen was the domliest dom I have ever known, and yet I never had sex with him.

Why is he on the list? I don't usually include people I haven't actually fucked. As anyone who has seen the film *Clerks* knows, as soon as you start tallying up all the people who you've sucked, wanked, or been reduced to orgasmic tears by, the list can end up being an uncontrollably long one. I say 'you' might find this, but in all honesty I mean me. The admin would be unthinkable.

However, I include number fourteen because the things he has done to me are significant. They deserve more credit than the catch-all title 'play', which includes dalliances in clubs with strangers or being spanked by kinky girlfriends at a party.

Number eight so wholeheartedly approved of him that he was willing to sit outside fourteen's house in his car, waiting for me to emerge, beaten and flushed, then slip into the passenger seat and hitch my skirt up around my waist. As eight drove me home he'd tell me I was dirty, and make me slip wet fingers inside myself and spread my thighs to show him how much I'd enjoyed being used by someone different.

Whatever I did with fourteen, I ended every evening feeling like I'd been thoroughly fucked.

He liked to find places that were private but public. Hidden nooks and doorways where he could press me into the wall and order me not to make a sound. It's incredible what a pair of leather gloves and a calm demeanour could do to stop me from making the noises I'd usually revel in.

One night, on the hunt for one of these places, he found what looked like an abandoned room just outside the entrance to a block of flats, just a door in a wall that took us into a place no bigger than a cupboard, with broken glass bottles on the floor and no lights.

He put his hand over my mouth and whispered to me not to make a sound, then yanked my skirt up and my knickers down and touched me until I was trembling and could barely stand.

Every time someone walked past the door, or I breathed too loudly or made any noise, he grabbed my throat and stopped me breathing until they'd gone. He kept doing this, then stopping, then doing more, then stopping, until I was so weak and frustrated that I was crying, and had we been somewhere noise was permitted I'd have been begging him to fuck me.

When I got to that point, he pushed me down until I was squatting on the floor and shoved his cock into my mouth, maintaining his total silence and calm.

He held my hair with his leather-gloved hands and shoved himself right into my throat. It didn't take long—after a few minutes, just as I started to choke and bruise, he came hot and hard into the back of my mouth.

Ever the gentleman, he walked me to the train station and held me up when I stumbled.

That delicious frustration is something that dominant and kinky guys have a knack for handing out.

Fifteen made me wait too. Not for a fuck, but just for release. He'd fuck me slowly and I'd have no idea why he was holding back. Then at some point towards the end I'd realise I was shaking with need, tensing every muscle in my body and trying to push the first waves of orgasm through from my chest down to my stomach. He wanted me to wait for it so that I'd appreciate it when it came.

Fifteen was dominant too, but not as calm as fourteen. He'd beat me hard with belts, and sneer at me when I squealed too loudly. When we were playing, he'd fuck me with his hands so quickly that I'd tense up and writhe, then he'd pull his hands away at just the point when I thought I was getting somewhere.

But then we'd start fucking and he'd hold back. He'd kneel between my legs and put just the tip of his cock inside me. When I begged him for more of it, he'd pull away, making me arch my back to get more of him. Eventually, with his hands gripping my thighs, he'd pull me down further onto his cock as I wriggled and forced myself onto him. When he'd settled in, and I'd drawn a breath to calm myself, he'd lean right down onto me and fuck me with long, slow strokes.

He made me wait for it, and work for it. If I gripped him and thrust my cunt up further onto him he'd tut, and push my chest back down. With slow, intimidating control, he left me shuddering with frustration and squirming as I tried to fill myself with all of him.

When I started making muffled sounds of frustration, and gripping his back to pull him harder onto me—deeper, and further into me—he'd pick up the pace. Not enough—not *nearly* enough—but slightly faster, so I could get more from him by pushing my hips up to meet him. I needed him to speed up. I couldn't get there without it, but I knew that if he'd just do it quickly for a few more seconds I'd be there, and the need to be there is so deliciously painful. It aches right through my cunt - the need to come. It hurts.

I'd cry out.

And I'd grip him harder.

And I'd writhe, and fuck him harder.

And I'd say, 'Please. Please.

Pleasepleaseplease.'

And then for one brilliant, wonderful moment he'd do it—slam his cock into me with force and power and anger and lust and speed.

And I'd fall back, my body tense, my cunt twitching. My back arching as I came all over his cock, and he felt me shuddering all the frustration out of my body.

When I was done I'd pant and smile and my eyelids would droop with exhaustion. He'd pull out, wearing a serious frown and a look of concentration. He'd sit on my chest, with one hand on my neck and one hand gripping the base of his huge, still dripping cock, and tell me to open my mouth.

I shouldn't have been so obsessed with fucking other guys. As any serial dieter will tell you, the more you think about the object of your craving the larger it looms in your mind. The more I thought about new boys, other boys, the more important they became for me. Not more important than eight, but significant enough that they eroded some of that empathy that number one had given me a taste of. I knew eight liked it when I fucked other guys, but I'd become more casual about it, forgetting that the proud erection he sported when listening to tales of my expeditions was always balanced with a stab of heartbreak that I wasn't there with him.

Number eight was still almost the same person I'd fallen desperately for at the beginning of university. He had the same effete clumsiness, the same beautiful sad eyes. He still had the same ability to demolish my arguments and leave me either aroused by his eloquence or laughing at his wit. What's more, we'd done so much together that it was impossible to untangle who I was from all the strings that seemed to belong to both of us. That song I really love—do I actually like listening to it, or do I just like it because when he plays it to me he does a big wide grin and lights up with joy at the absurdity of it? I'm a pervert, sure, but would all the things I find arousing seem stone-cold dull if I couldn't relay them to him in bed later?

The new boys I met were deliciously other. I liked them for the qualities they had that were different to number eight. And I liked the effect they had on him too— listening to me telling him about how slowly fifteen had fucked me, and growing hard in response behind the steering wheel.

But despite his ability to become aroused by my selfish shenanigans, there was something fairly significant hovering between us. I couldn't quite put my finger on what it was. Or rather, I repeatedly tried to put my finger on what it was and ended up starting rows with him that had no beginning, middle or end. They'd start with 'you don't love me' and pass a few times through 'why aren't we married yet', occasionally looping around 'you're always looking at other people' and end—far too often—on me telling him we didn't fuck enough.

I've never understood why people insist on the distinction between sex and love. Sure, you might not be able to swing from the chandeliers when you're ninety years old, but you're certainly not going to stop fancying your partner just because they've got wrinkles.

Sex is one of the most important things that humans ever do together. We eat together to bond, we hug, we kiss, we flirt to build relationships, we fight to protect ourselves or show someone our strength. And we fuck people, and we love them.

Sex and love don't always come together: I've got plenty of friends with whom I can have a casual fuck and then wander off afterwards, only remembering to send a 'thanks for a lovely evening' text when I'm washing the jizz out of my hair the next morning. In fact, I've got some friends who are close enough that I'll fuck them but not affectionate enough that there'd even be a kiss at the end of that text.

The sex I had with fourteen and fifteen wouldn't have warranted a kiss at the end of a text. But number eight was there at the end of the evening, giving me kisses and love and affection and occasionally the passionate nineteen-year-old sex that I hoped would last us into our nineties.

'Why are you so obsessed with fucking the guys?'

I'm... sorry, what? This genuine question, asked to me by a kinky friend of mine, had me utterly stumped.

'I... What do you mean?'

'Well,' she explained, with a tone of weary frustration, 'most people come to parties to get spanked. They come to have a bit of risqué fun, and possibly beat up or get beaten up by a stranger. But, even when you get some really good play, you bitch and moan if no one will actually fuck you.'

Huh.

She was right. I *did* bitch and moan. My rant about why a particular club—which was billed as swinging and fetish—never had a supply of condoms was one that I had bored plenty of people with before. My reluctance to join in group scenes because they didn't press exactly the right buttons was, again, well documented. But until she mentioned it I didn't really think there was anything wrong with that. After all, spanking people is sexy, right? What's wrong with wanting it to lead to sex?

I was surprised to discover that not only was sex quite infrequent, there was a vague sense that actual sex—just fucking—wasn't on.

Sure, you could play a scene where you got tied up and dominated and humiliated and made to do things you never thought you'd do—and at this point I'll just give a little wave to the woman who taught me how to safely thread needles through the delicate outer layer of skin on my boy's tumescent cock—but actual *fucking* seemed a bit of a no-no. There were clubs filled with equipment and people willing to use it but to my mind we were all missing a crucial trick, and that is the trick where I bend over a solid oak workbench and the men take it in turns to fuck me.

It's not that I think we should all fuck—although there's a part of my brain that would be delighted if that were to happen—it's the fact that I felt wrong because I wanted to. If, as I occasionally did when being spanked, I responded to a guy's request that I count the strokes with 'Why don't you just fuck me?' there was an awkward silence. Once a dominant asked me 'And what exactly do you want, young lady?' It was only after I'd actually answered that I realised he was expecting me to say 'Punishment,' or 'I want you to beat me.' It turns out the answer was *not* 'Your cock in my mouth.'

Very occasionally, a gentleman would oblige me with a gentle stroke of my cunt, dipping his fingers into me slightly to moisten them before pulling his hand back and slapping me, hard, leaving a trail of my own arousal across my skin. Sometimes men, number fourteen being the prime example, would oblige me with a taste of their cock. But sex itself was trickier to have: I was often told that, well, it's just not what we're here for.

Number eight felt similarly disheartened. He'd accompany me to clubs and we'd spend the evening winding each other up into a frenzy of sexual rage, me dripping and desperate for him to fuck me and him itching to do the same. I'd find excuses to stand in front of him, my hands busy behind my back gently stroking at the bulge in his trousers. He'd place the back of one of his hands on my skirt, pushing through so I could feel him running it down the crack of my arse and forward to meet my crotch. And all the time we smiled and chatted and watched people get spanked.

The party that marked the final nail in the coffin of our group spanking escapades was a house party thrown by a friend. The theme was 'fucked-up orgy' or something similar, and I'd been promised that everyone there would be open minded, sexy, and willing to fulfil whatever fantasies I was capable of remembering once I'd drunk the best part of a bottle of wine. Clad in corset, knickers, stockings and not much else, I ventured in, with an eager number eight bouncing along in front of me.

The party, as it turned out, was almost as debauched as we hoped it would be. I got very spanked. Number eight got spanked, spanked people, and at one point had a group of giggling corseted women tracing his nipples with their immaculately manicured fingernails. He was having a good time and I—ever the grumpy pessimist—*almost* was. The problem was not with the party, which had booze and music and fun and more than a few people who were so sexy I wanted to eat them. The problem was that, despite the rather pornographic invite, there didn't seem to be any actual sex.

I had hoped for something similar to teenage parties, where number one and I would be able to build each other up to the brink of lust and then rush off to someone's bedroom to hump quickly and efficiently on their bed. I didn't mind if it was number eight or not. He'd told me I could do what I liked as long as he was having a good time. I took this to mean 'go nuts, try your best to fuck someone', so that is exactly what I did.

A stocky, bald, switch-y guy, who was more used to being spanked than taking control, escorted me away from the hub of activity and into a quiet corner. I'd been watching him for a while, admiring the solid curves of his body and the precision with which he did everything: taking a sip of his drink and wiping the bottom of the glass so as not to leave rings on the table, sitting down at an angle without disturbing the girl who was being spanked over the chair next to him. He seemed interested in what was going on, but aloof, as if he was waiting for just the right moment before joining in. As he pulled me away I hoped that moment was now.

'I like you,' he said, grabbing the back of my neck. 'You've been looking at me.'

'Yes, I have.'

'Why?'

'I want you to do things to me.'

He stared straight at me, unblinking, then started stroking the back of my neck. He moved forward, putting his lips right next to my ear. 'What sort of things?'

'Bad things.' I was just about ready for him to spin me around and slap me on the arse, or leave me quietly, to ponder what pain he might cause while he went off to fetch an implement with which to cause it. But he did something much odder: he kissed me. A deep, wet, hurried snog, the kind you do right at the end of the school disco because you're worried your parents will come to pick you up soon and the fun will have to stop.

I snogged him back, just as eagerly. I grabbed at the waistband of his trousers, fumbled with the buttons and shoved both of my hands in: one at the back, to cup the smooth hardness of his arse, and one at the front, to grab his even harder cock. He pulled back a bit and grinned. Resting his forehead on mine, he looked at me again and I shivered at the intimacy: spanking guys rarely did this. They kept their distance to maintain their control and poise. This guy? He wasn't interested in poise, he was just interested in getting laid.

'Where can we go to fuck?'

I suggested one of the bedrooms and we started an exploration. The first was out of bounds because a group of girls were tying a guy up and dripping hot wax on him. In the second, a few people were sitting chatting. We went in and promptly started making out on the bed, in the hope that we'd get them to leave. As we snogged, I rubbed myself against him, feeling his unusually thick cock pressing against my crotch. But they wouldn't go. The conversation continued around us, the group either unaware of how desperately I needed this guy in me, or hanging around so they'd get to watch the spectacle.

The guy dragged me off the bed and into the final bedroom. Peace and quiet. A single bed in the corner and the rest piled high with boxes. This clearly wasn't a designated 'party' area, so we were free from interruptions. I pulled down his trousers and pushed him up against the wall, taking the luxurious opportunity to squeeze him through the fabric of his pants. I could feel the drops of wetness spreading as his dick leaked enthusiasm through the cotton. All the while his jaw was working, giving me those teenaged snogs that I hadn't realised I'd been missing.

And then the door opened.

'Sorry to disturb you guys, it's just that so-and-so has just been sick and she really needs a lie-down.'

Neither of us said no: we're British, after all, and are therefore not only polite but aware of the perils of excess alcohol. We left the room, ran straight into the bathroom, and I bent over the bathtub.

'Fuck me.' It wasn't a question or a request, more a way of encouraging speed. Bathrooms at parties are never a great place to fuck, as there's always the possibility that so-and-so will...

So-and-so did. A knock at the door.

'Could you please hurry up in there because I'm going to be... Oh God.'

I pulled up my knickers as he fumbled with the lock, and we were dumped back out into the hallway.

'It's not our night, is it?'

Frustration like that is simultaneously delicious and terrifying. I was ready to tear down the walls just to get this guy somewhere—*anywhere*—that I could fuck him. At that point a simple spanking wouldn't have done anything to alleviate the itchy feeling that I just needed something inside me. Spanking would spark the craving, but it wouldn't stop it any more than looking at a picture of a cake would stop someone being hungry.

I don't think I care so much about coming—it's not a need to come. It's just a need to feel something solid inside me, to relieve the throbbing ache deep inside my cunt. A desperate urge to squeeze my muscles and clench tightly around his dick as he forces it fully into me. A need to be fucked.

When my friend asked, 'Why are you so obsessed with fucking guys?' I couldn't think of an answer. I wanted to say because it scratches an itch, or because they make me horny, or spanking just doesn't quite hit the spot, but none of those would have conveyed the deep and urgent need that I felt running from bedroom to bathroom and back again with a guy I barely knew just to get that one, satisfying second as he plunged himself into me and I could let out a satisfied shudder.

So when she asked that question, I could think of nothing better than to tell her that story. Although she was happy with a spanking, she understood why I wasn't.

'Perhaps those kinds of parties just aren't for you?'

'Yeah, perhaps you're right.'

This guy and I, we never did get to fuck.

I couldn't be in a relationship that had anything like that amount of frustration. Too many times I've heard people say, 'Oh, you're married now, no more sex for you,' or 'Seven years together, eh? I guess your sex life's probably fucked but at least you're comfortable.' And I wonder why we write off sex so easily, as something that's nice while it lasts but not worth mourning when it's gone. I wonder if the reason sex in a relationship dies out is simply because we expect it to. We're so busy building the strong, everlasting love that we think we'll have when we're ninety that we forget about the rock-solid passion that kept us together when we were nineteen.

Number eight and I could not have survived without sex. As people we'd survive, sure. Stick a chastity belt on each of us and you could probably watch us live out a full and healthy life with only the occasional scream or public breakdown. But survived *together*? No. Sex wasn't just a fun thing for us, it was the foundation of everything we loved about each other.

But there was never quite enough of it. You know how it is, when you've been together a while: your evenings spent fondling each other on the sofa in front of a film, desperately hoping for a sex scene that'll push things over from 'casual touching' to 'full-blown fuck' turn into evenings spent eating popcorn in front of it, hoping that the credits roll before it's technically past your bedtime. We'd fuck when it was bedtime, but not before. I'd paw at him in the kitchen while he was cooking dinner only to be batted away: 'Not now, the sauce will curdle.' I'd welcome him home from work in knickers and nowt else only to be told 'Wait. Just... wait. I'm tired.'

He kept me happy, and he kept me comfortable, and the occasional passionate and imaginative things he did kept me hanging on for him, drooling if he'd so much as look at the drawer where we kept our toys. But too often he'd sigh and say he was tired, and turn his back on me in bed, and I'd cry like I was sixteen again, begging number one to let me come one more time before we slept.

So why did we stay together? When every argument ended in the same cul-de-sac:

'You don't love me.'

'I do.'

'Why do we never fuck?'

'We've fucked four times this week.'

'So why don't we fuck more?'

'Because... I don't know. I'm tired. I'm sad. I just want to hold you.'

As we went to leave the party, and I had to kiss a frustrated goodbye to my unfucked stranger, I turned to get number eight, to check he was ready to go home. I was more than ready to go—to get in a taxi and speed home as fast as we could, his hand in my knickers all the way, feeling the arousal that this stranger had conjured up. I pictured his strong, slender hands rubbing gently at me, keeping me hovering just on the edge of coming until we fell into the flat at the end of the journey and he could take an orgasm from me the second we started to fuck.

But as he gathered his things his shoulders slumped and he just looked sad. My explorations with the stranger had taken up most of the time that eight and I should have spent together, touching each other and playing and whispering commentary to each other as we watched other couples go at it. I'd had an amazing evening but he, it seemed, hadn't. The part where we were supposed to go home and fuck didn't seem as natural when we hadn't spent the evening together.

He peered at me, with red-rimmed, tired eyes, and a look that said: *I just want to hold you.*

CHAPTER FOURTEEN

In Which We Confirm Our Suspicion That Girlonthenet Is Actually A Total Arsehole

What counts as cheating? A snatched kiss from a stranger in a club at 2 a.m.? A lustful look across a crowded train carriage at someone who isn't your partner? I don't know. It depends on who you're with. For some couples, it's not cheating to have full sex with complete strangers, it's just an independent and fun night out which you can tell your partner about as you rinse off someone else's come shot. Other couples will be more traditional: kiss a colleague at a work do and it could be grounds for divorce. Some people count physical cheating as more significant than emotional cheating, others wouldn't mind if their partner had a cheap shag but would be heartbroken to find out that they'd shared an intimate bottle of wine with the woman who could be their next wife. What counts? Kissing? Touching? Telling unflattering stories about your partner to the new person you fancy?

One thing I know for sure: despite the open nature of our relationship, fucking a guy without telling number eight? That counts.

Number sixteen was a good friend. At least, he became a good friend swiftly after we had sex. I'd met him through work, which was about the only clichéd thing about our time together. The first time we had sex was almost an accident. I don't think either of us had entertained the notion until one night, after downing enough tequila to knock out a rhino, we ended up snogging at the climax of 'Summer Lovin' in a dirty karaoke bar at 2 a.m. He was as surprised as I was.

The sex we had was unfamiliar to me. He didn't beat me with his belt or call me a dirty girl, he didn't rip off my knickers and bend me over the coffee table. He pulled me into his bedroom and undressed me while we kissed, then as I lay down on the bed he rested between my legs and shagged me with a rhythmic, comforting normalcy that felt weirdly like a holiday. It's the sort of sex I imagine brand new couples have on Friday nights, after they've met in a bar or a club and decided to retire to one or other's house: an unpretentious shag, revelling in the sheer joy of putting part A into slot B and rubbing them together because it makes you both feel good. Not making love, but making fun, like playing tennis or sharing a plate of fajitas. This kind of sex is what makes the world go round.

I don't want to make him sound boring; number sixteen was anything but. In fact, he introduced me to yet another thing that could give me that spontaneous kick-in-the-gut: number sixteen made noises. He spoke to me, he moaned, he said 'Oh yes,' when I did something nice. He told me he was hard, that he loved how it felt when he was inside me. He told me how wet I was. He asked me if I liked it. He sucked in big gulps of breath while I had his cock in my mouth. He sighed. He moaned a bit more. He groaned and gulped and finally he climaxed with vocal, lusty relief.

Good Lord, the world could do with more vocal boys. I love the challenge of doing things to make them go 'aaah' and if I get that feedback I'm going to keep doing it again and again. If I could request anything from the gentlemen of this world it'd be to turn up the volume. You don't have to shout it from the rooftops, or terrify the next-door neighbours by wailing like a mourning widow, just let go a bit, get carried away. Don't lie there in silence, humping me stoically with a face of concentration like you're solving a particularly difficult crossword puzzle.

After we'd finished, as I rummaged under his bed to find my socks, he asked me if I was going to tell our friends, or number eight. Until that point it hadn't occurred to me not to. Of course what I'd done was cheating in the traditional sense, and it probably wasn't something that eight would welcome with open arms—any previous sleeping around had been done with not just his prior consent but his enthusiasm. But he understood me, too. He understood how I loved the thrill of the first time with someone new. Knew I loved to whisper stories about it in his ear while I squeezed my legs around his hips to feel his matching arousal. I'd have happily told him, apologised for the impromptu nature of the thing, and then rubbed him to a sticky climax under the duvet as I made noises like sixteen had.

But number sixteen was more traditional than that, and the thought of telling anyone made his eyes wide with terror. From his perspective, and crucially that of his girlfriend, sex was most definitely cheating, and it would not be brushed off or discussed in lustful tones.

'I don't want anyone to find out. I don't want my girlfriend to find out.'

So I agreed to keep my mouth shut. The stakes didn't feel quite the same as they had when I found out number one had cheated on me. Given that we'd already fucked, the horse had well and truly bolted with sixteen. Although the thought of eight finding out that I'd lied brought me out in a cold sweat, although I could almost feel the pain and rage he'd experience if he knew that I'd kept something from him, the damage seemed already done. Number sixteen's girlfriend was distant. I'd never met her and couldn't even recall him telling me her name. But the pain would be just as real for her if I came clean about the noisy night I'd so casually spent with a guy she was looking to marry. I could cope with being the incorrigible slag, the girl who got drunk and dragged guys home from karaoke bars at 2 a.m. I could, at a push, cope with upsetting number eight. But I wasn't sure I was ready to destroy a friend's relationship when he was begging me so hard not to.

'I understand.'

And he breathed a sigh of relief. I put on my coat and closed the door quietly after me, heading home in a blur of hazy lust and blossoming guilt. It wasn't the sex that counted as cheating, it was the lie. As I boarded the night bus and made my way to the back seats, I told myself what all bastards tell themselves to justify their bastardry: that what number eight didn't know wouldn't hurt him. I examined the only real secret I'd ever kept from him, and I felt alone.

Since we'd been together I'd never felt this far removed. Even when we were miles apart and communicating sporadically by text, the fact that we were still linked meant I'd never felt like an individual unit. How could I possibly be alone when he lived with me, every day, in my thoughts and plans and fantasies? He knew everything about me, from what underwear I wore to the fact that I preferred my orange juice without bits in. When my eyes wandered in a crowded restaurant he could scan the room and immediately identify not only the guy who had caught my eye, but the specific reason he'd caught it: 'Jeans hanging off his hips, your three o'clock, yeah?' 'Yeah.' He'd read my abysmal teenage poetry and watched me get fucked by other guys and laughed at me as I sat knitting in front of the telly.

So that first big lie, the first secret? It made me feel alone. But it wasn't the all-encompassing black hole of loneliness that I'd expected—a small part of that break felt amazing. The tiny section of my brain that now belonged solely to me felt deliciously different. It told me things I hadn't realised before: your world is big. It's interesting. You don't need to be afraid of this. Being alone isn't always lonely and sad and sobbing over romcoms while your partner's out having fun: it's independence and freedom. It's buying whatever the fuck you like from Tesco and not having someone complain that you didn't use the voucher. It's sitting on a train with no one beside you, fantasising about what you could do with the guy opposite. It's lounging in a bar in a town you've never been to and reading an amazing book. It's deciding, at the last minute, to leave your boyfriend for the weekend and go home to see your family, and not having to feel guilty about it.

I've never been the sort of person who takes my boyfriend everywhere. I'm occasionally envious of couples who can spend every waking minute together without wanting to push the other one off a bridge. They're friendly with their partner's siblings, confident chatting to their in-laws, and unconcerned about spending Christmas with each other's family. I've never been like this. Although I've introduced boys to my parents, I worry that they'll feel left out, like they don't fit in. This leads to awkwardness and a simmering resentment that I have to explain running jokes, or baby them by providing cups of tea because they don't know where my mum keeps the teabags. And I certainly don't want them at home for Christmas—what if they ruined my family traditions by doing something unconscionable, like insisting we open the presents before we've had lunch?

My family is simultaneously lovely and incredibly intimidating. They won't disapprove of people I love, but they will, in casual banter, call them cunts, and expect them to laugh. They'll quote obscure jokes from *Blackadder* and expect you to feed them the punchline. If you're accompanying us to Wetherspoon, they will insist on buying you drinks then frown on you in private if you didn't get your round in. And when we're home, half-cut after a night spent exchanging gossip over cheap gin, they'll hammer out Andrew Lloyd Webber numbers on a rickety old piano and expect everyone to know the words, or at least slur a vague approximation of them. You don't need to hit the high notes, but you do need to refrain from laughing. And that, when my mother and I perform drunken duets, is certainly no mean feat.

So although number eight would occasionally accompany me home, chat nicely with my mum and get drunk with my old school friends, I spent most of my time on these trips flapping around him and making sure that he wasn't feeling left out. Not to mention smiling desperately at him as I launched into the second verse of 'I Don't Know How to Love Him' and hoping he wouldn't collapse into fits of giggles.

On the weekend our relationship died I went home on my own. Not because I didn't want him there, or because I was planning on spending the weekend dragging strange boys into dark corners for furtive snogs. I went alone because it suddenly felt like I could. The tiny part of me that was shining with new-found independence decided that I could leave eight for a weekend and the world wouldn't collapse—it might just get a bit bigger.

This particular weekend was a special occasion. Amy and I, still friends despite ten years apart—it's hard to shake the bond you've developed by getting touched up on different levels of a bunk bed—were throwing a reunion party for a boy we'd known when we were younger. Amy wanted to play hostess and sparkle and show everyone a good time, while I was curious to see this boy again: the boy who'd been my First Love.

Have you ever wondered what you'd say to your younger self if you could travel back in time? I have. I have a list of things I'd tell fourteen-year-old me, should scientific advancement ever give me the ability to meet her. I'd tell her to pull her socks up, do some revision, ditch the friends who copied her maths homework, and for the love of God never *ever* take up smoking. But I also used to fantasise about advising her on First Love. I'd tell her to stop mooning after him, to understand that her melancholy desperation would do less to attract his arousal than it would to make him shy away. Hundreds of times I've relived the fantasy of squeezing back into my younger body and taking it in hand: brushing the hair out of my face, putting on my most confident smile, and sashaying past First Love until he pants 'fuck me fuck me fuck me', then falls to his knees in an agony of unrequited lust.

The reunion party that Amy was throwing was the closest I'd ever get to having that time machine. I rallied the small part of me that felt independent, and the slightly larger part of me that had learned how to make men look longingly at my arse, and I pushed thoughts of number eight to the back of my mind. I didn't expect to have sex with First Love; there was no reason why adult me would get any further than teenaged me had. I might be more confident, with bigger tits and better hair and a lot more stories with which to try and tease an erection out of him, but I was still the same nerd underneath: the girl he'd rejected. The only difference was that I didn't fear the rejection any more.

Seeing First Love again really did feel like going back in time. All the good things—his smile, his wit, the chunky watch that he wore on his right arm—they were all exactly as I'd left them. He hadn't aged as much as either Amy or I, who both felt a bit haggard in comparison. Where we'd gathered extra weight and worldly cynicism, he'd just got a bit taller, a bit bigger, and a lot more muscular. When he hugged me close he squashed my tits against his chest, and I smelt the same smell I'd drooled over as a teenager.

We went out on the town, to pubs that had changed ownership and décor at least three times since we'd sneaked into them underage. Sips of our drinks were punctuated by ten-year-old stories and jokes:

'Remember when Darren showed us his dick in the park by your house?'

'Yeah. Impressive for his age.'

Giggles, another drink.

'Anyone know what happened to Jenny?'

'She's around. She doesn't come out though: kids.'

Murmurs of disapproval tinged with a pity that was almost definitely misplaced.

'Didn't Andy get married?'

'What, Andy that you fucked? Nah, he's still single if you want his number.'

We weren't as interested in each other's current lives. You have a job now? Friends? You're living far away? Don't talk about it, please, you're killing the atmosphere.

When the pubs closed we wandered the streets near our old school, swigging booze we wished we'd been ID'd for and visiting all of the places we'd ever hung out.

'Remember that corner, Amy? Where you and Darren first pulled?'

'Shut up, you. I only pulled him to give you time alone with... what was his name?'

'Rob.'

First Love interjected: 'You were with Rob? How did I never know that?'

I grabbed the bottle from him and took a long swig. 'You probably weren't interested.'

He laughed, and grabbed me around the waist. 'Haha, are you still sore that I never fancied you?'

'Yeah, you bastard. My poor teenage self was riddled with lust, and all you ever did was rub your boner up against me once or twice.'

'Christ, yeah. I was a pricktease. Or... whatever the right word for it is with girls.'

We all laughed, and stumbled in the direction of Amy's house to continue reminiscing in her back garden. Her boyfriend was inside, bored of our impenetrable chatter, and her neighbours were good enough to turn a blind eye to the barking laughter coming from next door.

At three in the morning, exhausted, Amy took us inside and showed us where we were to sleep.

'There's only one bed, I'm afraid. Do you mind sharing?'

First Love and I looked at each other, flushed and tired and high on stories of how young we used to be. We both shook our heads.

'No, no problem.'

I raced to the bathroom, brushed my teeth with a thoroughness familiar to all smokers who are hoping they'll get to kiss a non-smoker. When I went to bed, and let First Love take over in the bathroom, I was confronted by that age-old dilemma: what do I wear in bed with someone who I am supposed to not have sex with, but am secretly hoping I might? Just knickers looks too forward, but changing into a full pyjama set might put him off. I settled for knickers and a t-shirt then lay down, abandoning all pretence that I didn't care if First Love touched me.

Lying wide awake in the bed, I heard him come into the room, strip down to his boxers—no PJs, a good sign—and clamber in next to me. His breathing wasn't shallow, and I could almost feel the weight of him making his decision.

It probably took ten minutes for him to move his hand slowly across the bed. I heard the rustle of the bedsheets as he got closer. Eventually, his hand reached my waist and I shifted backwards towards him.

'Fancy a cuddle?' he asked.

'Hell yeah.' I shifted back further, leaning into him, pushing my arse up against the positively gigantic bulge in the front of his boxers. He moved his hand down to my knickers and pulled them down. He lifted one of my thighs and, with his hands wrapped firmly around me, pushed himself inside. A few moans, a few thrusts, a twitch and a stifled 'mmm' later, First Love became number seventeen.

Did I feel bad for cheating on eight? I'd love to say no. I'd love to say that I was happy and carefree and confident that, although certainly not the best decision I'd ever made, my choice to fuck the first guy I ever fell for was cathartic enough to be worth the subsequent fallout. I'd love to say that, but I can't. Because—and I won't pull any punches here—I felt like a total cunt.

It seemed like a good idea initially, and a perfectly natural thing to do. After all, short of inventing my actual time machine, the closest I'd ever get to satisfying the miserable, lovesick young version of me was to do as an adult what I'd never managed as a kid. That's how I tried to justify it, anyway. But desperate self-justification is the last refuge of the world's worst kind of bastard, and I was one: a bastard's bastard. A gold-plated, top-of-the-range bastard with an extended five-year warranty.

Sleeping with number sixteen could, at a push, be written off as a drunken lark. If I'd told number eight that it had happened it may well have been something that brought us together further, forcing us to have the conversation we'd been on the verge of for the last couple of years:

'You know how you like to fuck other guys?'

'Yeah?'

'Stop it.'

'OK.'

But number seventeen? Despite my attempts to justify it—a golden opportunity! Once in a lifetime!—there was nothing that made First Love more significant than any other. What made him special when I was fifteen made him decidedly *un*special when I was in my twenties. Much of the excitement and allure of the younger First Love was there because I'd never slept with a guy—I didn't know what they were like. Countless years of screwing others, blowing doms in doorways and getting spanked at sexy school should have taught me one thing: men, like women, are only ever human. When First Love became number seventeen he stopped being Mr Right and instead turned into just another human. Some guy I'd fucked. A number.

If you gave me the opportunity to travel back in time now, I'd give myself some rather different advice: don't fuck First Love. Wank yourself silly imagining the alleyway scenario if you have to, and stare longingly at him as he plays football with the other guys on the school field, but whatever you do don't fuck him. If you fuck him you'll break the spell.

If breaking the spell wasn't disappointing enough, as soon as we'd finished and I saw the arcs of spunk spray onto his washboard stomach, I realised that I'd conclusively closed the book on someone much more important: number eight. Who missed out on the title of 'First Love' but was overwhelmingly my Greatest Love— someone funny and bright and beautiful, who more than loved me back. Rather stupidly, I'd failed to realise that *doing* what I want isn't necessarily the same as *getting* what I want. Running off for the weekend to have sordid nostalgic sex with seventeen was fun in the short term, but in the long term it meant I'd broken whatever it was I had with number eight.

So I sat on a train heading back to London with a demon sitting on my right shoulder telling me how badly I'd fucked up. Telling me that I might as well just pack things in with number eight, because if I couldn't stay faithful to him even when I was allowed to have sex with other people, then there was no hope for me ever. The angel on the corresponding shoulder sat in mute silence. If she'd spoken up it would only be to tell me I deserved everything I got, and she'd have been right.

Suddenly being alone didn't feel quite so brilliant. The sense of independence and freedom that I'd glimpsed before was replaced by a weird, hollow scream.

I could fuck number sixteen and write it off as a mistake, something I did once to get it out of my system. Sure, I'd slept with him, but we were just friends, yeah? Just mates. It wasn't significant. First Love was as significant as you can get—we hadn't fucked by accident. On the train on the way home, I ran through all of the things I'd done that weekend—shaved my legs, plucked my eyebrows, packed the clothes that made me look just thin enough that I'd impress yet still show off the curves of my arse. I'd told myself that I hadn't set out to fuck him, just to catch him, then run away freely like I'd anticipated I would with number eight all those years ago. On the train I recognised that for the big fat ugly lie it was: I'd set out to fuck my First Love, and I'd succeeded.

But in succeeding here I'd failed more significantly elsewhere. My minor victory in sleeping with First Love was actually a distraction from the far greater problem: number eight and I were over. While I'd been out collecting shiny souvenirs, everything else I'd valued had gone.

As the train sped steadily home, back to number eight and the conversation I didn't want to have:

'Hey, darling, I fucked someone else. Well, two people, actually. Sorry! How about a blow job?'

I realised that, just as there's no way of telling this tale in a memoir without sounding heartless, there's no way of having that conversation without breaking someone's heart.

It didn't happen at once. Neither of us was sensible enough to recognise the value of a good, clean cut directly through the centre. There wasn't one conversation in which I confessed, he broke, and we sobbed in each other's arms before waving a teary goodbye. We drew it out, made it last, smashed ourselves repeatedly into each other in the hope that we could make something work.

But we couldn't.

'What if we just both saw other people?'

'Or what if we went to counselling?'

'What if we got married?'

'Ooh, how about we pretend this never happened?'

'Shall we just forget about this for now and fuck?'

Of course. Always. The only thing that would placate the wrenching pain of knowing that things with eight were over was to fuck him. We talked during the evenings and then fucked at night, clinging to each other in the hope that this—this desperate, unnatural passion that had refused to die even after eight years of overuse—would be enough to keep us together.

But it wasn't.

There are many things we can learn from experience: how to talk to people, how to make people happy, how to play video games without just mashing buttons and hoping for the best. But one of the few things I don't think we'll ever learn is how to break up with someone we love. Everything I was used to—the smell of him, the taste of him, the way he'd crank up the volume on the car stereo and throw his head wildly from side to side when a particularly exciting pop-punk track came along—my life suddenly seemed impossible to live without these things.

I realised just how much I'd placed on that initial meeting, and the hope I'd held on to since I saw him walk into the first lecture. 'This is the man I'm going to marry.' How pathetic. How ridiculous. How utterly childish. As if love at first sight not only existed, but was exactly as shining and perfect as it pretends to be in films. As if the fact that I wanted him so badly would be enough to stop either of us from ever fucking up. I'd meant it, as well. Don't let my swearing cynicism distract from the fact that I am a complete and utter idiot. I wanted to marry number eight, eat breakfast that he made for me in the mornings then kiss him goodbye as I left for work. I wanted us to have joint bank accounts, a mortgage, cherry tomato plants in the garden. I'd pictured what our children would look like, and the patient, gentle movement of his hands as he taught them to play Xbox. If I closed my eyes I could see the weathered lines in his face when, aged fifty, he'd come at me with Viagra-powered lust. This was the love that we should have had. This was the logical conclusion to all the things we did together, and the things he did for me.

Eventually I couldn't separate the things we'd actually done—did we repaint the bathroom, laughing at Radio 4 comedy and splattering each other with magnolia, or did I just imagine that?—from the things I just thought we *should* have done—he wanted to go to a gig and I said no. Or did I say yes? Did he hold me while they belted out the final song, and we got chips and hummed it on the way home? Every memory of the last few years was branded with his face, and it made it almost impossible for me to do anything myself. Because I was so flooded with memories of what we did, I couldn't remember what it was that *I* did.

'Do I have any hobbies?' I asked my long-suffering best friend.

'Yeah, of course,' he replied, topping up my drink and grinning a reassuring grin.

'Like what?'

'Well... you like Japanese stuff,' he said after a worrying pause.

'But do I only like Japanese stuff because *he* did?'

'Oh yeah. Hmm. You like punk music.'

'Again.'

'Shit.'

We sat for a while, sipping vodka Red Bull and staring around my almost empty flat. What were my hobbies? Who was I? What did I do? Was there any part of me that hadn't sprung up in the period since I was eighteen, and wasn't therefore inextricably tied to eight? Eventually we settled on a depressing array of meaningless junk: Murakami books were out, as was Japanese food, as were most of the bands I liked, because eight had introduced me to all of them. In their place: drinking vodka, going to stand-up comedy gigs, and the serious masturbatory habit that had been with me since childhood. These were the only things I could identify that weren't significantly changed because of his absence.

It spiralled into idiocy. Even the things he did that drove me up the wall became things I couldn't live without. I can't possibly cook myself a decent meal—what will I do without number eight here to give me pointless instructions on how to measure rice? There's no point turning on the TV, I'll only be able to watch the shit that he never wanted to watch with me. Opening a bottle of wine before 6 p.m.? There's no fun in that if there's no one around to tease me for being a lush.

I expect things were the same for him. He'd sit around his flat, wondering whether to go for a run then deciding that it probably wasn't worth it given that there'd be no me to perv on him as he did post-run naked press-ups on the living room floor. Or feeling like a game of Grand Theft Auto would be wasted if I weren't nagging him to either do the washing up or at least let me suck his dick to try and break his focus.

But eventually it ended, as these things do, and the nostalgia for our relationship was replaced by a nostalgia for the way I used to feel about our relationship when I was in the throes of heartbreak. At the time it felt like the End Times. I wanted to approach people on the street and say, 'Excuse me, but would you mind *not* going about your daily business, please? My heart's just been broken.' I was pretty miffed that the dustbin men kept collecting rubbish and the shops stayed open beyond 6 p.m.—didn't they *know* that number eight was gone? Didn't they realise I was in mourning? Standing in supermarket queues, I felt like nicking the shop floor microphone and announcing that the shop was closed—how could these people do something as mundane as buying bread when my heart was crumbling into an overly dramatic pile of dust?

Reliving the months when we were trying to untangle our lives brings back the vague memories of how it felt like the end of the world, but time fades even the most painful experiences. And it wasn't like it was new. It had felt like Armageddon when I found out that number one had cheated on me, but I got through it without breaking down in a supermarket. As time faded my memories of eight, and subsequently the memories of mourning the loss of eight, I wondered whether I'd grown up a bit. Having been through two heart-wrenching break-ups, perhaps now I'd be immune to this sense of cataclysmic, end-of-relationship grief.

After all, how many times can the world end before the end of the world stops feeling significant?

The answer, it transpires, is at least three.

CHAPTER FIFTEEN

Dear All The Men On The Internet: You Complete Me

I was recently singled out at a comedy night, during that part of the show where the compère chats to audience members in order to make hilarious jokes about their lives. He asked how long I'd been with the boy next to me, and where we initially met.

'On the internet,' I replied, and the audience pissed themselves laughing.

How quaint. I felt like turning round to them and asking just which century they were living in. Perhaps people's squeamishness about internet dating is a hangover from a time when, in the infancy of the internet, those brave enough to use it to meet potential partners were people of a slightly pervy persuasion, who'd find it hard to meet a match anywhere else. For these people, patiently waiting for a dial-up connection seemed a hell of a lot easier than polling everyone in their local pub to find out who had a matching balloon fetish. But internet dating, while perhaps a novelty ten years ago, is now not only an acceptable way to meet someone but a borderline necessity, especially in a city like London where people you meet on the street are as likely to spit on you as chat you up. Laughing at someone for meeting their squeeze online is like laughing at commuters who trust the mysterious forces that power tube trains, or refusing to visit a doctor in case they might be a witch.

Where else does one possibly meet people? There's work, I guess, but the idea of having loud, angry, jizz-dripping sex with a colleague then subsequently having to take them seriously in meetings brings me out in a cold sweat. What's more, you can never quite guarantee that when you break up with each other—as you almost inevitably will—they won't go showing Dave in IT those photos you took in the bathroom.

How about on the way to or from work? After all, American sitcoms are teeming with people who are willing to stride nonchalantly up to an attractive stranger and ask them for coffee. It's something I've considered before, particularly when there's been a guy on the tube wearing a tight t-shirt and sporting tattoos that I just want to lick. But this sort of behaviour will probably have to remain in America, at least until we have a huge cultural revolution. Approaching an English person on public transport is not the best way to kick-start a sexual relationship: they assume you'll either rob them or introduce them to Christ.

So how about a pub? After all, English people are at their most gregarious and cheerful when ever so slightly pissed. But unfortunately with drunkenness comes a serious lack of coordination, making even the most graceful people look like clumsy chimps. More importantly, being drunk affects your own judgement, making you more likely to cop off with people your sober self wouldn't look twice at. I've attempted pub chat-ups before, but the vast majority of them have ended either in someone backing away, terrified, as I regale them with tales of my previous fucks, or red in the face as I rail at them having realised that the Man of My Dreams is vaguely pretentious, worryingly rude or, on one notable occasion, racist.

Nightclubs are barely worth mentioning: the possibility that you'll accidentally screw a bigot is much higher, given that you are unable to hear a bloody word anyone's saying. Moreover, the only nightclub approaches I've witnessed have involved one person dancing seductively towards another and attempting to rub their genitals on their leg. This is exactly as sexy as it sounds, i.e.: not.

So where else but the internet? The internet is by far and away the best place to locate people who seem like your type. What's more, it's useful for screening out those who definitely *aren't* your type, those who'd either annoy or terrify you. No more bombshells at 2 a.m., when you've been chatting up what seems like a hot person for an hour only to hear them say, 'I actually find sex hotter when neither of us orgasms.' Or 'You know, I think it's important that the man retains the role as head of the household,' or even 'You know, you'd be really pretty if you lost a bit of weight.'

You can cull people without having to go through the tedium of an initial conversation. Did you shorten 'your' to 'ur'? We're probably not going to get on. Listed 'clubbing' as one of your hobbies? No thanks. Included a hilarious joke about how 'fat chicks need not apply'? Even if I'm not having a fat day, you're definitely on the 'no' list. Sure, I've probably ended up ditching a few potential partners with whom things could have worked out, but there's nothing like a search list full of new opportunities to make one realise that there are plenty more hot nerdy guys in the sea.

And, of course, the same is true from their point of view as well. No man I meet online need worry about whether I'm too tall, too loud, or, as one guy rather excellently put it, too 'drinky'—I most definitely *am* all of those things, and I state it up front in my profile so as to avoid that awkward moment when we meet in a bar and he looks around for a discreet window to escape through. Even if you don't make it past the first awkward pint, neither of you has invested much effort, so neither will be heartbroken if things don't work out.

Number 21 was one of those guys. We met on a dating site, he was attracted to me because my profile mentioned the word 'sex', and I liked him because he seemed reasonably nerdy and willing to put in the effort to send a joke that made me laugh.

We met in central London, retired to the nearest pub, and proceeded to get incredibly drunk. Things went well. He was exactly as funny as I had expected him to be, ever so slightly more nerdy than I had anticipated, and, most importantly, incredibly keen on having sex with me. There were no strings attached—he had a girlfriend who also dated other people, so he wasn't in it for the long haul. I invited him back to mine expecting some reasonably fun if ever so slightly drunk first-time sex.

Before I explain what happened, a quick word about first-time sex: it's crap. Not crap as in 'unenjoyable'—all sex is pretty enjoyable as long as we're both reasonably horny and sober enough to put the right bits into the right pieces. However, first-time sex is never going to come close to the amazing sex you have with someone you've been fucking for a while.

You're both excited, and happy that you've managed to ensnare someone hot, but despite your enthusiasm for that first shag you will probably fuck it up, because you have almost no idea what this new person actually likes. You might know from pub chat that they like blow jobs/spanking/being pissed on/that bit where you stick your fingers in their ass just before they come/etc. But you haven't a sodding clue about the nuanced things that give them that genuine 'unngh' feeling.

New people, be they male or female, will make noises that you're not used to, say things that you aren't familiar or comfortable with or, even worse, conduct the whole thing in a stony silence that leaves you wondering if they'd rather be chewing broken glass. They might have problems getting hard or wet. They might be less energetic than you're used to, or they might try to twist you into acrobatic positions that you're unable to do because you don't have the same yoga background as their ex.

So why do we bother? Well, because it's fun. Despite the technical failings the overall experience is usually enjoyable. And, more importantly, it is usually worth putting in the groundwork to establish something that could be spectacular. OK, so he didn't really get that bit quite how you like it, and he asked you to stop blowing him because you were 'overenthusiastic', but in ninety-nine per cent of cases he'll also have done some stuff that blew your mind, or at the very least made you go 'oooh', and entice you back for another go.

Number twenty-one fell into the one per cent.

We got straight down to it as soon as we walked in the front door. He pushed me into my bedroom, tore off my top, and threw me down on the bed in just the way I'd asked him to. He rolled on a condom, told me I was a dirty bitch, then plunged it into me.

Oh fuck yeah. I sighed with pleasure. He moaned. I pushed my hips up to meet his, relishing the feeling of him deep and hard inside me and then... he bit me.

'Ow.'

'Yeah, you like that?' He bit me again—hard. His teeth sank into my neck and I was worried that he would actually draw blood.

'No, actually I really don't.'

'Oh, OK.'

Approximately thirty seconds later, he bit me again.

'Dude. Stop biting me.'

'Oh yeah, sorry. Force of habit.'

We resumed fucking, and I said no more about it, until around the two minute mark, when he grabbed a fistful of my hair and started yanking it like he wanted a chunk to take home as a souvenir.

'Ow.'

I'm not averse to hair pulling. In fact, I'd go as far as to say it's fucking hot. I love it when guys, in the middle of a shag, grab a big handful of my hair and twist my head to one side. If someone's fucking me from behind, tugging on my hair to force my head back is deliciously almost-painful, and adds to the feeling that he's in control. I'm just a toy for him to play with, forcing me this way and that according to his whims.

But this was no normal hair pulling, less of an attempt to control me than a genuine attempt to tear it out at the roots.

'Please stop pulling my hair.'

'But... I thought you liked being dominated?'

'I do, but I also like having hair.' I'll admit it: it's not the sexiest way to let someone know of your likes and dislikes. I wouldn't have blamed him if he'd pulled out, fished his pants off the floor of my bedroom and announced that he was leaving. But to be honest that would be better than what he actually did next: he pulled my hair again.

'Ow. Fucking OW.'

'Sorry.'

I fumed. I gritted my teeth. I tried to block out the fact that—actually—his penis felt pretty good inside me thank you very much. And, about three minutes later, he came. A shuddering, shaking orgasm accompanied by an extremely pleasant-sounding grunt. Done.

It wasn't horrible, it wasn't terrifying, it was just rude and painful. I enjoyed fucking him, for the bits that could count as fucking. But his complete lack of care about whether I was actually enjoying the biting and the hair pulling made for a spectacularly crap shag. After he left, I brushed down the bed, collecting an entire hairbrush-full of my own hair, and I never spoke to him again.

Was that my worst online date? Oh hell no. That was just a bad fuck. The date itself was still good enough that I was willing to invite him into my house, my bedroom and subsequently my vagina. As I revelled in my new-found freedom, putting on an incredibly good show of not being homesick for number eight, I filled my diary with dates, many of which were far less successful than number twenty-one.

One of the massive downsides about being an unashamed, tell-everyone-I-know slag is that guys all expect me to fuck them. In fact, even my friends are surprised if I tell them that I went on a date with a guy, he was nice, and yet still we didn't fuck. Why on earth wouldn't you fuck him—what went wrong?

There are three reasons I might not sleep with someone on the first date. Firstly and most conclusively: the guy intimidates me. Despite being a loud-mouthed harpy, I'm not immune to being a bit nervous around certain men, even ones I might otherwise fancy. I can be desperate to take someone home and into my bed, but if he pushes things a bit too far I'll worry that I might never be able to get him out of it. I wish that 'too far' was subtle enough that I'd have difficulty explaining it, but unfortunately, it isn't.

The following are all things that otherwise normal and lovely guys have actually done either on, or sometimes before, a first date:

Asked me if I'll fuck them within the first five minutes—no, I'm only three sips into my pint.

Suggested that we meet in a secluded area of Hyde Park at midnight—no, and I'm calling the police.

Told me that their fantasy includes anal stretching—ouch.

As above, only with vomiting blood—double ouch. It's best to leave extreme things until we've got to know each other a little, and even extremer things off the table altogether.

Let me know, 'just in case', that they've booked a hotel—I'm fine with booking hotels, by the way, just not before you've met me. The subsequent assurances that there is 'no pressure' are directly contradicted by the fact that a hotel in London costs more than most people earn in a week.

Told me that they aren't planning on leaving their wives for me. Which, while understandable, is irrelevant in a situation where we've so far only exchanged names and brief hellos.

Even if a first date goes well, I can be immediately turned off by whatever follow-up happens after that. A text that says 'That was great, we should do it again if you're up for it' is lovely, and exactly the sort of thing I'll send if I enjoyed myself but didn't quite manage to charm my way into your tight cotton boy pants. But a post-date text that implies either that a) we're perfect for each other or b) you're going to pursue me relentlessly until we meet again is a turn-off no matter how well we got on. Asking for a second date is the only reasonable way you'll get one, nagging is the quickest way to ensure you don't.

The key thing with date follow-up is to be ready for a 'no'. Even if you think the date's gone well, it might be that the other person disagrees, and is simply trying to find a nice way to say 'not for me, thanks, but good luck in the future'.

Some people take this kind of rejection so badly that there should be a course they can go on before anyone lets them within two clicks of a dating site. One gentleman responded to my 'sorry, but good luck in the future' email as if it were simply an opening move in a game of chess—an attack that he had to parry and counter in order to change my mind. He sent me a point-by-point rebuttal of my reasons for not accepting a second date, and concluded with an emotional flourish: 'I cannot in all conscience let you walk away from something that could be spectacular.'

Much as I admire fiery emotional rhetoric, *I* couldn't in all conscience let this man make me feel guilty because we went for a couple of pints and I didn't immediately ask him to marry me. I repeated my wishes of luck, and politely declined. Imagine my surprise when this man, whose last email had implied that we might be soulmates, opened his next email with: 'You fucking stuck-up fucking bitch'. He sent me four more increasingly alarming emails over the course of the evening fuelled, I suspect, by both gin and resentment, culminating in the terrifying question 'How about I turn up at your work and tell them all what a fucking bitch slag you are?' I tried to sleep on it, but kept waking with visions of this man sitting in the reception of my office building holding up a sign that said 'bitch slag' and me being marched out of work under strict instructions to either date him or have him arrested. As I staggered in to the office, bleary-eyed the next morning, a new email bleeped through on my phone: 'So sorry about last night. I got drunk and I shouldn't have said those things. Can we try again?'

So in case you're wondering what counts as 'pushing things too far', it starts at 'I've booked a hotel room' and works its way up to something resembling that.

The second reason why sex might not be forthcoming on a first date is that there are practical issues. Disappointingly, life doesn't always conspire to produce gigantic fuckfests on a weeknight. Sometimes I'll plan a date when I'm horny, then turn up to it tired, drawn and desperate to go to bed. Sometimes I have to work early the next day, sometimes I'm ill, sometimes I'm on my period and just not up for having the 'I'm menstruating but I still want to do this if you're not going to be all squeamish about it' conversation.

On a first date with a rather shy boy, the fact that I fancied the life out of him was overshadowed by exactly these practical issues. I was intrigued by him. He was warm and gentle and funny and despite throwing a few howlers into our initial discussion—'I'm not really that into reading.' Long, uncomfortable pause before I said, 'Shall I get my coat?'—he interested me. This, I assure you, had almost nothing to do with the fact that he was one of the nerdiest people I had ever met, and therefore sexy as hell, coupled with the fact that he was bald, which I happen to have a quite spectacular thing for.

I wasn't working early or on my period, I was just accidentally double-booked. Drinks with this shy guy were curtailed because I was due to meet another, much less shy—and therefore guaranteed to fuck me—guy later that evening. Cursing my inability to correctly annotate my diary, I left him nursing his remaining half pint and said a very apologetic, and early, farewell.

The look he gave me when I left almost made me stay. He'd been nonchalant, bordering on stoned for most of the date, and despite the fact that we'd spent two pints joking, I wasn't convinced he'd had a particularly brilliant time. But as I stood up and gathered my things he looked kicked-puppy sad. He didn't beg me to stay, he just asked:

'Are you sure you need to go so soon?' and the look on his face was one of disappointment. It said, *This is never going to happen again, is it?* Hot though he was, I'd booked a fair few dates for the next few weeks, and I wasn't quite sure that this shy, casual guy was quite right for me. If you'd asked me that night if I thought I'd see him again, I suspect I'd have said no.

The final reason for not sleeping with someone straight away shouldn't come as a revelation. It's a boring end to the 'no sex' triumvirate, but the most common reason of all. Sometimes, despite their brilliance, I just don't fancy them.

Statistically, even for hyper-horny slags, people we fancy are in the minority. No matter how pervy you are, there'll be very few people in the world that you actually want to fall to your knees in front of. We walk through life bumping into, brushing past, and being checked out by countless hundreds of people with whom we'd never plan on leaping into bed. Did you fancy the guy who served you in Sainsbury's? That woman on the number 25 bus? That group of hipster youths smoking roll-ups outside the cinema? Probably not. It's not unusual for us not to fancy someone: it's the default position.

And yet for some reason when we're actually dating, we find that it's hard to get these words out. We offer myriad ridiculous reasons why we might not be able to see someone again: I'm busy; I've met someone else; I'm back with my ex; I'm a secret agent who has been called away on a classified mission and if I don't make it back please mourn the beautiful thing that we might have had. Blindingly obvious though the truth is, we'll say anything to avoid having to actually state it.

These seemingly white lies are far more hurtful than the truth itself. If you turn down a second date because 'I'm just really busy at the moment' you imply that your date is so tedious and unimportant you can't clear one evening in your diary to have a drink. Tell them you've met someone else and they hear 'someone better'. Highlighting individual issues is even worse: 'You live too far away'; 'I couldn't cope with your vegan lifestyle'; 'Your profile says you want kids and I'm not sure I do'. You've opened the floodgates for them to offer alternative solution after alternative solution only to be continually slapped in the face by your repeated 'no's.

Saying 'I don't fancy you' on the other hand has the benefit of being true, non-judgemental and also pretty final. No one can argue with an 'I don't fancy you', because it's not something that anyone can change. Likewise it doesn't involve critiquing them as a person: a guy can be sensitive, caring, thoughtful and funny yet still fail to tick your 'sexy' box. If they don't make you salivate or weak at the knees, there's not much anyone can do to push you together.

So, a plea to everyone who is dating, or likely to date in the future: let's give each other the courtesy of being honest. It's the nicest and simplest thing to do, it avoids confusion, and, most importantly, it saves time. Let's tell more people—politely, and with a sorry smile—that we just don't fancy them. The time we save can be spent running another search for someone who *does* fire us up.

I Like My Men Like I Like My Coffee: In My Mouth First Thing In The Morning

You have a new message from MiceDrivingCats:

Sorry if I was off when we met. I'm not good at meeting new humans under pressure. I'm just one of those in the generation that's more comfortable with the internet. Let's hope Twitter is never struck by lightning—the social web will collapse around it leaving millions destitute and out of touch. People will be forced to express opinions to individuals, not collectives. Pictures of the night before will have to be emailed around, like people used to do in the 90s. They will have to recognise the people in the pictures all by themselves, like primitive animals!

Reply, from GirlOnTheNet:

I am terrified by your image of the future. Instead of scraping our web usage data, Google and Facebook will have to resort to conducting strip searches in the street to ascertain what they should tell advertisers to sell us. And ego-Googles will consist of individuals standing on a high vantage point and screeching through a megaphone 'Do you know who I am?!'

The shy boy was less shy once we'd had a drink together. He'd send me cute comments and funny stories and ask me how I was. I didn't usually like messaging back and forth; I'd usually email guys just enough to establish that we might be compatible, then insist on proper chatting in the pub. After all, investing significant time deciding whether you fancy someone's online persona is time utterly wasted: people always seem cooler on the internet. But both the shy guy and I were too busy to arrange a second date. When I dropped the conversation, he'd pick it up, with a persistence that would have annoyed me in anyone else, but in him I found flattering. I checked my messages daily, pleasantly surprised if there was one from him. And, in the meantime, the dates with other guys started filling up my diary.

Number twenty was initially incredibly promising—a smart, funny scruff of a guy who was infinitely more laidback than me. After a couple of messages back and forth, then one quick drink, he invited me back to his house so we could talk about sex without shocking the people on adjacent tables. He was fascinated by my past experiences in fetish clubs, and I was fascinated by his claim that he never wanked to anything—*anything*, mind—other than videos his female friends had made for him.

'What sort of videos?'

'Just, you know, of them masturbating.'

I was gobsmacked. That felt like a lie. I'm a pretty open-minded girl, but masturbation is something that even I, an unstoppable wanker, feel nervous about doing in front of someone.

When I touch myself in front of someone I feel a bizarre urge to do it wrong, to do it like they do in porn. To spread my cunt wide and fuck myself with my fingers so the watching boy gets a good view. To wank so that it's difficult to come, so that I last. Home alone I can go from nought to soaking orgasm in the time it'd take to fire up whichever fantasy is currently ticking my boxes, but in front of others I'm embarrassed to do anything other than what girls do in porn.

Number twenty swiftly convinced me to give it a go, with a few kisses that resonated deep in the pit of my stomach, ten minutes or so of extremely competent fucking, and eventually a request that was so politely worded I could hardly have refused. As I lay back on his bed, willing myself not to make fake sex faces or moan in ways that I never would if I were alone, I rubbed at my clit while he knelt over me.

He clearly liked watching. He rubbed himself as he looked on, his cock growing thicker, straighter, redder as I sped up. When I neared the end, and my thighs twitched with the first waves of my own orgasm, he came, shooting jets of spunk all over my face, my neck, my hair and a substantial portion of his bedding.

I couldn't believe I hadn't realised before that this would be an amazing thing. Being the sole focus of someone's arousal, where they're not turned on by your touch but simply by the sight of you is deeply erotic. I understood now why his friends might have been keen to make videos for him. As I sprinted out of his flat to catch the last tube, I wondered why I hadn't believed him.

But great though he was, he was clearly a one-time-only sort of guy. This wasn't exactly a heartbreaking revelation. I'm not sure how long I could last with a guy who couldn't come unless I was putting on a show for him. It'd be an exhausting bit of play-acting, like telling your partner you were French on the first date, then having to maintain the accent as it developed into a long-term relationship.

Scanning through incoming messages on the dating site, I found a couple of other guys who were interesting, and generous enough to want to date someone whose profile consisted mostly of sarcastic jokes.

Number twenty-three was so nerdy that he swapped tips with me on how to optimise our dating site profiles, like eager webmasters at a Google conference trying to make sure when you call up results for 'hot lovers in London E3' your profile comes top of the list. After a marathon five dates without so much as a peck on the cheek, followed by a quick session of gentle sex, we realised that we probably weren't going to be tearing each other's clothes off on a regular basis. In looking for sex we'd managed to accidentally lay the foundations for a pretty decent friendship.

Many people have told me that you can't have sex with your friends. This categorically isn't true. It's one of those rules, like 'never sleep with your colleagues', that was made to be broken. Although I don't usually sleep with colleagues, I've known people who have met their partners at work and enjoyed long and happy relationships, not to mention some extremely explicit and adventurous sex. But not sleeping with your friends is the same: although we're warned against it—'What happens when you break up?' 'What if one of you gets a new partner?' 'One of you will get hurt!'—we're also offered countless examples of friends who have got together and gone on to be happier than two lovebirds at a particularly feathery orgy. If it's such a dangerous mistake to make, why are people setting us this bad example?

The answer is that they're not—no one else's relationship is ever really an example to us. We can learn from others, but ultimately whether something works comes down to how individuals handle each situation. You might be uncomfortable with the idea of fucking your friends in case it turns into a Ross/Rachel drama, but someone else might be happy to shag a mate and it'd be as easy as an evening together watching box sets of *The Wire*. The rule isn't 'don't sleep with your friends' but 'choose wisely which friends you sleep with'.

Number sixteen and I were more than happy to have a friends with late-night-sex-benefits relationship—incoming text: 'It's Friday and I'm bored. Fancy a beer and a shag?'—but number twenty-three preferred to keep things platonic. This was a fun new feeling for me. Having had few platonic male friends since I broke up with eight, I enjoyed being grown up about things, and also being the one he came to for opinionated advice on how to woo a new lady.

And in the meantime, the shy guy was still hovering in the background.

MiceDrivingCats:

I'm dying to find out what happened with all those things we've been talking about. Drinks soon?

GirlOnTheNet:

Soon, but not this week. I seem to have some sort of horrible disease, no doubt caught by standing too close to besuited coughing people on tube trains.

MiceDrivingCats:

Get well soon (and all that), I hope it's not plague (that's for luck, 100% of the people I have said that to later turned out not to have the plague).

We were both busy, and he didn't nag me for a second date. He just kept messaging, being both available and interesting, until I realised that I missed him if he didn't. When I got an email from the dating site—'Hey, GirlOnTheNet, you have a new message from...'— I was hoping to see his name.

Meanwhile, life in real life was happening. Despite spending more time on internet dates than was strictly healthy, I did occasionally leave the house to do things other than have borderline strangers masturbate on my face. And I met guys in these real life situations too, the only difference was that, given I didn't have their email address and a laptop to hand, I had to rely on the old-fashioned way of chatting them up: talking to them face to face.

After initial bouts of nerves, when I'd stare miserably at a nice-looking guy across the room, wiping drool from the front of my shirt and trying to work up the courage to say anything other than 'umm', I eventually discovered that not only do men generally not bite, but chatting them up is not nearly as terrifying as I'd let myself believe.

Not that I'm good at it, of course. There are some people who are genuinely good at chat-ups: women stunning and confident enough that they can stride up to a man in a bar, click their fingers and whisk him away, with just a brief pause while he trips over his tongue on his way back to her house. Likewise there are probably guys who can do more with a raised eyebrow and a sexy smile than I could do with a whole arsenal of try-hard chat-up lines.

Dating sites and self-help books offer innumerable winning formulas on how to become one of these people. There are even courses you can go on that promise shy nerdy types that after a couple of weeks and a few hundred quid they'll have passing strangers falling at their feet and all but begging them for sex. They offer to turn you into one of these charming, charismatic sex-magnets. But they overlook the salient fact that these sex-magnets aren't actually magical. These people are probably trembling with nerves inside, no matter how confident they look to the naked eye. If they're speaking to someone they genuinely like, the risk of being rejected is enough to make even the most confident singleton a bit uncertain.

All they've done is mastered a few tricks to hide their nerves and uncertainty.

The first trick: be casual. Striking up a conversation with a stranger, while perhaps not natural to most of us, is not rocket science either. You don't have to learn lines, gestures or a complicated secret handshake, you just have to do what you'd want someone else to do in that situation: be friendly, polite and casual. This is how things worked for myself and nineteen. I met him in a bar after a conference we'd both been to. I said hello as I ordered a round. He was all gregarious smiles and chatting, and by the time my drinks had been poured I realised I liked him, so I offered him a drink too. Our mutual friends all joined together and squished onto a big table, then at the end of the evening he took me back to his hotel where we had sweet, casual, uncomplicated sex followed by a blow job and breakfast in the morning.

As this was one of the first times, post-number-eight, that I'd approached a stranger without the aid of a dating site, I was delighted to discover that it wasn't difficult. He didn't need me to do an IQ test, or perform a complex mating dance. There was no awkwardness, no stress, and no requirement that I spout pre-planned hilarious chat-up lines in order to get his attention.

Which brings me neatly onto the second trick: there is only ever one good chat-up line. That line is:

'Do you fancy a drink?'

Lay aside the sentimentality of 'You're so beautiful,' avoid ironic clichés like 'Did it hurt when you fell from heaven?' and don't risk the potentially intimidating directness of 'Fancy a fuck?' The best chat-up line is tried, tested and, although not guaranteed to succeed, it's at least guaranteed to never make you look like a complete tool: 'Fancy a drink?' Your subtext says 'Hey, I think you're interesting, and I'm willing to invest up to four pounds to find out if my initial assessment was correct.' But if they say no, your pride remains intact because they haven't directly rejected you, they might just not fancy a sodding drink.

Next trick: pretend to be confident. Very few people are genuinely confident, they're just better than others at pretending. That perfect person sat at the other end of the table making jokes with the waiting staff and holding court with his wit and charisma? Total coward. Deep down he's probably worrying about whether he's spilt soup down his shirt or if you'll notice that he's farted in between courses: he's just good at pretending. No one wakes up one morning to find they've developed confidence, just as no one wakes up thinking, I'm a grown-up now. We're all frightened children deep down, and it's nice to realise that everyone else is as insecure, immature and incompetent as you are.

Number twenty-two, despite his outward displays of confidence, seemed distinctly nerdy underneath. I tested my theory by simply asking him—after a reasonable period of good-natured chat—if he fancied a drink and, subsequently, a blow job. It turned out he did.

Despite my mind telling me, Don't go and talk to that guy, he is far more attractive than you and likely to shoot you down without so much as listening to you stutter your way through a 'hello', I'll happily strike up conversation. Occasionally I even come across as a normal person, despite having to remind my heart to stop beating so fucking loudly and my hands to behave like proper hands and stop accidentally pouring wine down my face. I come across as confident not because I actually *am* but because I recognise that *no one is.*

It's easy to say all this, though: be confident, be casual. But there will be people who quite understandably are unable to shake off years of shyness just on my say so. So if all else fails, and the casual confidence just won't come, remember how it worked in school: get one of your friends to talk to them for you. The old 'my mate fancies your mate' trick worked well with number twenty-four, who I met when he was best man at the wedding of a friend of mine. After an afternoon's worth of polite small talk and lukewarm white wine, I slurred at the groom: 'Hey, is your best man single?' At which point the groom channelled the spirit of Cupid and shouted across the room: 'Oi! You're still single, mate, aren't you? *She* wants to know.'

I didn't say it was classy, I just said that it *worked.* To my delight, the best man was not only single, he was more than willing. I gave him my number, and after the party he took a cab to the Travelodge where I was staying and fucked me in the arse against a rickety dressing table.

So, while honing my theories on how to chat up men without causing them to run for the hills, and occasionally refreshing my inbox to see if I'd received a new hilarious message from the shy guy, things were looking pretty fun. Number eight was still burning a hole in my heart, but the hole was getting slightly smaller and less blistered by the day. The residual ache thoroughly put me off entering into anything mature enough to be classed as a relationship. I didn't want to create yet another brilliant thing only to smash it again on the rock of my sexual incontinence. But I was quite keen to find a boy or two who I could see more regularly.

First time sex is all very well—it's carefree and fun and there's no worry that the person you're shagging might turn round and hug you, or propose marriage, or any of those other things I was keen to avoid. But a regular, friendly shag can be a much better long-term bet. For a start it saves you having to gather the time and confidence to approach new people. Secondly it means you don't waste any evenings sitting in the pub with people who are entirely unsuitable, pretending to each other that you might have a lot in common and then parting with a 'see you later' that you both desperately hope is a lie. Finally, sex you have with a regular partner can be dirtier, filthier and more intense.

Meet number twenty-five. On paper he was the perfect guy for me: insanely funny, confident, cheeky and covered in tattoos. I could practically taste the punk rock oozing from his skin. The first time we fucked was like a fight, all grappling and wrestling and changing positions to test what the other one was made of. It was rapid, but not quick. We'd fuck for half an hour then break, panting, drinking pints of water and chatting while we recovered for the next bout.

He was testing to see what I could do, and the answer was mostly 'let out surprised yelps as he placed his fingers with precision accuracy and exactly the right pressure on my clit'. For my part, I was less focused on impressing him because I was far too busy *fancying* him: I'd have had posters of him on my bedroom wall if they were available. At one point while we were shagging, he slowed his strokes and looked down at me, only to catch me staring at his shoulder like it was a particularly tasty joint of meat.

'Are you perving on my tattoos?'

'Umm... yeah, a little bit.'

'Dirty bitch.'

Slam—he shoved his cock back into me with a force that made me wince.

He worked late, and would phone me from outside my house so as not to wake anyone. I'd creep out of bed and tiptoe to the front door, in a vest top and knickers, to see him waiting on the doorstep with a lopsided grin and a raging erection.

Did I mention that he was filthy? He was. I got a text from him, in the lead up to one of our evenings together: 'This evening, can I come in your hair and/or eyes?'

Never had the and/or dilemma been used for such beautiful purposes. Of course, of *course* you can. Could you piss on me too? Yeah? Fantastic. How about holding my wrists down and making me struggle while you fuck me? Tick in that box. Hold my mouth open and spit into it? Yep. Over the course of just a few sporadic evenings he had me doing things that had taken eight and I years to work up to. For the first time I felt I could see directly inside a guy's head, and the interior view was a close match with the decoration inside my own mental sex palace.

So why didn't it work? Why are there four more chapters in this book, when logic dictates that the happily-ever-after should happen here, as number twenty-five and I walk up the aisle to a suitable Green Day track, then honeymoon at a dungeon in Amsterdam?

Well, for a start there was the 'emotional attachment' thing. One of the reasons twenty-five was so good was that he didn't want anything from me other than a couple of hours to fuck and the odd email about the ways in which I wanted him to defile me. He was casual, irregular and decidedly uncomplicated.

But there were other problems, too. Things that made me wonder if this guy wasn't, in fact, not just a bad idea, but a bit of a shit.

There was a huge mismatch of attraction between us. I was very giggly and swoony, and would hang on his every word, watching his lips move with fascination and loving the shape of them as they mouthed my name. Despite knowing very little about him, I spent much of my idle spare time considering the shape of his body, the lines of his tattoos and the way he'd grunt with exertion when we fucked. If he was a punk god, I was his drooling groupie.

And he? Well, he felt exactly the same way, but not about me. He'd also hang off his every word, waiting impatiently as I talked to him until it became his turn to speak. When I occasionally tried and failed to get a word in edgeways it wasn't because he was deliberately ignoring me, but because he genuinely couldn't conceive of anything I'd say being more important than the ramble of thoughts that would tumble relentlessly from inside his beautiful head. I suspect he'd have found it easier to get hard looking into a mirror than at me.

The dilemma I faced was one that every girl and guy I know has been familiar with: do I stay with this person because I like them, knowing full well that they think far less of me? Or do I move on to someone a bit warmer, who actually listens when I speak? I was still keeping an eye on my inbox for new messages from the shy guy. Sure, he wasn't a punk-rock poster boy, lickable and filthy and ready to fuck me into a coma, but he was *interested* in me. Each message that came through nudged politely for more information, more chatter and just a little bit more of me. Was he a better bet than twenty-five who, while clearly keen to fuck me, would have been equally happy if I'd just drawn a pair of tits on the duvet cover? At least it would remain quiet in the post-sex afterglow, while twenty-five told long-winded stories about himself.

Eventually, number twenty-five made the decision for me. After a few days of agonising over whether I could spend any more time with a man who could barely remember my name, twenty-five stopped replying to my texts.

Just like that. One night he was coming in my hair and/or eyes, the next he was wondering how to tell me that he'd got a girlfriend. I don't think my heart was broken, but I was pretty annoyed. Because it means that despite the frantic, sweaty, tattooed rock-god sex, my abiding memories of twenty-five are of the cold silence that greeted the last two texts I sent him, a sense of confused rejection and a rather unattractive dose of thrush.

CHAPTER SEVENTEEN

APPARENTLY COPROPHILIA IS NOT AN ACCEPTABLE TOPIC FOR DATE CONVERSATION

OK, fine. I'll go out with the shy guy. I mean, it's not like I really *want* to or anything. Except I sort of do. But I don't. I'm interested, but he's shy, you know? He doesn't strike me as the sort of person who'll bend me over and beat six shades of sexy into me. But he intrigues me.

I'd been stupid enough to ditch the first date just a couple of hours in so I'd have time to get home and ready before twenty-five came round to fuck me. Given that twenty-five had officially fallen off the face of the planet, and I'd demonstrated the consistency with which I'm able to make appallingly crap decisions, perhaps dating the shy guy wouldn't be such a bad idea.

'So, you don't like books then.' I'm nothing if not an aggressive conversationalist.

'Nope, not really. Does that make me a bad person?' He raised an eyebrow, looking wholly unconcerned about the possibility that I might think it did. The languid, casual ease with which he chatted to me and stroked my ego had me drawn to him—the way someone who speaks quietly can have you leaning forwards and holding your breath so as to better grasp what they're saying. He pulled me in without ever even trying to.

'Not really. I just... It's a good topic of conversation, isn't it?'

'Is it?' Again, relaxed. There were pauses in the conversation—not long enough to get awkward but longer than I'd had on other dates. I expected him to be a bit nervous like I was, to chat to fill in the blanks. But he seemed as comfortable with the pauses as he was with everything else. He was so relaxed I half expected him to lie down when things got quiet.

'OK,' I said 'What *is* a good topic of conversation?'

He thought for a minute, and then asked me: 'What would be the worst thing you could do on a first date?'

Good question.

'Hmm... I guess, something horrific and awkward, maybe watching a grotesque film. How about watching *Hostel* at someone's house, and then halfway through the film they start getting an erection?'

He laughed. 'Good one. That's definitely a good one.'

'How about you? What would be *your* worst first date?'

'No question: meeting their parents.'

One—nil to him, I think. He seemed interested enough in my answer that we spent the next half-hour discussing the merits or otherwise—mostly otherwise—of cheap horror films. Although we'd been messaging regularly, the fact that it had been so long since that initial aborted first date, I expected we'd have to start again from scratch—nervous hellos, shy smiles and a long build up before I could broach the subject of whether or not we'd be able to fuck. Instead within the space of ten minutes we'd gone from 'What are you drinking?' to me explaining, in quite unnecessary detail, the specific digestive functions of a Human Centipede.

'This is horrible, isn't it?'

'Yeah.' he shrugged. 'But it's interesting how you want to keep talking about it.' He smiled at me. 'You're definitely not doing well at persuading me you're not a serial killer.'

'I'm not a serial killer.'

'If you say so.'

Everything about him was relaxed. I don't think he'd have flinched if I'd taken an axe from my bag and swung it at his head. He'd have made a joke about it, stepped slowly to one side, and probably asked me if it was his round.

I wasn't used to guys being this calm. The men I'd fucked on dates had been excitable and agitated. Number twenty-five was positively spasming with energy every time I saw him. Most of the guys I'd known before would twitch and fidget and leap up and check their phone every five minutes to see what was happening in the world. This guy? He just sat, calmly and patiently, and talked to me about everything I wanted to discuss. Unflinching, unblinking, smiling throughout. Compared to the whirlwind of the rest of my life, it was like slipping into a warm bath.

Three pints into our second date I was desperate to find out the most important thing: could we fuck? I wasn't looking for someone to marry. The swiftness with which my fantasies of marriage/mortgage/babies with number eight had come crashing down put me off, and it didn't feel like I'd be likely to say the 'm' word again. But I did need to get *that* feeling when I saw him. Excited butterflies when I get a message from him are all well and good, but I wanted that crucial bit extra: lust, desire and electric shots of arousal that'd pass between us as he handed me a pint.

'Fancy some chips?' I offered, ever the classy seductress.

He shrugged, then nodded. I could have asked if he fancied torturing then eating some kittens and he'd have given the same response. 'Sure. Is there anywhere round here?'

'There's a chippy near my house.' And for a second I saw eager enthusiasm in his eyes, a sort of 'tell me you're not joking'. He wasn't keen on chips, but he was certainly interested in my house, and that made me weak and numb with arousal.

We huddled into each other on the night bus; he was all big shoulders and warmth. We grabbed some chips then settled down in my lounge, neither of us quite ready to make the first move in case we ended up disappointed. Eventually, I took the paper out to the kitchen and he followed me, affecting a clumsy face-bump that was the beginning of our first kiss.

I'd hoped that the first kiss would lead to him dragging me by the hair to my bedroom and shagging me like I was in trouble, but sadly it didn't. I had to take a bit of initiative, and I led him in there myself.

But at that point things went downhill, as he slowly, gently, calmly made love to me.

Oh God, I sound so horribly ungrateful. I know some people love it—the face touching, the eye contact, the tender words and gentle kisses and long, slow strokes. The smiles, the whispers, the soft focus.

But when twenty-six fucked me slowly all I could think was Well, *he's* not that keen. Having spent so long thinking about him, I wanted him to be desperate to have me. I wanted him to hurl his chip-paper to the floor and demand immediate satisfaction, to be so hot and hard that he'd frot against my thighs as soon as he got close enough.

Guys, don't peel my clothes off slowly while you kiss every inch of my delicate skin; moan and swear and writhe as you tear off your trousers, wondering why it takes as long as six seconds to get your cock out and into me. If we're shagging for the first time, or the second, third, fourth, or twenty-second, you need to be lustful, and hot, and focused so hard on coming that nothing can distract you. It might seem like foreplay, but to be honest if I've dragged you back to mine at the end of a second date, if I've spent the last two hours boring holes in you with my lustful stare, there's only minimal foreplay required; if I weren't already turned on I wouldn't have brought you here.

I shouldn't be mean to the gents who do this. There are many people for whom this is their ideal fuck. Amy, who is still hovering in the background of this story, recently confessed that she thought she'd found The One—a guy who, while remarkably ordinary looking, was the best shag she had ever had. So good that she watches him walk around the room and almost swoons like a Victorian maid.

'Why's he so good?' I asked.

'He makes love to me. Actually *makes love* to me. I didn't realise that "making love" meant until I got with him. He's gentle and soft and it's just like in the films—he actually *looks into my eyes*! And he strokes my boobs really softly. He even kisses my neck. It's amazing.'

Good Lord I'm glad she likes this. Because there are guys who like it too, and I'd rather hand them Amy's number than have to disappoint them by rejecting their delicate caresses. While Amy's busy with the lovemakers, I'm free to hunt down the guys who'll to mount me like a dog in heat. The guys who, when they read Amy's description above, thought it sounded like a horrible nightmare. He looks into your eyes? You mean you're actually *facing each other*?

When Amy asked me why I liked *my* guy I replied: 'He fucks me like he hates me.'

'You're weird, you know that?'

Well, yes. But aren't we all? I understand why no one wants to hop into bed with a near stranger and start doing things that terrify them. I didn't expect twenty-six to slap me, choke me, or call me a filthy whore. I just wanted something a bit more forceful, a bit more powerful. His huge arms and big shoulders had written cheques that the slow, languid lovemaking just wasn't coming close to cashing. I bucked against him, lifted my hips up to meet him, put both my hands on his arse and pulled him in to meet me. And as we picked up the pace his breath caught in his throat and he came inside me, leaving me squirming with need.

When we'd finished he put his arms around me and drifted off into a peaceful sleep. I retired to my side of the bed and lay awake, cursing Amy for being right about my weirdness, and wondering if I'd ever stop.

Sex isn't everything. It's not the be-all and end-all. Despite almost constantly thinking about what I want to do to boys—or, more specifically, what I want *them* to do to *me*—I understand that when you're with someone for more than a hump in a car park there are other things that are more important. Mutual respect, fun, the ability to have a massive fight about politics one minute then a giggle with each other the next: sex isn't everything.

But it's surely *something*, right? It's not unimportant. Twenty-six had, more than anyone I'd met since eight, been exciting. I wanted more than just sex—the fun and friendship and playfulness as well. But time spent chatting and laughing and going to the zoo is a very different prospect if it's interspersed with scenes of frustration as I beg him to hurt me, squeeze me and do something—*anything*—other than make love. I knew he was turned on, but the gulf of difference between 'turned on' and 'so horny for you I'll fuck right *through* your knickers given half a chance' was a wide one to cross.

Grateful though I was that this beautiful guy was not only willing but eager to get naked with me, the demanding girl at the back of my head was reminding me just how impossible it would be to stay with him for longer than a week if he fucked me gently. I was warm to him, but he didn't give me that feeling—he *couldn't* give me that feeling—because he kissed me softly and held me as if I would break.

We were on our third date. A picnic. It was sunny and warm and I drank cans of cider while he smoked weed and looked for excuses to move closer. He wanted to hold me, and I wanted to see his thick cock stretching against the crotch of his jeans. He stroked me gently, and I wished he'd stop arsing about and just put his hand down my top. I was thinking over our first shag, and the smooth, languid way he'd fucked me, staring into my eyes to look for signs not just of arousal but affection. He was apparently thinking the same thing, because eventually he threw out the question:

'So, am I your boyfriend yet?'

'I'm sorry?' When in doubt, pretend you haven't heard. He asked again, and I laughed nervously. To be fair, it's not an easy question to either ask or answer.

When we were kids, you'd send a friend up to ask the object of your affection if they'd 'go out' with you. If they said yes then, hey presto, you were boyfriend and girlfriend. You'd remain that way until one of his mates approached you to tell you you were dumped—piece of cake. But as an adult, how do you move from a date to a relationship? I know friends who'll call someone their boyfriend after a certain number of dates, others who'll crack out the 'b' word after the first shag. Me? I like to wait at least a year. Maybe two. After all, until you say the 'b' word there's no risk you're going to break things by sleeping with other people or disappointing them by forgetting their birthday. If something remains casual then you don't have to worry about how much damage you're almost certainly going to do to it.

Having been with number eight for so long, and come to the realisation that not only was this guy completely perfect for me, but that we would never be able to build one of these 'permanent relationships' that other people seem to have success with, because of my pathetic inability to keep my knickers on and my mind focused on one person, I wasn't much keen on beginning that whole thing again with someone I would inevitably disappoint, especially someone with whom I wasn't sure I could build even half of the passion that eight and I had relied on to keep us going. The girl who'd nagged number eight about marriage, who'd thought that 'commitment' sounded like a nice thing to do together, was long gone. The girl who replaced her was cynical, dismissive and less likely to walk down the aisle than straight off Tower Bridge.

As I sat with twenty-six, I thought about what being his girlfriend might actually entail. Evenings in the pub, picnics where we sat stroking each other and disgusting each other with references to horror films. Him explaining to me, as he had earlier that day, the ins and outs of the sexy nerdy things he did in his day job. Pie, mash, beer and laughing in the pub. All the good stuff. But also gentle sex and affectionate cuddles and nights in on the sofa watching DVD box-sets, growing more and more frustrated that we'd been here for two hours and hadn't yet fucked. Would I be able to sit next to him and let him stroke my thigh as he was doing now, without wanting to pull off my jeans and hold his hot palm against my crotch? When I put it like that the answer was obvious.

'I'm sorry, I can't be your girlfriend.'

He looked surprised, and a bit sad, but he didn't move away.

'That's OK, you don't have to be my girlfriend. Can I ask why, though?' His simple acceptance of everything was disarming. This wasn't someone who was going to tell me how I should act and what I should do, and that made me more keen to do things that he would like, to say the words that he wanted. I didn't want to see the melancholy resignation in his eyes. But I had to.

'You're amazing. But you're...'

'A nerd?'

'No, I love that you're a nerd.'

'Bad at spelling?'

'Well, there is that.'

He laughed. 'So what is it then?'

'You're gentle. You're fragile. And you like me.'

He nodded. 'I do like you. Is this one of those "it's not you it's me" things?'

I thought about it for a while, and as I did he lay down and put his head in my lap and I wanted to stroke his neck.

'I think it is one of those things, yeah. I don't want to have an actual relationship, with bells and whistles and regular dates. I'd disappoint you. I just want to fuck. And I want to fuck in a horrible, dirty way, which might disappoint you as well.'

To his credit, he took it well. He made all the right noises, and said 'that's fine' and 'don't worry' and 'I'm not going to hold it against you'.

And then he took me home, pushed me to my knees, forced his cock into my mouth and called me a good girl.

The change from gentle lovemaking to holding me down and telling me I was dirty happened in the space of that one afternoon. Twenty-six had gone from being someone I was sad I couldn't have a relationship with to someone whose company I craved. I'd clear my whole diary just to spend an afternoon with my face buried in his crotch. Getting a text from him that said 'Come round tonight so I can fuck you bent over the sofa,' would leave me dazed for an hour while I tried to push the image out of my head. While I was putting my make-up on in preparation for one of our dates, my oozing desire for him would drip steadily into my knickers. By the time I arrived at his house and rang the doorbell, I was soaked.

I could barely remember what our first time had been like, because I was too busy filling my waking thoughts and fantasies with this new and more dominant version of him. The first desperate blow job, when I choked and trembled for him as he fucked my throat, gradually led to other things. His gentle strokes were batted away, so he'd reintroduce them as rough squeezes and gropes. He'd start exploratory discussion about what I might be willing to do, and be surprised and delighted when I greeted him with enthusiasm.

We established that yes, I loved it when he fucked me in the arse and no, I wouldn't laugh at him if he asked me to fuck him in return. He realised that he could spank me one minute then beg me to hold him the next. Gradually he started doing things without asking permission.

Remembering stories that I'd told him, he'd throw in new things: pinning me down on my front and whispering in my ear while he fucked me, pulling out before he came and letting his spunk spray hot and hard into the crack of my ass, putting his hand over my mouth when I squealed and telling me to 'sssh' in a deliciously controlling way. We'd watch porn together, and I'd ask him: 'Is this what you watch?'

'Not always.'

'I want to watch what *you* watch.'

And he'd change the video, replacing a gentle, soft-core video of a girl masturbating with a group of men fucking her nice and hard. I'd put his dick in my mouth and hold one of his feet tight in my crotch while I listened to the noises, and waited for him to twitch with pleasure.

'I love fucking you by that corner in your room. It means I can brace both my hands against the wall and really go for it.'

He'd look down at me while I was bent over, and I could feel his eyes watching me as his cock slammed home. Each thrust felt like a spectacular punishment, forceful and bad like I'd done something very wrong, taking my breath away with each stroke.

And every time I gasped or squealed or spoke he fucked me harder, as if he was mocking me for calling him gentle, teasing me for not believing he could do this. I could hear the grin in his voice as he asked if I wanted it harder, asked if I liked it, asked how it felt. It was not 'making love' any more, it was not even fucking. It was 'being fucked', and it felt exquisitely good.

He relished being the one in control, making me perform tricks he'd only ever seen before in porn and he leapt into my world of angry sex and stained bedsheets with an enthusiasm powered by the thickest erection I could ever have wished for.

It was as if, as soon as he'd accepted that I wasn't his girlfriend, he no longer had to worry about horrifying me enough that I'd refuse to be. It wasn't a Madonna/whore complex, not exactly—he just hadn't met anyone who was so certain about what they wanted and was unashamed to ask for it. But his delight couldn't quite silence his confusion.

'You're weird,' he said one night, as I rolled away from him, rubbing his cooling spunk into my stomach.

'Why?'

'Because you don't seem bothered by dirty things.'

'What? But I *love* dirty things. I couldn't be *more* bothered.'

'Exactly.' He explained that his previous girlfriends had enjoyed the warmth of his arms around them, and enjoyed the occasional gentle shag. But the dirtiest thing he'd ever done was fuck a couple from behind, with the occasional nod towards a threesome in the so-distant-it'll-never-happen future. When I asked why, his answer was telling:

'I didn't think they'd like it.'

And they call *me* the weird one.

'Well, did you ever ask them about sex?'

'Sometimes. But not in this much detail. Just a "Do you fancy a shag?" conversation rather than a "What would you like me to do with this cucumber?" conversation.'

He wasn't an idiot, of course. Lots of people fail to have the very specific 'What would you like me to do with this cucumber?' conversation. People skirt around issues, and hint at things, but getting up the courage to ask people directly can be almost impossible.

We should talk about sex more. I accept that it can be tricky to work the conversation round from 'What shall we see at the cinema?' to 'Can I piss on your face?' but there are certainly moments where a mention of fisting won't be entirely out of place. You don't have to dictate the entire evening:

'OK, first I would like you to gently rub my left breast, then place my nipple into your mouth. After this you shall remove my knickers, slap me on the thighs and say "Spread 'em", whereupon I shall moan a little bit before you commence penetration.'

You just have to open up:

'I like it when you control me.'

'I need you to hurt me.'

'That thing you did last Thursday? I need you to know that was amazing.'

Women's and men's magazines are full of sex tips, from tying your lover up with silk scarves to running ice cubes over their nipples. We're told to try new positions, new techniques and enough 'revolutionary' new toys that it's a wonder we have any cash left for condoms. But the best sex tip of all is rarely mentioned: talk. Just talk. Tell your partner what you actually want, rather than what you think they want to hear.

I'm guilty of holding back sometimes myself. The first time I was with number twenty-six—when I was wracked with miserable disappointment that he was more inclined to stroke my face than slap it—I should have said something then. I should have said, 'Hey, you know what would be amazingly hot? If you spat on me and called me a bitch. Because I'm just not into this gentle thing.' I didn't because I didn't want to upset him, and have this shy, special guy run for the hills. But as soon as we started talking properly, the floodgates opened up.

'Take it right down to the back of your throat. That's it. Good girl. Suck a bit harder, yeah. Oh God. Ok, that's good, keep doing that. Open your mouth wider, I'm going to fuck your throat. Do you want that?' A muffled yeah. 'Good. Open wide. Oh yeah. Hold still.'

During sex, after sex, over a pint in his local, we'd talk. Occasionally strangers would overhear our conversation. I like to think that they'd discuss some similar things on the way home, each half of the couple opening up a little bit about what they liked.

'Did you hear those two in the pub talking about throat-fucking?'

'Yeah, filthy bastards.'

'I want to try it.'

'... Me too.'

So, heed my rallying cry: talk. Tell someone about this super-hot dream you had, or what you last masturbated about. Give them the courage to say the same thing to you. Apart from anything else, it'd make me look less weird when I throw anal douecheing into a casual pub conversation.

As twenty-six came out of his shell, he asked me questions. He wasn't asking my permission, or for me to educate him like a slutty teacher in a comedy porn film—he just wanted to know how things felt for me.

'Could you put your tits in my face so I can suck your nipples while I wank?' Nothing would give me greater pleasure.

'Can I tie your ankles to the bedposts then fuck you in the cunt?' Be my fucking guest, kiddo.

'Does this hurt?'

'Will you tell me when to stop?'

'Did I go too far?'

'Do you actually like this?'

Understandably, being a gentle and loving guy who wouldn't normally hurt a fly, let alone tie it to the bedposts then beat it until it actually cried, twenty-six wanted to make absolutely sure that this was something I enjoyed rather than endured. I'd have been pretty stupid if I ignored my 'just talk' advice, so I thought I should give him a brief but effective overview.

'Yes. Yes, I actually like this. I like this so much it makes me ache inside if you won't do it to me. I like being slapped, spanked, held down and throat-fucked. I like it when you choke me, and I like it when you call me a whore.'

Someone once asked me if the reason I was submissive was because I had low self-esteem. This, as I hope you can understand having read what I can only describe as a narcissistic, self-indulgent wank about my entire life to date, is definitely not true. What's more, it harks back to that old assumption that sexual things are rarely done because the girls actually enjoy them. Linking submission and low self-esteem assumes that the girl doesn't really want pain in the same way as she might want a cuddle and a chocolate brownie. She takes the pain because she feels like she deserves punishment—she's bad/wrong/fucked up etc. Number twenty-six was about as far from misogyny as you can get, and yet he still carried around a few beliefs about women that wouldn't be out of place in a 1950s *Guide To a Happy and Sexless Marriage*. He genuinely believed that buttsex and beatings were exclusively products of male fantasy—things that women did to please guys and porn directors included to provoke a money shot, and was shocked when I told him that far from being enticed into BDSM by an over-eager boyfriend, I'd discovered it myself many years ago when an imaginary wench disobeyed an imaginary pirate, and my mind made the good things happen.

Do I need to be hit because I feel worthless? Because, deep down, I'm a bad girl who deserves to be punished? No, I don't 'deserve' to be punished any more than I deserve a pat on the back and a free lottery ticket. I'm surprised and delighted when a dude gets it into his head to beat me to the verge of tears and then fuck me like a ragdoll. It's not what I deserve, it's what I emphatically and wholeheartedly *want*.

Compare and contrast with the pop-psychology explanations offered for why some men like to be beaten. The stereotype is of a guy who is powerful during the day so wants to spend his evenings submitting, to take the pressure off and blow off steam on the other side of the power spectrum. I'm sure there are people who fit into both of these camps: powerful men who are cowering slaves by night and distressed women who submit because they hate themselves. But they're by no means the majority. If they were the BDSM scene would have disappeared under the weight of so much sadness before it even got its stiletto-clad feet off the ground.

We don't rationalise other sexual preferences like this. Do we feel the need to explain away one guy's desire for blow jobs because he thinks his cock is dirty and needs to be cleaned? No. We say he fucking likes blow jobs.

We work on the rule of thumb that people are having sex because they want to. If, when a girl tells you that she wants to be spanked, you assume some complex psychological trauma to explain away her 'unusual' desires, you make the wild and significant assumption that she doesn't like it.

Number twenty-six was surprised that I liked it. His initial gamble—that having mentioned his gentleness I'd be stunned into arousal if he took me roughly—paid off a thousandfold, but it took a bit more practice before he was willing to accept that sex wasn't just something I was doing because he wanted it, it was something that I actively *needed*.

So while twenty-six focused on trying to make me go 'unngh', I turned my attention to trying my hardest not to accidentally fall in love with him.

Love makes my friends do weird things, like deliberately go on tedious, all-inclusive holidays. Like buying joint-owned kitchen equipment and spending Friday nights cooking unpronounceable dishes with falafel and quinoa. I was pretty suspicious of love. I'd loved number eight so desperately that even remembering him would bring me out in nervous shivers. We'd deliberately avoided being friends because when we tried to be friends we'd end up in bed together, then spend the next day tearing ourselves to shreds trying to find a way we could make our relationship work without killing one another.

Loving someone new felt like deliberately setting a trap for myself, and I wanted to avoid it at all costs. In the beginning I shifted away from number twenty-six whenever he tried to hug me. If he complimented me I'd change the subject. If he asked me to stay over I'd feign illness, and babble about how I had to get home to do some unspecified 'thing' and it was best for everyone if I just hopped on a night bus.

But it didn't work. Without even trying he snuck into my heart. Sitting with him on the sofa, with my feet tucked under his legs became the highlight of my week. I'd sit on the train reading emails he'd sent to me and, rather than simply focusing on the filthy parts, crossing my legs and wishing I could run for a quick wank in the bathroom, I'd re-read the actual words. 'Pub tomorrow, about 7?' And grin to myself.

I started hugging him. And hugs turned into cuddles turned into nights asleep in his huge arms, feeling the warmth of him on my back.

But when I left his house the old worries came back. Love is a fucking bastard. It makes me irrational and needy. It tempts me into shit decisions. Problems I'd previously have stamped on become reasons to run to him for a hug. Challenges stay unchallenged, because he makes them easy to forget. It makes me lazy. All I'd ever want to do is sit with him, on him, by him, until my bills went unpaid and my washing up started to evolve new breeds of bacteria. Until the sun went down and the world was destroyed and everything I'd worked for crumbled to dust.

I didn't want to love him; I loved me—normal me. I loved the me who could tell boys to fuck off when I was busy, who had enough motivation to pull myself together when I was miserable and do good things when I wasn't. Love can make me blind to a lot of things, but I wasn't yet blind to what I could achieve if I weren't sitting so comfortably in his arms.

So I made myself go out. I made myself see my friends. I made myself tell him 'No, I can't come round tonight, I'm busy.' And he shrugged it off in his casual way, and told me that he liked me happy. He liked me independent. He liked knowing that although I was still seeing other guys, he was the one I thought about when I crawled into bed at night, touching my cunt through my knickers and wishing he were there with me.

And I told him fuck you. I told him shut up. I told him I didn't want to be tied down.

And eventually, I told him I loved him.

CHAPTER EIGHTEEN

So I Accidentally Had Sex With A Few More Dudes

My mother will be horrified to learn that I like speaking to strangers. Strange men, who I meet briefly, then retire with somewhere to fuck. Love is all well and good, but the kick-in-the-gut is often most easily accomplished in the first few moments with someone new.

There are lots of things we miss out on as adults, and it's only when reminiscing about being a teenager that we realise what we no longer do. Snogging, for one. When was the last time you snogged an adult? Really snogged, I mean, with spit and tongues and rapid jaw movements, waggling your head from side to side and hoping you didn't bump their forehead with your glasses, or accidentally dribble down their face.

There's also the minor issue of adults being a bit bored of tits. If I seem to be fixated on this it's because I am. Sure, they'll give you a quick feel when you're snogging, they'll take off your top and do some cursory playing during sex, but it's been a long time since someone tried to furtively get mine out in the back row of a cinema. I miss the days when guys would stare at them, squeeze them, suck them, bite them, and all but worship them as the

Second Coming of Christ if you let him get within a couple of feet.

Finally, fingering. Adult men rarely finger me any more, because they've learnt that they can get a much more immediate and visceral response by rubbing my clit. Which is all well and good—legend has it that men used to be unable to find a clitoris, so is it any wonder that they're now so keen to prove they've located it?—but I miss the way younger guys would shove their fingers into me, relishing the sense of victory that comes with achieving third base. Compared to the perfunctory, half-hearted rummaging that's an adult guy's way of saying 'I want to fuck you and I believe this is the correct way to begin that process,' it's immense. The physical feelings might not be quite as good, but the enthusiasm's there. Given the choice between an enthusiastic yet incompetent fingering and a guy fumbling with my clit like he's trying to start the pilot light on a knackered-out boiler, I know which one I'd pick.

We might dabble in all these things as grown-ups, but they no longer hold the excitement that they once did. Why would we spend thirty minutes making out on a sofa when with a quick spit and a 'brace yourself' we could be fucking within the next ten seconds?

As sex itself becomes easier, the peripheral things grow less appealing. And that's a massive fucking shame. As much as I love it when you're pounding away at me, we can't have sex all of the time: we have jobs to go to and buses to ride and friends to meet in the pub. So why not cast your mind back to your teenage years and remember what we used to do at school, on buses, and in the pubs that we weren't legally supposed to be in? Touch me up in secret, snog me in public to the disgust of our fellow passengers, slip your hand down the back of my knickers until you can feel the wetness of my cunt.

The Japanese have a word for that feeling of nostalgia: *natsukashii*. It's not a sexual word, but an emotive one. When you remember a good childhood friend, or walk the streets you used to walk to go to school. If you look through old photo albums and imagine you can smell the familiar scents of a house you used to live in. *Natsukashii*: good old whatever. Good old school, good old friends, good old getting-fingered-at-the-school-disco.

Short of hopping in a time machine and rewinding ten years or so, the closest I'll ever get to this feeling is sex with strangers. Those who keep me aching and waiting and wondering whether or not they'll make a move. Number twenty-six could have me begging him for a fuck, tears streaming down my face as he forced his dick into my throat, but he couldn't make me feel those butterflies of pre-sex anticipation.

Twenty-seven was just such a guy. He wasn't just a stranger, he was a *young* stranger. A nineteen-year-old punk who reminded me of the guys I'd wanted to go out with before I met number one. He had a quick mouth and a dirty smile and a veritable Sistine Chapel of tattoos all over his torso. He showed me his newest, a motto stamped in Gothic lettering on his wrist, and I imagined the hand attached to that wrist wriggling its way into my knickers.

I was twenty-seven—eight years older than him. His youth pushed my thoughts of domination to one side and had me craving instead that eagerness that I remembered from school. I wished there was a bunk bed to which we could retire, so he could work his hand painstakingly up my body in the hope that he'd get to touch a tit before the credits rolled on a film.

But the free-and-easy fumble I'd had in mind didn't work out exactly according to plan. The youth that was so exciting to me when we were in the pub, where he could be confident and gregarious surrounded by his friends, became a worrying and unattractive proposition when I got him alone at his house. He offered me a cup of tea, then seemed uncertain how to proceed. He was less keen on groping me than learning from me, awaiting my instruction like an eager student. The sex we had was fun, but looking around his bedroom at the stained mattress, beer bottles and unrecognisable album covers, I felt older than I ever had before. I was a filthy old woman fucking a student, and the past I was nostalgic about was, to him, the present. It'd be a good ten years before he got nostalgic about fingering.

Number twenty-eight was much more like it. Tall, charming and prone to self-deprecating jokes, I'd met him through the dating site too. His username made him sound like a porn star, but I was delighted to find that he was incredibly normal. He drank real ale and made me laugh, then snogged me in a phone box on the way back to the train station. As we waggled our heads from side to side like they do on *Hollyoaks*, I rubbed his dick through the fabric of his trousers and felt proud at how hard he was.

Twenty-nine couldn't get hard at all. I gave him soft, gentle blow jobs, I asked him how he liked things and tried to recreate exactly what he described. I talked dirty to him, stripped off and buried his head in my tits. I moaned and writhed and sighed and did my best impression of a woman who was in no way disappointed to end an evening unfucked.

Eventually, after half an hour of trying, he rolled over and gave up.

'I'm so sorry, I just can't.'

'That's OK,' I lied. 'We drank quite a lot before we came back here.'

'It's not that,' he said 'It's just that, well... I had a wank before I came out.'

I put on my 'decidedly pissed off' face. There are loads of legitimate reasons why this could happen. I'm not going to haul a guy over the coals because he's having trouble getting hard. Apart from anything else, hot coals to the bollocks aren't known to be a particularly helpful remedy for impotence. But although there are many perfectly reasonable excuses for being unable to perform— you're pissed, nervous, on medication, of a certain age—having cracked one off earlier in the evening is definitely not one of them.

Don't get me wrong, I love a good wank as much as the next sex-crazed harpy, but if your onanism interferes with the sex you've promised me, I'm going to kick off. If you've masturbated before we go out, you don't deserve my soft blow jobs and assurances that it doesn't matter—it does.

Other guys have done this to me before, and told me it comes from the film *Something About Mary*. Ben Stiller rubs out a quick one before he dates Mary so as to prevent him either sitting through the date with a rock-on or having post-date sex that climaxes before he's got his pants off. That film should come with a warning: 'This film contains scenes that will disappoint girls who actually want to shag you.'

You might be able to wait until morning and be ready for another go, as twenty-nine was. But by that point the fun is usually over, the thrill of breaking the will-they-won't-they tension with a rock-solid erection is no longer achievable. I know that you want to fuck me, because you spent half an hour the night before rubbing yourself semi-rigid and trying to thumb yourself inside. By the time morning comes round I think of you less as a powerful sexual being and more like a cow that requires milking.

My date with thirty-one was far more successful, and ended with him ejaculating spectacularly down the back of my throat, after what I can only describe as a breathtaking blow job. Breathtaking not because I was particularly good—I was at least five gin and tonics down, so it's safe to say that I wasn't—but because he took over the entire thing. It was less like a blow job and more like being used as a particularly treasured sex toy, and bloody good it was too. We parted ways after the first date, though, as the only thing that was compatible about us was that his dick fit snugly in my mouth.

Thirty-two was lovely, but suffered similar problems as twenty-nine, which were compounded by the fact that I idolised him. He was older, wiser and far nicer than I could ever aspire to be. When confronted by his inability to stay hard, my fragile ego shattered into a thousand pieces and I nipped home early for a hot bath and some tearful self-abuse.

Thirty-three was similarly great, and had a deliciously long, straight cock. But he...

Oh, fuck it. I was going to say, as I said to him, that he lived too far away to become a regular fuck. I'd get frustrated riding the tube out to his house, every minute that took me closer to him was three minutes in the bank for the long journey home on the night bus later. The distance was an issue for me, but did a distance of forty-five minutes in one of the most well-connected cities in the world ever actually prevent two people from shagging? No. There was nothing wrong with thirty-three. Or thirty-two or thirty-one for that matter. Or the guys who arrived a bit later—the one who laughed at the choking sounds I made as I tried to swallow his cock, or the one who couldn't get off unless I was vigorously rubbing his nipples. None of the men who feature in this chapter had flaws so insurmountable that I couldn't have mounted them if I made an effort. They were all fun, interesting, different, hot guys, who were generous enough to bestow their fuck upon me, and I picked them up then put them down again like a bored child rifling through a toy box.

What a shit.

I didn't want to be with number twenty-six, because I was worried I'd end up breaking up with him one day. I was terrified of making him in any way significant, because the significant men who'd come before him had ended up broken. But in the meantime I was shuffling through a whole range of other perfectly lovely guys who I ended up rejecting for spurious reasons. Those to whom I said goodbye after the first shag were the lucky ones. Thirty-three had a rather worse time of it, as I strung him through at least three dates and a few lovely shags before breaking the news that I was an arsehole.

'You're telling me you don't want to fuck me any more because I live in Zone Four?' A justly raised eyebrow and disappointed frown.

'Yeah. It's just... by the time I get here after work I'm knackered and then we fuck and I feel bad because I leave straight afterwards to get home.'

'But I'm only round the corner from the tube station!'

'You're right over the other side of London!'

He threw his hands up in exasperation, and told me we should remain friends, despite my idiocy: 'But let's meet for beers in the centre of town next time, shall we?'

'OK.' And, sheepishly, I left.

So why did I keep sleeping with other guys? Why, when twenty-six was sitting waiting for me in his flat, casually stroking the erection he'd keep intact until I got in, did I not just hop on the first train to his house and ask him to spend the rest of his life fucking me?

Because I enjoyed it.

Disappointing though it's proven to be when I explain to people why I liked sleeping with strangers, there isn't a deeper issue here. I don't have low self-esteem, I'm not craving a father figure, I'm not trying to make up for a childhood incident in which I was told I was unattractive and worthless. I slept with guys because I *liked sleeping with guys*.

That nostalgic excitement, although it often wears off quickly after the first few shags with someone, is a feeling well worth chasing.

We accept that men like this. We make jokes about the fact that men want sex and women want chocolate, and we'll roll our eyes if a male friend seems to fancy anyone who walks past with a swing in their hips and a figure-hugging outfit, but when women do it we're confused.

There must be an alternative motivation for women to want sex, surely? It's well documented, in all of the shit films we watch and cheesy soaps and books and plays and adverts: men want sex and women want money/status/comfort/a father figure/a really lovely pair of Christian Louboutins. Men can talk about getting laid, but woe betide a girl who starts talking with the glazed-eyes, drooling lust of a genuine pervert.

What was good about the guys I fucked? I fancied them. What was wrong with them? Nothing that's easy to explain to someone who thinks that girls give sex as a favour. None of them were mean to me, rude, bigoted or stupid. They all just, at one point or another, stopped giving me that drooling lust.

Does that make me a slut? Yep. But is a slut a particularly bad thing to be? Nope.

I've slept with a fair few guys and I'm not ashamed. I'm glad that I fucked each and every one of them. The hot ones, the not-so-hot ones, the ones who struggled getting it up, the ones who hurt me in a delicious way, the ones I loved, the ones I hurt, the ones I cried over and the ones I cried for.

Whether I'm a slut will depend, primarily, on what your attitudes are towards women who like fucking—I'm heartily in the 'for' camp—and how many people you've slept with yourself. The 'slut ratio' when I was a teenager was generally taken to be your age, meaning that you were a slut if you'd fucked more people than you'd had birthdays. By this reasoning, it's only the guys in this particular chapter who tipped me over the edge. But there are people who'd consider it the height of sluttery for me to have fucked just two or three. A hundred years ago it would be unconscionable if a woman fucked someone other than her husband. What counts as excessive promiscuity is completely subjective, so there's not much point in equivocating about exactly which of my fucks turned me into a slut.

But I don't think whether I'm promiscuous is the important question here at all. I'm not ashamed of sex. If I were I'd have joined a nunnery years ago. What's important is not how I shagged someone, but how I treated them. Most of the guys I've fucked have ended up relatively unscathed: twenty-five, for instance, who was so unhurt that he texted me a few months after he'd initiated radio silence and asked me to send him a picture of my cunt. Twenty-seven who, despite being adorably intimidated by me, spent the next week bragging to his friends and all but drawing them diagrams of what we'd been up to. Even seventeen, the one-time Love of My Life, managed to shake off the pain of rejection and was shagging someone else on the floor of my living room within a week of us hooking up.

But others didn't fare so well. Twenty-nine, who sent plaintive email after plaintive email asking if we could meet again. Thirty-three, who couldn't understand why I was giving him bullshit excuses to avoid another date. Those I was dishonest with, those I hurt and those I cheated on. The ones who came looking for a girlfriend but got a quick fuck and a pat on the arse instead.

So am I a slut? Of course. But that's just a word we use for a girl who likes sex. Am I a *bastard*? That's a much more significant question.

CHAPTER NINETEEN

All Of That Time In Hell To Spend For Enthusiastically Sucking The Cocks Of The Married Men

'Does it bother you that I fuck other people?'

'Umm. That depends.'

'On what?'

'On what you mean by "bother".'

We were sitting in twenty-six's lounge, eating pizza in between shags and, as usual, avoiding the unspoken question of where I'd been the night before.

'I mean, does it upset you?'

'Of course it does.' He stayed calm, as he always did, and made no attempt to make his upset sound less trivial. He didn't want to hurt me, but he didn't want to lie to me either. Just one of the many reasons why I wanted to curl up in his lap and never ever leave.

'So why do you let me do it?'

'It's not my job to "let" you do anything. You do what you want—that's who you are.'

'You know... you're allowed to fuck other girls if you want to.'

'I know.' He nodded, then stared at me thoughtfully. 'I just don't want to.'

When I was much younger I used to kiss my friend's boyfriend. Which sounds sort of innocent, and not like a significant affair, but in the interests of full disclosure I should point out that I mostly kissed him on the dick. He was lonely, I was lamenting number one's inability to maintain a permanent erection, and we just sort of fell together. He'd drop his girlfriend home, drive me somewhere secluded, then I'd suck him off in the front seat of his clapped-out car. On the drive back to my house he'd tell me how guilty he felt.

I felt guilty too. I was spoiling something that had been good for my friend, something that she'd miss when it inevitably disappeared. I was also breaking all of the significant promises I'd made to number one. To compound matters, being a screamingly jealous harpy myself, I was engaging in a whopping hypocrisy. As I quizzed number one on the girls he might or might not fancy from his college, fleeting visions of this other guy's dick would pass through my mind, and I'd have to work hard to stop myself asking whether I was being a two-faced prick. Because the answer was an unequivocal 'yes'.

But the other side of guilt, of course, is that it's deeply sexy. What happened with number two in the garage didn't happen just because we were horny and there was nowhere else to go—part of the thrill was in potentially getting caught. Adrenaline is a pretty strong aphrodisiac, and—like fucking someone in a park at night, or rubbing their cock in the back row of the cinema—the sexual kick is stronger when you know you might get caught.

Number thirty was married. Not just married in the technical sense, a 'my wife and I have separated and it's for the best because we fell out of love with each other' situation. He was married with a child, which is about as married as you can get. He was also horny as hell. The first time I met him he played footsie in the pub with me, and made eyes at me over drinks that the others in our group didn't notice. He was tall, with big wide shoulders, a selection of well-placed tattoos and dark brown eyes that didn't so much say 'come to bed' as 'pull down your fucking knickers'. His wife would have been a lucky lady, if it weren't for the fact that he cheated on her.

The first time we shagged was at a hotel, and from then on we developed a regular routine: go out for drinks, pretend we're not going to have sex, tell each other it's a bad idea to really build up that lovely guilt, then run to the nearest private place and make frantic, desperate lust with each other.

Did I feel guilty? Of course. But that's not what you're after, is it? Guilt does things to me that make my knickers wet, so of course I felt guilty. I also felt that other emotion that normal people are supposed to feel when they've done something wrong: a darker, less sexy type of guilt. In the minutes after I'd fucked number thirty I'd wonder how his wife was, and whether she ever suspected that he was with someone else.

Where the fuck has the empathy gone now? Sure, there's a general sense of upset that I can feel when I imagine his wife waiting at home, but ultimately nothing strong enough to make me say, 'Hey, you know what? We should stop this. We shouldn't see each other any more. We should be... what do they call it? Oh yeah—decent people.' I wanted to say that, but I didn't. Because the risk to me was so slight. While twenty-six was upset by my desire to fuck other men, he'd have been more upset to feel like the one who was holding me back. His sadness was a wistful but practical one: a pang of misery if he knew I was in bed with someone else balanced by the knowledge that I loved him more for his acceptance of it. His heart would ache but not shatter, and it was *his* heart that I cared about.

The wife, on the other hand, was so distant as to be almost abstract. If her heart broke mine wouldn't break in tandem, because I knew nothing about her beyond what my biased and distracted lover deigned to tell me. The 'my wife doesn't understand me' argument, while usually dismissed as the plaintive mutterings of a guilty adulterer, serves a dual purpose: it gives the mistress a get-out clause. What I'm doing is bad, sure, but if his marriage is rocky then perhaps it's not quite the out-and-out evil that my conscience tries to persuade me it is.

Ah, fuck it. There's no excuse. I'm not trying to pretend there is one. There's just lust, immorality, a pathetic lack of willpower, and a bunch of complicated desires that rarely make any sense. We all do bad things, some of us more than most. Let she who is without sin hurl abuse in my general direction. I'd definitely deserve it.

I tried to assuage my guilt by withdrawing, and making sure that I never pushed things. Stupid though it sounds, I felt like the whole scenario became less bad if I resisted, if I didn't text or call or email. When we went for drinks I maintained the illusion that we were only going for a drink, right up until the point that he asked me to come with him to do furtive, sweaty things.

If I don't make the first move, it's not my fault, right?

Thirty-four, no less married than thirty, made the first move too. I don't even think I knew he was married until after we'd kissed. By the time we got to my bedroom, I was almost peeling him off me. He came in less than a minute— a glorious, flattering round of applause.

Both of them were wonderful. Neither were, understandably, for keeps. But because they were both expecting something new, different and exciting— something they didn't get at home—they were willing to go that bit further to impress me. Positions I was rusty at, tricks they wanted to try. I'm certain that part of the attraction for them was exactly the nostalgia that drew me to strangers: the thrill of conquering someone new, and having them do things you weren't expecting, things that weren't routine. And, of course, the adrenaline rush of doing something really *really* bad.

'You're a naughty girl, you know.' My ears pricked up, thinking he was gearing up to start again. But then he added, sleepily, 'You shouldn't tempt me like this.'

'I shouldn't... what?'

'Tempt me. You know, I *am* married.'

I did not like that. There's a certain amount of blame that I'm more than willing to take. I'll berate myself for fucking a married man in the same way as I'll curse all the other morally reprehensible things I've done: wishing death on commuters who take too long to swipe their Oyster card during rush hour, using flatmates' shampoo when I'm too poor to restock, shouting at my best friend for no better reason than I'm drunk and he's there. I'll accept the blame for my moral failings, but tempting you is not one of them.

I *am* a naughty girl. I'm an evil, amoral wench who's made some incredibly bad decisions and done some really awful things. But just as I'll stand by my own mistakes, I expect you to stand by yours. Whatever temptation I pose,

I'm not holding a gun to your head and telling you to get your cock out.

The guy I went on a date with, who told me he wouldn't leave his wife, had said something similar.

'I know I shouldn't be here with you, but I just couldn't resist.' It was meant playfully, as a light-hearted compliment, but it made me nervous. I like to think I'm pretty powerful, a loud, roaring, Siberian tiger of a woman. But do I have the power to make men do things against their will? Clearly not. Witness my inability to get twenty-six to do any washing up, or get eight to mastermind a guy-heavy orgy for my twenty-second birthday, or get any number of guys to get their round in when the bar's crowded. I'm persuasive sometimes, but irresistible? No.

Tell me you love your wife. Tell me she doesn't understand you. Tell me she's all but thrown you out and you're only with me so you don't have to spend the night under a bridge. Tell me whatever you like to make yourself feel better, but don't tell me it's solely my fault.

If I sound judgemental here it's because I am. I know what it's like to need a fuck. I know the aching pain of being horny with no release. I know what it's like to lust after someone you can't have, and I know how hard it is to resist temptation when a once-in-a-lifetime, no-strings-attached, my-partner-will-never-know fuck comes along. I know this because I didn't resist, either—two, sixteen, seventeen, the guys I slept with even though it hurt twenty-six. I wouldn't turn down a guy because something silly like a promise made to my boyfriend got in the way. I slept with him and then pathetically tried to justify it later.

I won't blame you for your decisions if you don't try to lay them at my door. I might have slept with you, kissed you, told you I'll keep it a secret, but you've done all of this too. As reckless and amoral and bad as I am, there's one thing I haven't done: I haven't made a promise to your wife.

Should I have made those promises to number twenty-six? I'd certainly promised him a couple of things: that I'd always be honest, that I'd always be safe. But never monogamy. Although he'd have cried with joy if I'd agreed to stop sleeping with other people, something was holding me back from making that leap. Monogamy implies the sort of boyfriend/girlfriend relationship that I wasn't quite ready to handle.

The problem with having a boyfriend is that there are so many other expectations that go along with it: taking him to meet my parents, bringing him out with my friends, remembering his birthday, mentioning him conspicuously to my work colleagues.

Having a boyfriend brings some benefits—it's a nice easy shortcut to get you out of *those* conversations, you know the ones.

You're mingling with family members at Christmas, handing around festive greetings and plates of slightly battered mince pies, updating grandparents, aunts, uncles and cousins on your latest life status. Job: check. Roof over your head—usually phrased as 'And where are you *based* these days?' as if people in their mid-twenties are occasionally shuffled around London to make sure no one spends too long in the same postcode: check. Hobbies: check. And then the question: 'So, when are you going to get a boyfriend?' That question in itself is pretty odd. I can see why having a job is important, and a home and hobbies. But asking me 'when are you going to get a boyfriend?'—not *if*, *when*—rests on the gargantuan assumption that the life I lead is incomplete. I think some family members imagine that life after number eight involves sitting at home every night crying into a romance novel, lamenting the gaping, boyfriend-shaped hole in my lonely, miserable heart. I say, 'I don't want a boyfriend.' They hear 'I can't get a boyfriend.'

This implies that no one in the history of the world has ever or could ever make an active choice to be alone, because being alone is a Bad Thing. But of course, those of us who *are* alone know that it's not. Being alone is a joyful, wonderful thing. We get to go out when we like, stay in when we like, spend time doing crap DIY, writing blogs or committing ourselves to whimsical projects. We get to drink all the gin in the cupboard, eat whatever food we've scraped from the back of the fridge, and then have a victorious wank right in the middle of the lounge.

So of course, bringing a boyfriend along to family events provides a neat escape from having to answer that question. Unfortunately, it leads to a whole load more questions. He'll be quizzed on his job in a veiled attempt to work out how much he might earn, and I'll have to deal with the dreaded 'm' word. It's a short step from 'Are you seeing anyone?' to 'When are you going to get married?' as if marriage is the ultimate goal in any 'seeing someone' relationship. When faced with this question I'm often tempted to answer: 'We don't want to get married, but we're hoping that next week we'll get that threesome he's always wanted.'

And that's before we even get started on the 'When are you going to have children?' fiasco. I have no idea why it is acceptable to ask anyone this, but it seems to me like perhaps if we're going to ask the question we should direct it at the men as well. None of my male relatives have had to bat away the question of children, because it's assumed that making the decision to have babies is entirely a girl thing. And it's the women who, as their bodies age beyond twenty-five and therefore start hurtling towards decrepitude, are responsible for making sure kids happen.

At twenty-nine years old I am now officially 'pushing thirty', which apparently means that I should be clawing my way into the heart of any available gentleman in the desperate hope that he fertilises my rapidly dwindling stash of eggs so I can spit out a child or two to give my parents something to coo over.

This isn't going to happen. Even *thinking* about trying for kids brings me out in a cold sweat faster than you can say 'episiotomy'. Perhaps, years into the future, I'll change my mind. But for now the thought of getting pregnant makes me want to hug close to me all the things I love—my independence, my freedom, my time alone, my beautiful flat with all the things in it that aren't covered in sick and dribble. Don't get me wrong, I'm not down on parents. I will happily get pom-poms out and cheerlead their valiant efforts to continue our species. Those who can cope with the dribble and sick, and smile through it without dry-heaving: I salute you. Because there's no way in this world that I'd want to do it.

'Time's running out, though,' they say, to which I am usually too polite to respond: 'I don't give a flying fuck.' Time's also running out for me to watch *Celebrity Big Brother* or convert to Scientology. I'm not going to rush to do either of these things—they are undesirable things to do, and they aren't going to become any more desirable just because there's a limited time in which to do them.

Even without marriage and children rearing their respectively veiled and dribbling heads, calling twenty-six my boyfriend felt like a stretch. I didn't want to be tied to seeing him every day, I didn't want for my default evening to consist of sitting on a sofa with him eating pizza and watching box sets. I wanted all the fantastic things I loved about single life.

Being single is brilliant. I can see people I like, avoid people I don't, fill my diary with dinners and dates and drinking. If I'm in the pub and having a bad time I can go home, safe in the knowledge that I haven't 'thrown a strop' and dragged a partner home with me. If I'm bored of an evening, I can flip through my black book and see who wants to come over. I can love people, fuck people, get drunk and be sick in the gutter and moan with hungover shame in a pile on the sofa the next day, and none of this will be of significance to anyone other than me.

If I'd made twenty-six my boyfriend then I felt like all of that would suddenly become terrifyingly significant. I'm not just going for drinks with friends, I'm going without him, and he'd be understandably hurt that he hadn't been invited. As it was, with an openly 'together but not going out' status, we'd both be secretly pleased if the other invited us out, but not significantly distressed if they didn't: why on earth should he invite me to his friend's birthday party? It's not like we're *together* or anything.

My final and perhaps most important reason for staying single, the reason I wanted to keep at least an arm's length of distance between myself and number twenty-six: love hurts. A relationship is the all-or-nothing option. You give everything you have to someone who has the power to destroy the lot on a whim.

If you're in a relationship, then I'm impressed. You're willing to lay your heart out on the chopping-block of their affections and trust them not to pound it into a miserable, bloody slab of pain. Those pop-psychologists among you might be wondering if it's because of number eight— because I'd invested so much in my dreams of our saccharine, so-happy-it-hurts lifelong relationship, then subsequently pushed a wrecking ball through all of it, doing that with someone else was a little bit terrifying. And you'd be correct. You'd have hit the nail right on the head, then hung an embroidered picture on it bearing the words 'I told you so.' I couldn't commit to twenty-six because commitment symbolised all of the things that I was certain to cock up, leaving not just him but me sobbing into a pile of Kleenex and swearing off love for ever.

At least when I'm single I know that my misery is my own. If I'm wretched it's because I've made myself so, and I'm probably in a reasonable position to fix whatever's wrong. But when my decisions have the power to make someone else miserable too, the stakes are doubled. The risk is greater. The potential for my ham-fisted, slick-knickered idiocy to crush another person looms scarily over every conversation we have. I don't hear ' Do you want to be my girlfriend?' but 'Here is my heart. Please take it,' and, just as when I hold a baby and am immediately pierced with the fear that my arms will stop working and I'll drop the poor thing on the carpet, my hands tremble and I want to give it back. I'm not responsible for this. I'm not grown-up enough for this. Take it away.

What's more, even given the likelihood that if something goes wrong it'll be my fault—as it almost inevitably will—there's an even scarier possibility: that someone else could make a decision that brings my whole world crashing down around me. That, in protecting their hearts, guys will take number one's route, and use unwitting attack as the best form of defence. That I'll wake up one morning to find twenty-six either gone or, worse, tearfully confessing the ways in which he's wronged me while I try and fail to suppress the howling agony of betrayal.

If I make relationships sound dramatic and tragic that's because I think they are. There's nothing relatable or true about relationships in which everything goes well, where you live day in, day out with no trauma or passion or tears. No one actually lives 'happily ever after', they live 'up-and-down ever after', more likely to waltz off into Homebase than into the sunset. During the course of the average relationship you might buy your partner roses twice, but you'll buy their toilet paper a thousand times more. You'll probably hear 'Fancy a cuppa?' more often than 'I fancy you.' And although there'll be days when you wake up in the morning, look over at your partner, and the vision of his dribbling, sleepy, pillow-imprinted face will make you want to hug yourself with joy, there'll also be nights where you wake up sweating after a dream that he's left you and the world no longer makes sense. *That's* why I don't want a relationship. The power to destroy twenty-six is far too significant a thing to give to me—like handing the nuclear codes to someone who hasn't mastered counting yet. And it's not a power I'm ready to give anyone else either. When I wake up in the morning I feel safe knowing that the only person with the power to destroy me is me.

If you're waiting for the comeuppance then I'm delighted to tell you that you won't have to wait for long. What I didn't realise is that avoiding a relationship with someone doesn't actually stop any of that emotional stuff from happening. I refrained from using the word 'boyfriend', I made myself go out without twenty-six, and told my friends and family that he was 'just some guy', ignoring their raised eyebrows and brushing off any feelings I had towards him. But that didn't stop me actually *having* feelings, it just meant that I didn't acknowledge them.

Like a smoker who says they can give up any time they like, I maintained that I could break up with number twenty-six if I wanted to, and it'd be no more painful than falling down and grazing my knee. Never again the heart-wrenching agony of prying the separate sections of my life away, as I'd had to do when I broke things with number eight, or the sudden blow-to-the-head pain of finding number one had cheated on me. With twenty-six I'd decided that we were always going to be casual. Because if things were casual, he definitely couldn't hurt me. Until he did.

It was a Saturday, in the summer, when the world inconveniently insisted on ending for the third time. One of those unusual British Saturdays where the sun is actually shining and you don't feel like you need to take a raincoat 'just in case'. I'd not seen twenty-six for a week, and the build up of excitement had been fanned by a number of increasingly urgent and desperate texts from him:

'When can I see you?'

'I need to see you.'

'Please can I see you?'

I'd put him off for a couple of days, because it was a busy week for fucking other guys. Drinks and dating had taken up enough of my schedule, and I thought that leaving it a bit before I saw twenty-six would achieve the twin objectives of keeping him at arm's length and also getting him horny enough that he'd jizz in his boxers the second I walked through the door.

We met in a pub: his local. The aim being that we'd have a casual drink or two in the sunshine while talking filth to each other until we couldn't bear not to tear each other's clothes off, whereupon we'd scurry back to his house and make a satisfying mess on his living room carpet. I dressed up, because after a week apart that's always a fun thing to do: 'Know how sexy you remember I was? Well, get a load of THIS!' I wore tiny shorts and a top that was just see-through enough that people would wonder if I knew that my bra was showing. I straightened my hair, smeared on some make-up, and half-walked half-ran to meet him.

In the pub garden I nursed a pint and all but hugged myself with excitement. After a week apart we had a full twenty-four hours together: enough to pack in at least three times the sex we usually had, interspersed with chatting, drinking, and sitting on his sofa watching porn. A perfect Saturday.

When he arrived I didn't even have a chance to work out that he was nervous before he hit me with his news.

'I slept with someone else.' And his hands trembled. His mouth went dry. There was a long silence.

I forced myself to smile, and ran through all the times I'd told him he should sleep with other people, all the times I'd assured him that despite being jealous over number eight I was no longer a jealous person. I chose and discarded a million different things to say ranging from 'Good for you,' to 'Did you use a condom?' and tried my hardest not to say the one thing I actually felt, which was 'ARGH.' Eventually I settled for:

'OK.' Accompanied by some vigorous nodding to underline just how completely OK it was that the guy I loved had spent the night with someone else.

Was it in his bed? Was she better than me? Who was she? Did she do things differently? Did he love her? Was he planning on doing it again?

'Are you sure you're OK?' He looked worried, and reached over to grab my hand.

'Yep. Totally. Fine. That's fine.' And, as if to cement just how completely fine I was, I shook his hand. Then I stood up, tripped over my handbag, ran to the bathroom and vomited.

Not, in fact, OK then.

Luckily for me, twenty-six had the uncanny ability to know exactly what I was thinking despite me doing my best to cover it up by saying ridiculous things like: 'OK' or even 'I'm actually really glad you've had sex with someone else because now I feel like we're on a more even footing.' When I returned from the toilet he was pale.

'You're not all right with this, are you?'

'Umm. I... No, I am, I am. It's just a surprise. But it's completely fine for you to have sex with other girls.' Which was, quite frankly, the only thing I *could* say in that situation without sounding deranged. Although I wanted to scream at him, to sob in the middle of the pub and ask him why he'd break my heart like this, I had to accept that not only had we never had an exclusive relationship, but that in sleeping with someone else he was doing something that I'd actually encouraged him to do.

There was a long pause, as he waited for me to tell him what I was actually thinking.

'So there we are. Shall we talk about something else?' My hands were shaking now too as I picked up my drink and tried to drown the urge to scream with weak lager shandy.

Unconvinced that I was as satisfied with this conclusion as I was desperately pretending to be, he eventually offered: 'I won't do it again if you don't want me to.'

This had exactly the opposite effect to the one he'd intended, and rather than calming me down caused me to feel even more nauseous. I didn't want to tell him not to— how could I? I was out with other guys at least once a week, and still excitably checking my emails to see if I had a new online match, or an email from one of the guys I still saw on and off. Telling him I didn't want him to do it again would be inappropriate, hypocritical and unfair.

'I don't want you to do it again.'

'OK.'

Shit.

CHAPTER 20

Love Is Like A Box Of Chocolates:
It's Fun To Start With
But Eventually Makes You Feel A Bit Sick

It's looking pretty likely that I'll cock things up again, isn't it? I mean, on the surface everything's brilliant—the man of my laziest, comfiest dreams is in love with me, and willing to pander not only to my jealous rages by agreeing not to sleep with anyone else, but also my selfish need to fuck anything that winks at me. Hooray! Happy ever after!

Except, rather obviously, that's not a happy ever after at all.

There's something creepy and troubling about relationships that are unequal. I'm not talking about relationships where one of them has sexual power and the other doesn't. I've met more than my share of happy couples who have a power exchange relationship and it works bloody well for them. One of them will cook, clean, keep house and provide sexual favours as and when required while their partner lounges happily on the sofa lifting a finger only when it's necessary to change the TV channel or distribute some sexy discipline. Those relationships aren't unequal if both of the people in them are happy to be: they're complementary. Nothing would be more miserable than forcing the dominant one to spend time in the slave boots, while the slave looks on helplessly, unsure when to say 'jump' and which way up to hold the whip.

The creepy relationships I'm talking about are those where one partner gets the final word and the other gets no word at all. One person desperately wants a voice, a choice, and the other won't let them have one.

'We're not having your shit music on in the car.'

'I'll look after the money.'

'You can't sleep with anyone else, but I can.'

Although the selfish horny slag inside me wants to live in a magical dream world with twenty-six, where I can fuck him on demand and receive his warmth and love and comfort, while maintaining a stable of—yes, I have planned this—five other friendly, lustful boys to shag me, a servant to do the cleaning, and an extra one to do the little things that want doing, such as fetch me a beer and stretch out my jeans when I'm having a fat day, the reality of it would be creepy. Sleazy. Painful.

Because the more twenty-six assured me that he could 'cope' with me sleeping around, the more I realised that I didn't want to make him 'cope' with anything.

Eight had coped with me. With my frotting strangers one minute and flying into jealous rages the next. With my tantrums and lusts and demands. Number one had coped with me, when I'd forgotten our anniversaries or brushed him off for a furtive shag with number two in a garage. The guys I'd met on dating sites had coped with me throwing them out to get the night bus home after we'd fucked. Other guys had coped when I told them we should be friends. But I didn't want twenty-six to 'cope' with any of the shit I'd dealt out to the others. And certainly not with that sinking, nauseous feeling that I'd got when he slept with someone else. I wanted him to be happy not *in spite of* me but *because of* me.

I used to joke that the reason he commanded my attention in a way others couldn't was because of his dick. His dick is wonderful—thick, straight, almost permanently solid, straining at his jeans as he grips my arse, or slips an idle hand down my top. But I joked about it because the truth was much harder to actually spit out of my wretched emotionless mouth. It's not his dick: it's him.

He's warm, he's kind, he's funny. He's beautiful. He has big arms and hands that envelop me like I'm tiny. He says utterly ridiculous things in an accent that makes me drool. He wraps me in big sweaters and brings me coffee, like this kind of calm happiness is the most normal thing in the world. He swings quickly from gentle to passionate, and every time he does it takes me by lustful surprise. And when I get angry or unreasonable he nods, and listens, and tells me I'm not mad, then holds my big, mad head in his gentle hands and makes me feel like a normal person again.

We're not identical: we disagree on everything from what we're having for dinner to whether the US is going to turn into a right-wing religious nation—I say it won't, and he is wrong. I maintain that cheap instant coffee has a much better taste than posh coffee that's made with a filter: he maintains the opposite and is therefore, again, wrong. I like being tied down, he'll be the one doing the tying. He likes playing Xbox; I like sucking his cock while he plays Xbox. But everywhere else that really matters, we're equal. When he speaks I listen. When I speak he listens, then gets confused by my tendency to overthink and panic about everything, calls me a dickhead and tells me to stop worrying. When I call he comes running, and when he calls I'll probably hop in a taxi because I'm too lazy to run. When I say 'I love you' there's no hesitation, no pause before he responds in kind.

I'm buggered if I'm going to insist that this amazing guy should sit at home listening to his heart creaking under the weight of my infidelity, then greet me with a kiss and a smile when I return to him covered in spunk. We need to be equal. And for us to be equal, I need to shut up, grow up and pull my fucking knickers up.

So, with a conviction that I genuinely wish was true, I tell him:

'I don't want to fuck other guys any more.'

There's a long pause as he takes a drag on his cigarette and raises a sceptical eyebrow.

'You don't *want* to?'

'No.'

Another pause.

'OK, I do. But that's not the point. When I go out with other guys, it's a gamble—they might be brilliant or they might be shit. They might fuck my mouth in an alleyway and have me weak at the knees, but they might also bite me and pull my hair and make me annoyed.'

'So, I'm a safe bet?'

'Yep.' Wait, that doesn't sound good. That sounds a bit callous and insulting. I'll make it better.

'You're a great shag.'

'You say the sweetest things.'

Hmm. That was probably wrong as well.

'And I love you.'

'I love you too.'

I think I won that back, but I hadn't quite explained the real problem.

When I told twenty-six he was a great shag, what I meant was more significant than just 'Well, that was fun, now it's bedtime.' He didn't stop me wanting other guys, or staring at them as they crossed a crowded room, but there was something extra there that might make resisting other guys slightly easier: he gave me that kick. While I'm not averse to fantasising about other guys covering me head to toe in their spunk, the idea of twenty-six doing the same is equally, if not more, attractive.

I still want to shag other guys, but on any given night I'd much rather shag him. I want twenty-six to cover me in his spunk, to gentle my head as he slides his dick into my mouth and call me his girl and make me feel like I'm dirty and special and used and hot. The nights I used to spend on dating sites are now taken up with either fucking twenty-six, thinking about fucking twenty-six, or masturbating furiously while remembering particularly successful fucks I had with twenty-six. It feels good, it feels special. But because it's special, it also feels dangerous.

I was still worried that as soon as I acknowledged that whatever we had was special, I'd immediately do something to break it. I can like guys, I can lust guys, I can fuck them with a desperate, panting enthusiasm yet still remain healthy and in control. But then just a bit more—a few more nights spent sleeping beside them, a few more hugs that don't end in a fuck, a few more secrets exposed and intimate discussions—and suddenly it's all too much. I can't sleep, I can't think, and, worst of all, I can't *come* without thinking about him fucking me into submission. And I can't be in love this hard without overdoing it.

If I can't fuck or wank without thinking of twenty-six, then he's has become precious to me and is therefore doomed. He's special enough that most of the time I don't want to fuck anyone else. I barely even think about anyone else when I'm lying horny on the sofa thinking about what I might wank to. I know what I'm going to wank to—the same fucking guy who's in my head even after he's left my bedroom.

I've become monogamous, and accidentally created a relationship so precious that I'm in danger of smashing it. I'm at the merry stage of drunk and reaching for another pint and smiling because the night can only get better and I'm so happy and I'm dancing and I'm horny and I want more oh please let me have more and just another pint and another dance and I just want to stay here a bit longer and I'm definitely not going to be sick. I promise.

We're on the sofa, discussing fantasies in a casual enough way that he suspects we probably won't get round to acting them out.

'If you could do anything, what would it be?' I wait for the obvious answer.

'A threesome with you and another sexy girl, please.'

'Not a gangbang with me and three dudes of my choice?' There's a pause while he thinks on it.

'Nah. The stubble would chafe.' There's a pause and he pulls me closer to him. I bury my face in his armpit, breathe in the hot, post-sex-sweat smell, and wonder if we can fuck one more time before we go out.

'I don't mind if we don't have a threesome,' he adds. 'It's not compulsory.'

'I know it's not compulsory, I just... I want to do something you like.'

This was not a selfless thing. People say, 'I just want him to be happy,' and some of them really mean it. But I didn't mean it exactly like that. For a start, the idea of doing something for him that he'd always wanted, that he'd fantasised and masturbated and salivated over, gave me that 'unngh' feeling harder than I'd ever had before.

I also felt that a threesome might make us a bit more equal. Twenty-six wanted more stories under his belt, to do a few more of the things that gave him that kick too. So when my friends joked about sexy things I'd done in the past, he could smile proudly and remember the time when two girls had a pillow-fight over who got to be the first one on his dick.

Finally, and most importantly, I wanted to give him something. Something other than a miserable night alone waiting for me to come back post-shag and turn my attentions to him. I wanted him to have something amazing, and for me to be the person who gave it to him.

'A threesome it is.'

They don't happen just at the click of your fingers, though. A few weeks later, having laid some foundations—'My boy thinks you're hot', 'I think you're hot', 'Are you coming out this Friday?'—twenty-six and I go drinking with some friends in central London.

They're taking the piss out of us for being too horny. We're having gleeful snogs that are unsuitable for grown-ups right in the garden of the pub, and laughing at their squeamishness. My girl is there. A new girl. A friend. A friend with cut-glass cheekbones and soft, pale skin and an arse that twenty-six wants to bury his face in.

And she's interested. Interested enough that after two pints she kisses me—a playful, gentle kiss followed by a grin.

'Do you want somewhere to crash tonight?' I ask her, pulling her closer in to me.

'Yes.'

'We're staying at his place.' I gesture towards twenty-six, who has been admirably pretending not to hang off our every word.

'I know,' she says. Of *course* she knows. She doesn't intimidate me. She's my friend, someone I've watched as she walks into the room and snogged when I'm drunk and touched because I'm curious. Someone whose skin is softer than mine and whose smell is more girly. And she fancies twenty-six.

What's *that* feeling? It's new. It's not jealousy, but it comes when she touches him, when she strokes his leg and kisses him on the cheek and they share an intimate look that says, 'Later, we'll fuck later.' It feels a bit like fear, but it could equally be pride.

In the cab on the way home they're all hands. I sit in the middle, not to separate them but to bring them together, to let them know that this is OK. She slips a hand inside my bra and he puts an arm around my shoulder, leaning across to reach her. I've got one hand on the solid bulge in his trousers and the other around her waist, stroking her, feeling the fabric of her top stretched tight against her chest. We're all tongues and panting and desperate enthusiasm, and the taxi driver does a sterling job of pretending not to notice.

We fall in through his front door and he pauses, wondering if he should act the host. While he's debating over offering us drinks, I'm pulling off her top, kissing her neck, dragging her through the door of the bedroom, and she's giggling at my fervour. She's so beautiful, all curves and smiles and the pale-skin dark-lips beauty of a fifties pinup. I want him to see her naked, and I want to be the one who showed her to him. In my haste to be the one who undresses her, I forget to wonder whether I'm actually turned on by this. Whether I want to see her naked.

Twenty-six comes through as she's fumbling with my jeans and I'm pulling down her knickers. Her cunt is smooth and wet, and her tits are larger, heavier than mine. She smells like milk and talcum powder, and twenty-six breathes in happily as he grabs her around the waist.

She kisses him, deep and long and smiling. And I realise I should smile too. So I do.

We tumble onto the bed, him trying to touch as much as possible. He takes off his clothes and, while we kiss and fumble, he tries to press himself against both of us, to feel as much flesh as he can, both of us squashed into him: warm and smooth and smelling like arousal.

It's playful, fun and uncomplicated, save for the tiny voice in the back of my head that's asking whether I want to be there. Of course I want to be there, this is what I do.

I bury my face in her, kissing her cunt then holding my lips up for twenty-six to lick, and he fucks me while I try to make her sigh with pleasure. They're quick strokes, hot and angry, the opposite of the gentle way he made love to me the first time. He looks at her while he fucks me, and runs his hands over her soft, pale tits.

This was fun. This was good. This was exactly what I wanted to do—see the light in his eyes and the tremble in his hands as he did something he'd never done before. I was looking forward to the main event, when he'd fuck her as he looked at me, let me suck her nipples and rub her clit and make her moan while he pounded her with those same hard strokes.

But it didn't happen like that.

The boy withdrew from me, letting her take her turn on me by lapping gently at my clit. As he put on a condom, I stroked her hair and looked up at him, trying to catch his eye. I was waiting for the moment when he caught my eye and we shared a conspiratorial smile, a horny stare, a quick 'Are you OK?' I needed him to catch my eye.

But he didn't.

She knelt between my legs, with her arse high in the air, and he looked down at it as he fucked her. He gripped her hips with his huge hands, and pulled her back onto his cock, desperate to get as much into her as possible.

I watched him fuck her, and felt her mouth on my clit, and tried to make the noises I remembered making when I was enjoying myself. Small moans, sighs and any noise other than the sob that threatened to come out if I stopped concentrating. I tried to focus on her—her beauty, her gentleness, her delicate hands doing good things to me. I tried to stop myself counting the fuckstrokes in my head as he slammed into her. I tried to shut up the voice in my head that was telling me I wasn't happy.

Because there was no logical, rational reason why I wouldn't be happy. I was doing something hot, that I'd wanted to do, with two incredibly beautiful people who were both having a bloody good time. What exactly did I expect? That they'd both hold back, waiting for me to dictate exactly the way this should play out? That they'd have been provided with a copy of my exact script beforehand and be ready with their lines and cues?

Neither of these people had done anything wrong, other than fail to intuit *exactly* what I wanted. I wanted him to catch my eye. I wanted similar conspiratorial, playful smiles from her—the kind Kate had given me the first time. I expected them both to notice that I was uncertain. I never expected to feel so alone in a room with two people, and above all I didn't expect that when he came, forcefully and copiously, it would be inside her.

So I did what any stupid, selfish, borderline lunatic would do in that situation: I cried.

Later that night, after I'd awkwardly apologised and they'd shown me far more sympathy than I deserved, we went to bed. I heard her making up a bed in the living room, politely excusing herself from sharing with us. I curled up beside twenty-six, bit my lip and tried not to shake as tears streamed down my face.

'I fucked up, didn't I?' he asked. He was unsure of what to do, his tranquil attitude replaced by a pale nervousness. He stroked my hair, squished up tight against my back, and tried to whisper comfort and unnecessary apologies into my ear.

'You didn't fuck up. *I* fucked up.' And I had. Having spent the last year with him pretending that I didn't have any emotions, I wasn't quite ready for them to explode out of me in such an embarrassing way.

In trying to give twenty-six something good, I'd forgotten that sex isn't a present or a favour, it's something you do because you want it. When I realised that I didn't want it, I didn't know how to stop things from happening. How to say, 'Wow, actually I am way more jealous than I should be about this situation so let's just order pizza and watch a film instead.'

What an idiot. Worse than an idiot, because now whatever I had with twenty-six was already broken. Every time he bent me over I'd see him doing the same thing to her. Every time he came inside me I'd remember the time he didn't. And when he looked at me he wouldn't see a hot girl any more, a girl who did good things for him, who moaned when he fucked her on the living room carpet or squealed when he beat her or sucked him dry while he watched porn on the sofa. He'd look at me and see me pushing things too far, going out of my way to chase that kick-in-the-gut and then exploding with jealous misery.

The girl who slept around. The girl who fucked up. The girl who cried during a threesome.

'I broke things, didn't I?'

'What?'

'I've broken this,' I said. 'We can't be together any more.'

He sat up, and rested his head on one hand. 'Why?'

So I explained. The need to fuck, the need to chase that hot feeling, the fact that the feeling came from extreme things: piss play, beating, pegging, guilt, strangers and most importantly from doing these things so that guys could get off.

I explained that I needed these things more than I needed to be loved, because the other relationships I'd had, I'd broken. I explained why I'd chased the threesome, wanting to give him that hot feeling too but not realising that it didn't work that way.

I explained that, although I loved him, when the End Times finally came I'd not be holding a loved one close to me and whispering last words breathlessly into his shoulder, I'd be running up and down the deserted streets, hunting one last man to fuck.

When I explained this to number twenty-six, to his credit, he didn't say either yes or no. He didn't hold me gently and pretend everything would be all right, nor did he ask me to leave so he could be on his own to mourn his loss and stare deeply into the dying embers of our relationship. He said:

'Shut up.'

'What?'

'I said, shut up. Stop being weird about this.'

'I'm not being weird about this.'

'Yes, you are.'

'I'm having a genuinely emotional moment. I don't think I want to keep going with this when I know I'm going to break it. I'm *guaranteed* to break it. Look at all the things I've done that have shown me to be a fuck-up!'

'OK, you're a fuck-up. But the world didn't end, did it? You haven't stopped breathing. I haven't stopped breathing.'

'So?'

'So. Stop being weird about this. It went wrong, you're sad, I'm sad. We'll become happy soon enough.'

'Will we?'

'Of course. But only if you stop being weird about it.'

'Really?'

'Yes.'

'But I've ruined things for you!'

'You're such a twat.'

And then he pulled down my knickers.

If You're Fucked Up And You Know It, Clap Your Hands

There are lots of things in this book that I'm ashamed of. That cold, creeping dread that it's going to be published and people will stop seeing me as an anonymous internet sex kitten but a fragile, pathetic, emotionally stunted madwoman bores a hole of shame deep into my stomach.

But I'm not ashamed of the lust.

If we're talking about shame, we're talking about the things I've done that are actually wrong— the lies, the cheating, the hurt. The times I dumped guys who lived on the wrong tube line, or betrayed wives I'd never met, or failed to give hugs when people asked me for comfort. The times I crept back into bed with number eight and felt the weight of the secrets I was keeping from him. The things I said to him that made him cry. The evenings I spent with twenty-six, casually running through things I'd done the week before, and failing to notice that he was holding his breath, just waiting for me to promise that I wouldn't do it again.

I will probably do it again. Because I make mistakes.

I might do other things too—wank men off in doorways, nudge them into threesomes with ambiguously bi-curious guys we meet on the internet, trawl dating sites to see if there's anyone who might give me that kick in the gut. I have no idea if things with twenty-six will last, whether he'll still be sipping coffee with me and coming all over my knickers when I'm ninety. But I'd be stupid to pretend I'll never mess up again. I'd be stupid to act as if this is a done deal, signed, sealed and accompanied by a lifetime guarantee.

I could end this book on a high, with a moral lesson and a promise. A 'love conquers all' conclusion that'll have you reaching for either the tissues or the sick bucket. But I'm not going to do that, because it wouldn't be true.

As far as I know, the next significant chapter might consist of my loved ones upping sticks and fucking off, leading me full circle back to the spare room at my dad's house, crywanking myself into spinsterhood with not a date in sight. It might lead me into the arms of someone who gives me that lustful, horny kick even stronger than twenty-six does.

It'll definitely lead me into more things I'm ashamed of—deception, hurt, jealousy, and nights that end with me screeching tortured eighties classics through a karaoke mic then hurling cider-flavoured vomit into the toilet. But I'll never be ashamed of the love.

Humans are weird. We spend our lives trying to place ourselves in boxes marked 'good' or 'bad', without recognising that the good guys and bad guys don't really exist, there's just a few billion of us who fall somewhere between these two extremes. We're a miserable bunch of fuck-ups at the best of times: we cheat, we lie, we steal, we break hearts, we annoy our friends with broken promises and we embarrass our parents by writing sex books. We forget anniversaries and shout at boys we fancy and intimidate first dates and cry during threesomes.

But the weirdest thing of all is not that we are fuck-ups, but that we expect not to be. Despite the mountains of evidence to the contrary, we expect to be able to become good people: to laugh in the face of temptation, stand tall in the presence of fear, and, in my case, refuse the offer of a spanking from a hot guy I met on the internet. Twenty-six knows this. Eight knows this. And now you all know this too.

We aren't good or bad people; we do good things and bad things, we love and are loved, we fuck up on an epic scale on a thrice-daily basis. So let's not pretend that we don't.

What's more, let's not pretend that sex is one of the few things that we are able to get right, or that we can all agree on. We feign horror at people with unusual kinks, disdain for those who do things differently, and we pretend that we only read dirty books to see what all the fuss is about. We're having a conversation about sex that's shaped not by our genuine desires and experiences but by the people who write the tabloid headlines, the film scripts, and the playful 'one hundred ways to please your man' articles. This laminated, bleached, explain-it-to-your-parents-as-a-laugh view of sexuality doesn't capture how any of us really feel.

Just as we all fall somewhere on the spectrum between 'good' and 'bad', so we also fall somewhere between 'pervert' and 'nun'. But we don't want to tell people exactly where we are on the spectrum, because we think everyone else is 'normal', whatever the sweating fuck 'normal' is. None of us really knows where we are in relation to everyone else, because instead of talking to each other about real desires we're listening to giggling Ann Summers reps and guffawing ad men, and nagging tabloid columns that screech moral outrage over the latest three-in-a-bed romp.

But let's not pretend that sex is fundamentally shocking and shameful. One person's 'three-in-a-bed romp' is another person's 'boring Friday night in'. If we were as repulsed and amused by the sexual act as we sometimes pretend to be, no one would ever fuck.

Sex is disgusting and wonderful and messy and human, but it's not special—I'm not special.

I'm filthy and stupid and fucked up, but I'm not exactly unusual. Not everyone will want to have their knickers pulled down in an alleyway, or be spanked by a man twice their age. Not everyone will pursue their desires with the same relentless need, and not everyone will put themselves at risk just to get that feeling with a stranger. But no matter how we get it, we do all want something, whether it's a hand down our pants or an arm around our shoulder.

No matter how many times we fuck it up, we'll keep coming back for more of it.

So let's not be weird about this, yeah?

They're Not Wedding Bells, They're Alarm Bells Mate

Love rarely hurts more than when you're nursing hip bruises after a vigorous bout of bent-over-the-arm-of-a-sofa sex. Or when you're crouched in a concrete stairwell trying to administer the blow job of your life, fingers numb with cold and brain desperately trying to remember how long it takes a human to get frostbite.

Or maybe afterwards: when you're done and counting the scratches.

Until this particular trip, my most painful love-related injury happened after a sweaty threesome with eight and nine: the guy I loved and the girl we both worshipped. We retired to my tiny, shambolic flat after a night of drinking and karaoke, and collapsed together on the bed. Well, not really 'bed' - it was a futon on the floor, still unmade from the morning, but I was horny and excited enough not to care. The whole thing started with a hug. Me on him, her on me, all of us smooshed together, smelling like cheap, fruity cocktails and post-dancing sweat. It felt warm and friendly, in the way you wouldn't expect a threesome to if you'd only ever seen them in bad porn. Usually these bad-porn-threesomes are characterised by either blunt group lust or individual narcissism: like American Psycho's Patrick Bateman setting up a camera so he can watch himself shag. But this wasn't that – it was comfortable. We'd known each other just long enough that our fucking wasn't awkward, but not so long that it had become routine.

Playfully, we ticked a few extra things off our group bucket list. She and I sucked and licked at his cock while he looked down at us with an 'I can't believe my luck' stare. We shared giggles and kisses and squashed our mouths together around the head of his dick. Spit mingling and hands rummaging at each other while he lay back and watched.

We fucked in a circle – one half draped on the other, in turn lying on the next. The game was more about giving than receiving, and none of us cared much about what was being done *to* us. It was far more fun to concentrate on my own task – the crotch my face was buried in, and the taste of the next person's sweat. Listening out for their cries when I did something special to make them twitch and shiver. At one point she had her face pushed hard into my cunt – tongue pressed tight against my clit while he fucked her from behind. Each of his strokes shoved her more firmly onto me, giving me a jolt of happiness. I could hear her moaning as I stared him straight in the eye, watching out for those moments when he bit his lip to try and hold back.

I want to tell you in detail about the hotness of the fuck – the shining delight in his eyes, her groans and my intense pleasure at getting to share it all with both of them. But it was overshadowed, as these things often are, by real life. As I got into it more, and reached down to grip her hair and tell her to keep going, a kick of pleasure deep in my stomach made me tense up. Made me *sit* up.

And smash my head on the corner of the bedside table.

Pointed, polished wood, directly into the eye socket. An almost instant black eye, which would last for at least a week. It hurt, sure, but every time I saw it in the mirror I couldn't help but smile.

Where was I? Oh, yeah. Love hurts. But I like it when it hurts – I remember it more clearly.

Like those sofa-bruises, which are still clear in my mind even though the trip happened years ago. Twenty-six and I, in a rare moment of clarity and organisation, booked flights and planned a weekend away. He was due to go somewhere with work, and I was excited about the chance to get a passport stamp as a dirty weekend souvenir. He arrived before I did, and spent the first two days bunking off work in favour of emailing me about what we'd do when we got there. Sightseeing, drinking in smoky bars, fucking each other raw on the floor of the apartment: that kind of thing.

When I arrived he whisked me into a warm coffee shop and plied me with cake and thick hot chocolate. We grinned nervously at each other over the table – still in the early days where we wanted to impress each other, both of us secretly hoping we could skip from 'oh look at the beautiful city at night' to 'let's hole up in the apartment, draw the curtains and bang like our lives depend on it.'

We did the latter. For the first night, at least. I dumped my bag on the tiled floor in the living room and he grabbed at my hips and yanked me towards him, dick already hard. I fumbled at his belt with my hands, and he dragged me through the apartment, giving me those aching, sucking, biting kisses that you give when you're fucking *desperate*.

When we got into the bedroom he pushed me onto the bed. If it had been a film he'd have done it in one smooth move – shoving me with his body and slumping down on top of me, legs perfectly positioned to rub his groin against my crotch. It wasn't a film though – that's why it was fun. It was real and hot and angry and hard. He pushed me, then paused so I could adjust, and I slipped down my jeans just far enough then rolled onto my stomach. He yanked his trousers halfway down his thighs, cock sticking out of the mess of belt and open fly, then hurled himself on top of me and buried his scratchy, five-day-stubbled face into my neck. I wriggled against him. Play-fighting an escape. He pinned my hands down to the bed and asked me:

'How...' a gulp. A pause while he got his breath and bit back his enthusiasm. That question could so easily have been a limp-willed 'how much did you miss me?' or - worse - 'how are you?' A jokey prompt to ease a still-nervous and not-yet-dominant twenty-six.

But it wasn't that. Gloriously, cunt-wettingly, it was this:

'How hard do you want me to fuck you?'

Unngh.

How could I answer? By what yardstick do you measure the hardness of a fuck? One that has your cunt muscles twitching with eager agony, and your knickers slick with need? How do you tell someone that you want them to fuck you so hard it will hurt for days after? Like their dick is a punishment you cannot wait to take.

'Hard.'

'Yeah?'

'Yeah. Fuck me like I'm in trouble.'

And he did. On the bed in the tiled apartment with the weird décor, and a freezing wind blowing in from the open window, number twenty-six pinned me down by my arms while I wriggled and gasped and pretended to struggle, and he fucked me like his dick could make contact with the ache in the pit of my stomach. And it was wonderful, and weird, and all the things I like best.

But I'm getting distracted again - that's not how I got the bruises. It's not how I got the knee grazes, either. The knee grazes came the next day, when we were walking home from dinner.

We had to eat, of course. You can't live on spunk and faux-wrestling forever. Twenty-six would chew broken glass before experimenting with new food, but I'm pretty handy with a Rough Guide so I can find margerita pizza in almost any major city. So: a walk in the cold, pizza, a brief stop at a shop to gasp at how cheap cigarettes were, then a discussion on the journey home to relive the night before.

'Do you fantasise about that?' he asked, knowing the answer. 'The struggle. Is it fun?'

'Would you have done it if you thought it wasn't?'

'No, of course not. You're right, that's a stupid question. I just wanted to talk about it again.'

'Why?'

'Because it makes my dick hard.'

So we talked about the struggle. The fact that a fuck feels better if it's somewhere like a fight.

I mess that explanation up, I know: fucking like fighting sounds bitter and angry. It sounds... ugh... non-consensual. And every time I mention these fight-fucks – the ones I like best - I risk painting twenty-six as a villain. But in reality, those fucks are every bit as consensual as the wine I drink or the cake I'll cram happily into my face when I'm offered it at a birthday party. I enjoy the struggle and the viciousness every bit as much as I enjoy other indulgences. While I'll happily add caveats for those who aren't familiar with BDSM, or those who'd twist consensual fantasy into something ugly like rape, in this instance I'm not sure they're needed. You know now, right, that I love twenty-six? You've been with us since those first few messages, you can see how much we've grown. If anything, the only caveat I need is to tell you that by this point twenty-six had embraced it. The fight-fucking, I mean. He went from lovemaking angel to brutal sadist in the short time it took me to ask him.

And I'm so, so glad I asked him.

We talked about the fuck, got his dick hard as requested, then when we got to the stairwell at the apartment he pushed me roughly against a wall. Tore my coat open and slipped one hand up beneath my layers, and yanked down my bra. Freezing cold fingers gripped one of my nipples and I let out a half-laugh-half-cough at the shock of it.

'On your knees.'

He's more nervous than that one line makes him sound. In fact, he's terrified we'll be caught by a passer-by. I can't really tell this at the time, though, because I'm too busy choking back his dick, and hoping desperately that he'll come nice and hard against my throat. He pushes himself deeper until he's fucking me back against the wall, and my head knocks against the plaster. He pulls back, and I shake my head slightly and urge him further on. I like the tightness of his dick choking me, and I'm keen to have a slight bruise underneath my hair to prove what happened. A tender patch that I can touch tomorrow, and remember the exact feeling of my head pressed against the plaster as his cock twitched, pouring spunk down the back of my tongue and into my throat.

Distracted again, sorry. I'm supposed to be telling you about the sofa bruises.

The bruises came during the final fuck of the weekend – the last one we had before running to catch a cab. They were given, and received, very quickly. He held both hands flat in the small of my back to keep me arched just so, then shoved his dick into me and bashed my hips into the solid arm of the sofa. Within four or five thrusts he realised he'd get better purchase by gripping the sofa itself, pulling it tight in one direction as he fucked me. Each stroke was punctuated by my hips grinding against the arm, adding another bruise to the purple mishmash of marks that I'd be nursing for a week.

And that's how I remember it – that whole weekend. I had to think hard to recall the conversation about cheap cigarettes, or the smiles we exchanged over hot chocolate. But the hip bruises and knee grazes and black eyes of the past are always near the surface. What's more, they run into each other: a bruise here reminds me of a scratch there, and that in turn reminds me of another. If they never healed I'd be black and blue and red raw, and I could point to each square inch of my body and give you a brand new story. Here's the time that guy whipped me with wire, or this one beat me with a wooden paddle and a grin. Every time I try to talk about sex, I remember another pocket of pain. Another bruise or scratch. Another anecdote to either amuse, arouse or unnerve people.

And I never want to stop.

When twenty-six and I got back from our trip, the sex still hurt. Alongside cheap cigarettes and cool foreign snacks I brought back something else - an ache if I wore a belt, and bright colours painted over my skin. I still went round to his flat for struggle-fucks on the living room floor and throat-fucks in his hallway. We made new bruises, until eventually there was no space left for new marks or memories. The bruises fell in the same places, each and every time. There were no rough holds that made me gasp with surprise. There were no new men to scare me with desires I'd never heard before or fantasies I couldn't dream up.

There was just me, twenty-six, and the memories of faded bruises.

So what happens now?

BOOK TWO

Girl On The Net: How A Bad Girl Fell In Love

Part confessional, part drunken-rant-on-the-bus, Girl on the Net guides us through the lessons a thirty-something sex blogger has learned about sex and love.

This book takes us on a journey that begins with a happy ending and goes swiftly downhill from there, dismantling some of our myths about romance along the way. Girl on the Net weaves her own relationship issues and surprises through candid personal stories and weird facts gathered from three years of sex blogging.

This book explores key sexual issues facing men and women: porn, kink, commitment, the biological clock, why feminist men are hot, and whether sex and love should really go hand in hand, or whether happiness lies in following your true desire...

Find out more at www.girlonthenet.com/books/

30630604R00199

Printed in Great
Britain
by Amazon